POLITICAL CULTURE AND PUBLIC OPINION

POLITICAL CULTURE AND PUBLIC OPINION

Edited by
Arthur Asa Berger

Transaction Publishers
New Brunswick (U.S.A.) and Oxford (U.K.)

Copyright © 1989 by Transaction Publishers
New Brunswick, New Jersey 08903

All rights reserved under International and Pan-American Copyright Conventions. No part of this book may be reproduced or transmitted in any form or by any means, electronic or mechanical, including photocopy, recording, or any information storage and retrieval system, without prior permission in writing from the publisher. All inquiries should be addressed to Transaction Publishers, Rutgers—The State University, New Brunswick, New Jersey 08903.

Library of Congress Catalog Number: 88-20029
ISBN: 0-88738-753-5
Printed in the United States of America

Library of Congress Cataloging in Publication Data

Political culture and public opinion / edited by Arthur Asa Berger.
    p. cm.
  Includes bibliographies.
  ISBN 0-88738-753-5
  1. Political culture.   2. Public opinion.   I. Berger, Arthur Asa, 1933—
JA75.7.P65 1988
306'.2—dc 19
88-20029
CIP

Contents

Acknowledgments — vii
Introduction — 1

Part I: A Theoretical Overview
1. Choosing Preferences by Constructing Institutions:
   A Cultural Theory of Preference Formation
   Aaron Wildavsky — 21

Part II: Hierarchical Collectivism
Introduction — 49
2. Mass Communications and World Opinion
   Leo Bogart — 51
3. Looking Beyond Teledemocracy:
   The Politics of Communications and Information Technology
   William H. Dutton — 79

Part III: Competitive Individualism
Introduction — 99
4. Television, Culture and the State in Brazil
   Conrad Phillip Kottak — 101
5. *Thief:* At Long Last, a Good Movie about a Capitalist
   Aaron Wildavsky — 121

Part IV: Egalitarianism
Introduction — 131
6. Up Against The Wall:
   The Vietnam Veterans Memorial & the
   Paradox of Remembrance
   Carol Wilder — 133
7. The Politics of Culture: Feminism and the Media
   Muriel G. Cantor — 149

Part V: Fatalism
Introduction — 167
8. Welcome to My Nightmare:
   The Graffiti of Homeless Youth
   C. Cajetan Luna — 169
9. "1984": The Commercial
   Arthur Asa Berger — 175

Name Index — 187
Subject Index — 191

Acknowledgments

Let me thank, first of all, Irving Louis Horowitz, president of Transaction Publishers, who liked the idea of a book on political culture and public opinion and gave me a great deal of moral support while I worked on the project.

I also appreciate the efforts of the people who contributed original articles to the book: Leo Bogart, Bill Dutton, Muriel Cantor, Conrad Phillip Kottak, and Carol Wilder. I am grateful, also, to Aaron Wildavsky and The American Political Science Association for making it possible for me to use the Wildavsky essay.

My first book, *Li'l Abner: A Study in American Satire* (Twayne, 1970), had a great deal of material in it on political culture. It was based on my dissertation on Li'l Abner, which I wrote under the supervision of Mulford Q. Sibley, the distinguished political theorist who taught at the University of Minnesota. It was he who got me started on popular culture. I've never been able to escape from the subject, and the more I do (and I've been at it for almost thirty years now), the more there is to do. The task of analyzing our popular culture and mass media, which play so important a role in our political culture, is endless. It is truly a Sisyphean enterprise.

I hope that you will find this book useful and edifying. The essays in it are written by scholars from a number of different disciplines and provide an up-to-date and interesting perspective on political culture and public opinion, one that has both fascinating analyses and important theoretical implications.

Introduction

Any book dealing with political culture and public opinion may be expected to cover a good deal of territory, and this one does. It contains articles on everything from culture theory to graffiti, from mass communication and world opinion to the Vietnam Veterans Memorial in Washington, D.C., from new technology's impact on the political process to Brazilian television.

Defining Public Opinion

We all have a pretty good idea of what is meant by public opinion; it being rather obvious. However, as Leo Bogart points out in the introduction to his book *Polls and the Awareness of Public Opinion* (original title *Silent Politics*), there are several different ways to think about this concept:

> Should collective actions be seen as manifestations of public opinion or as critical events whose principal importance is their influence on public opinion? The answer to this question depends on whether public opinion is considered the sum total of all the ideas on a particular issue held by the individual members of society, or whether it is thought of as a mood or emotion that suffuses a society and manifests itself in a variety of ways on endless subjects, maintaining a life of its own quite apart from what individuals think. The first conception underlies the practice of polling; the second appears to be more congruent with the analysis of collective behavior. (Bogart, 1985, p. viii)

We might keep these two approaches in mind as we read the essays in this volume, for different authors emphasize one or the other of these perspectives when they deal with public opinion.

We are fortunate to have an essay by Leo Bogart on "Mass Communication and World Opinion" which deals with the "flow of ideas across international boundaries and the restrictions on that flow," as well as related matters such as the development of international polling, the relation between transient opinions and deeply rooted values in a culture and the relationship between information and opinion.

2   Political Culture and Public Opinion

The Meanings of Culture

The matter of political culture is a bit more difficult to define. There are, it has been estimated, well over a hundred definitions of the term "culture" that have been used by social scientists—though many of them are quite similar. Culture, anthropologists tell us:

- is distinctively human,
- is passed on from generation to generation (that is, transmitted by communication and taught), and
- has an impact on institutions and the behavior of people raised in its presence.

One of the most widely-used definitions of culture was offered by Edward Burnett Tylor in *Primitive Culture*:

> Culture ... is that complex whole which includes knowledge, belief, art, morals, law, custom, and any other capabilities and habits acquired by man as a member of society. (Tylor, 1958, p. 1)

Beyond these fundamentals, however, there seems to be a good deal of controversy and some anthropologists emphasize the material elements of culture and others emphasize the symbolic dimensions of culture.

Conrad Phillip Kottak, like Bogart a contributor to this volume, summarizes a number of factors associated with culture in his textbook *Cultural Anthropology*:

> Culture, a distinctive possession of humanity, is acquired by all humans as members of society through enculturation. Culture encompasses rule-governed, shared, symbol-based, learned behavior and beliefs transmitted across the generations. Everyone is cultured, not just people with elite educations.... Culture rests on the human capacity for cultural learning, use of language and symbols. Culture refers to customary beliefs and behavior and to the rules for conduct internalized in human beings.... (Kottak, 1987, p. 35)

These insights draw us near to an understanding of political culture, which is generally understood to deal with the beliefs, values and attitudes found in people which play a role in shaping the political order found in a given society.

One of the best definitions of political culture can be found in Lucian Pye's *Politics, Personality and Nation Building: Burma's Search for Identity*. In this work Pye points out that there are contending forces involved in shaping a nation's political culture:

> ... political culture is shaped on the one hand by the general historical experience of the society or system and on the other hand by the intensely private and personal experiences of individuals as they become members of first the society and then the polity. (Pye, 1962, p. 121)

Thus, there is the macro-level analysis of the development of the political institutions of the society and the micro-level analysis of the development of various actors on the political scene. He points out that the concept of political culture is actually wider than that of a state, and quotes Gabriel Almond who suggested that, "The United States, England, and several of the Commonwealth countries have a common political culture but separate and different kinds of political systems." (Pye, 1962, p. 122)

Pye lists a number of matters which should be considered when dealing with a political culture. They are (Pye:1962, pp. 122-24):

1. The scope of activities, issues, and decisions which are perceived by people as relevant to the management of political power;
2. The body of wisdom and knowledge of the people which makes it possible for them to comprehend and find meaning in, explain, and predict those behaviors which they perceive as being relevantly political;
3. That faith beyond substantive knowledge which is governed by the prophetic words of those perceived as appropriate spokesmen of the future;
4. The values assumed to be most sensitive to political actions;
5. The standards accepted as valid for appraising and evaluating political conduct; and
6. The legitimate identities people can assume in contending for power and the common identity which the polity provides for all.

These matters give us a good idea about the meaning of the concept. Pye adds that we must also be mindful of the technologies a society develops for "organizing and manipulating power" and that, in the final analysis, what we call political culture can be found "only in men's [and women's] minds in the patterns of action, feelings, and reflections which they have internalized and made a part of their existence." (Pye, 124)

The Uses of Political Culture

We investigate political culture because we believe that its concerns are of great importance in understanding why people create or shape political systems the way they do, how different political systems function and why people make the political choices they do. But rather than focusing directly on political institutions and decision making, the approach is indirect. We

4   Political Culture and Public Opinion

recognize now, for example, that there are political aspects to our popular culture and mass media, that the arts have a great deal to tell us, and so does our everyday life.

This study of political culture should be looked upon as a means of supplementing the approaches we have developed to help us understand politics, and not as a way of suggesting that culture is, somehow, primary and that culture shapes politics and relegates it to the status of being an epiphenomenon (though some thinkers believe this is so, just as many believe the opposite is true).

On Preferences and The Four Political Cultures Found in Democracies

The first essay in this book, by Aaron Wildavsky, is relevant here. Wildavsky's essay, "Choosing Preferences by Constructing Institutions: A Cultural Theory of Preference Formation," deals with the issue of how people determine their preferences and suggests that culture plays a major role in shaping these preferences—especially the *first-order* preferences such as cultural values. We are born into a given culture and generally operate more or less within the perimeters it establishes for us. There is more leeway in our *second-order* preferences, such as what lifestyle to adopt, and our third order preferences, such as what policies should be supported to enable one to lead a particular lifestyle. Our preferences can be derived, Wildavsky suggests, from our institutional arrangements and are endogamous, not exogenous. They derive, he continues, from our cultures.

There are, he adds, only "a limited number of cultures that between them categorize most human relations," and these cultures define themselves by the way they deal with two fundamental questions: "Who am I?" and "What shall I do?" Drawing upon the work of the British social anthropologist Mary Douglas, with whom he has collaborated, he suggests there are four political cultures which can be found in democratic societies.

What happens, Wildavsky argues, is that "individuals exert control over one another by institutionalizing the moral judgments justifying their interpersonal relationships so they can be acted upon and accounted for." This he describes as the "cultural hypothesis," and it is in "social relationships, roughly as categorized by political cultures," that he finds "the most basic value and factual premises that we can hypothesize as lying behind specific political and policy preferences."

To show the power of his model, he considers two important topics, ideology and risk, in considerable detail. Let me deal with one important insight he offers here, in his discussion of individualism. He suggests that when we talk about "individualism," we tend to join together and confuse two distinctive political cultures: the individualism of the competitive individualists and of the egalitarians. For the first group, individualism involves freedom from restraints or equality of opportunity (which tends to accentuate differences in people) while for the egalitarians, individualism involves equality of result, which tends to diminish differences in people and stresses the needs of the collectivity and people in general.

He concludes this essay in a section titled "Cultures Constitute Our Political Selves" by suggesting a research program for political scientists. He writes:

> On the level of ideas, a research program on political culture would seek to increase our understanding of how opposed visions of the good life are selected, sustained, altered and rejected. As social scientists following Robert Merton and knowing, therefore, that unanticipated consequences are a staple of social life, we want to understand what else we choose when we choose our political cultures.

He suggests a number of possible topics for research, such as "appraising the consequences of living lives of hierarchical subordination or of the purely voluntary association of egalitarian liberation . . . at different times, on different continents, with different technologies, languages, and customs. . . ."

He also concludes his essay with an invitation—and an implicit challenge—to social scientists of all persuasions. The research program he has suggested, he says,

> . . . would enable us to test the general hypothesis that how people organize their institutions has a more powerful effect on their preferences than any rival explanation—wealth, technology, class, self-interest, tradition, you name it. The field of preference formation is open to all comers.

This article was Wildavsky's presidential address at the 1986 meeting of The American Political Science Association. I used the Wildavsky essay because I think it does such a superb job of showing how significant political culture is and, by implication, how important it is that we study it. It also suggests ways of understanding issues that are discussed elsewhere in the book. If Wildavsky is correct, political culture is not something of minor interest but, instead, should assume a position of centrality in our study of politics.

The Wildavsky essay provides the classification system or schema around which this book has been organized. Each of the remaining essays has been placed, without doing too much violence to the truth I believe, under one of Wildavsky's four categories of political culture. We find, then, essays by Leo Bogart and William Dutton which fit best under the hierarchical elitism category and essays by Conrad Phillip Kottak and Aaron Wildavsky which fit under the competitive individualism category. The essays by Muriel Cantor and Carol Wilder represent the egalitarian thrust in our political culture while the essays by Luna and myself fit best under the fatalist rubric.

With this brief discussion of the organization of the book in mind, let me now say something about each of the essays in this volume.

Mass Communication and World Opinion

The second essay in the book, by Leo Bogart, has already been mentioned. It considers the matter of the flow of ideas around the world and related mattters involving public opinion and values. Bogart quotes from a UNESCO report which argues that "world public opinion" exists, though it is fragile and still being formed. The report argues that the role of the media is to affect social change and not just report on events.

However, this world public opinion breaks down quickly into "block opinions" which are, themselves, not monolithic. The so-called "universal values" of people—for peace, etc.—are interpreted by people in different cultures in different ways. Thus, if there is such a thing as world opinion, it certainly is, in the words of the UNESCO report, "still in the process of formation, and thus is fragile, heterogeneous, easily abused and still unable to be considered as an authentic power." There are also a number of other factors to be considered such as mass literacy and freedom of information. How valuable is information about public opinion in societies where there is rigid censorship?

The Problem of Polls

Public opinion existed long before polls were invented and there is the question, already mentioned earlier, as to how to define public opinion. Bogart opts for the cultural definition, saying "Public opinion may be found in the changing climate of discussion and debate rather than the sum total of individuals' answers to pollster's question."

Most of the polls are not directly political, or don't involve issues "that carry a strong emotional charge." That is, most polls tend to be about,

> marketing and consumer behavior, media exposure and content preferences, attitudes towards work, hobbies, interests, sporting and cultural events and all the other topics beyond politics, with which people are accustomed to pass the time.

There are, Bogart says, numerous cross-national poles that are conducted, which use identical (or similar) questions. These polls make certain assumptions about commonalities that are often questionable. Thus, one might ask whether mothers of young school children should work and find widely varying answers in first and second world countries, but in third world countries the question would be meaningless, since in most of these societies women traditionally work, though this is done in the framework of household economies and not outside employment.

In many cases, opinion is polarized and people tend to answer the polls in terms of ingroup and outgroup positions. In other cases, people have no sense that their opinion counts. And there is the problem of the relation between information and opinion. Of what values are opinions if they are not based on information—information that is shared (which brings the mass media into the situation)? Thus, Europeans may be asked about American presidential politics, may not have enough information about the matter to form an opinion about them, and thus answer that they have no opinion.

In certain cases, where matters are complicated and where technical expertise is involved, people tend to align their opinions with groups they are associated with (such as political parties or unions) or with authority figures in whom they feel they can put their trust.

One important aspect of public opinion research involves "exploring the degree of public ignorance or apathy on subjects that may objectively be of great importance, and which the public really should know about." The fact that large numbers of people do not know about something suggests that they do not feel it is of any importance to them and is, then, an indirect expression of opinion.

Opinions and Cultural Values

Opinions that do not deal with politics, Bogart tells us, tend to be "expressions of national character and reflections of national cultures and value systems. Opinions are themselves a part of the culture, controlling the direction and pace of change." Bogart cites the case of American culture, which has experienced profound transformations in recent years. The changes are "mirrored in changes of attitude as well as behavior," and are reflected in opinion polls.

Bogart locates American culture within a broader framework of European culture, even though America is geographically separated from Europe. And within cultures there are often numerous subcultures and often differing opinions within each of them. Cultures may not determine opinions, but cultures shape them. Furthermore, "just as subcultures exist within countries, so culture groupings transcend national borders and shade into each other." And all of these differences are reflected in opinions people hold, though these opinions are relatively volatile; they change much more quickly than the cultures which generate them.

For Bogart, culture shapes our institutions, but culture is much broader than politics. He writes:

> Political institutions are cultural creations, and in turn shape the culture, but cultural phenomena have far wider currency than political ideas. When there are common cultural heroes and interests, or a shared familiarity with the same universal symbols of consumption, this hardly means that there are also common political values. The names of Coca-Cola, Shell, Mickey Mouse, and Luciano Pavarotti resonate with identical meanings in widely-separated societies, but this has little bearing on public opinion.

The mass media play a particularly important role here, especially what Bogart describes as "the picture media—photography, motion pictures, and television," since they allow direct communications and there is a great "density of information that is packed into visual experiences."

Culture itself (by which Bogart means the arts, elite as well as popular) is the subject of opinions and is often shaped by political institutions. As Bogart points out, many totalitarian regimes use culture for their own ends, as a political weapon.

This discussion leads to an analysis of the international mass media, propaganda, the power of American advertising and media, and the controversial issue of the New World Information Order. Bogart concludes by arguing that, for a variety of reasons, world public opinion does not exist. He offers two research projects that are relevant to the topic. First, he suggests we investigate "the degree of commonality in mass media experience and in exposure to news of current events." And second, he suggests we explore "the degree of commonality around the world in values and beliefs," which would give us a "preliminary sketch of the outer limits within which opinions might be formed on an international scale."

The Impact of The New Media

The essay by William H. Dutton, like that of Leo Bogart's, has a global reach, but the focus is on the impact of new information technologies on the political order. There is a considerable amount of debate on what impact these technologies—what Dutton calls "the new media"—will have on the politics. Will the new media open up the political process to out-groups or will these media consolidate the power of the elites who control the new technologies?

Introduction 9

There are, Dutton suggests, four different views about the matter of control. The first is what Dutton describes as the "democratic marketplace" view, which argues that the needs and preferences of the public, operating through the marketplace, will determine how these new technologies will function. The second is described as the "technocratic" position, and it holds that the military and industrial applications of these media will be of primary importance in shaping their use. The third view, the "pluralist" position, suggests that control of these media is but one of the significant political resources and that competing groups of elites will shape the use of these media. Finally, there is what Dutton describes as "reinforcement politics," which suggests that the new media will reinforce the positions of those already dominant in society.

There are, he adds, a number of different positions scholars take about whether the media are neutral or inherently biased, and therefore holding the potential for power shifts in a given society. There are the "neutralists" who argue that it is content, not technology, that is of primary importance. Then there is the countervailing interest or dual-effects school, which argues that a given technology can work in opposite ways. For example, he cites Pool's work on the telephone, which suggested that it can be used to circumvent or heighten hierarchy. Finally, the dominant view maintains that the new media have a "democratic" impact while the opposed position suggest, they will have an "elitist" impact.

Political Uses of Information Technologies

Dutton devotes a considerable amount of attention to the way these new technologies can be used. He discusses four areas in which their impact has been substantial: political campaigns and elections, governmental communications, public telecommunications, and international communications. He shows how the personal computer has revolutionized political campaigns and discusses the implications of these changes relative to such matters as the role of local organizations and the kinds of expertise political consultants must now have.

In his discussion of international communication and the new media, he suggests that in an information-based world, the new "communication infrastructures represent nothing less than new trade routes." In addition, these new media have powerful implications as far as culture is concerned:

> Culturally, many nations have raised concern over the maintenance of their traditions and values in the face of mass media institutions that threaten to homogenize the public around commercial rather than domestic programming. This issue has surrounded radio and television broadcasting for de-

cades in nations such as Canada. However, the newer media of cable, satellites, and video recording systems raise this issue anew because they challenge existing institutions and mechanisms for ensuring national controls.

This is a stormy issue that continues to be debated. Studies of media flow reveal that the United States and a few other nations dominate what is shown on television and in cinemas. What effect all of this is having on third world (and maybe even first world) societies is hard to say. A study on the way "Dallas" is viewed in Germany by Herta Hertzog Massing (*Society*, Nov. 10, 1986) suggests, for instance, that Germans tend to view the program in terms of their own cultural values, which implies that the impact of the media might not be as great as we think.

Dutton believes that the new media are "malleable political resources that are most often designed and used in ways that follow and reinforce the existing structure of power." This suggests that while the new media tend to be used in support of the existing power structure there is also a bit of room for maneuver.

Television and Culture in Brazil: A Case Study

We now turn to an article by anthropologist Conrad Phillip Kottak on television and culture in Brazil. He writes:

> This article will illustrate, with primary reference to the world's most watched commercial network (Globo), that control by gatekeepers can operate on several levels, and various degrees and types of censorship can apply to commercial as well as govenment-funded or -run television.

Brazil's government has a long tradition of supervising television's content and controlled television by granting access to the airwaves. This censorship was most intense during primetime, from 6 to 9:30 P.M. when "Brazil's most popular television programs—the Globo network's national news (8 P.M.) and its three nightly 'soaps' or telenovelas—are broadcast. . . ." (Things changed considerably with the changing of regimes in 1985, as might be expected.)

These telenovelas generally last about six or seven months and have enormous viewing publics. Kottak cites a number of instances in which these shows, as well as political reporting and debate, were censored. The censorship tended to focus on violence and politics rather than nudity and sex.

Since the main purpose of commercial television is "neither to entertain nor to enlighten, but to sell products," market research and related disciplines are well developed in Brazil. IBOPE (The Brazilian Statistical Public Opinion Research Institute) was founded, in 1942, for example, and has a role similar to the Gallup organization in America. But unlike American companies, IBOPE keeps its findings secret and does not publish them.

Kottak offers an extended analysis of the dominant television network in Brazil, Globo, and its main rivals, the Manchete network and SBT (the Brazilian Television System) owned by Silvio Santos, which attracts the lowest segments of the Brazilian market. Globo also tended to cooperate with the authoritarian rulers of Brazil from 1968 to 1974, when authoritarian government control censorship were at their height. Kottak suggests that as a result, Globo is the second most important institution, after the state, in Brazilian society:

> Monopolistic control of multiple media, marketing savy, and federal intervention and support have combined to create in Rede Globo an empire that stands alongside, and is rivaled as a national institution only by, the Brazilian state.

And Globo maintains its near monopolistic position by getting extensive press coverage of its offerings "while other channels are ignored or castigated." It also tends to adopt a rather imperialistic attitude toward what it will cover and what it won't.

Kottak concludes with a fascinating discussion of the 1984 presidential campaigns in Brazil and America. In the Brazilian election, Globo supported the direct election of the president, going against the wishes of the military rulers of the time, "its most daring independent political act." (It turned out that the military were able to have the election done indirectly, via a nominating convention.) Kottak found a great deal of confusion in Brazil about the election. He writes, "In trying to decipher the Brazilian electoral process, I encountered an amazing amount of misinformation, which the media seemed to do as much to propagate as to resolve." And Brazilian television paid little attention to the results of this historic nominating convention, sandwiching it in during a Jerry Lewis movie.

Kottak's study is an interesting one because it shows how a medium can become a kind of "mouthpiece" of the government. Yet in the case of Brazil, where that medium, television, was censored for many years and where television is of monumental importance, the generals were not able to maintain control of the government. This case study gives us reason to think about the long-term effects of media and resist seemingly self-evident conclusions about media and society.

"Thief"

This review of *"Thief,"* which appeared in the twentieth anniversary issue of *Society*, provides us with an opportunity to see how Wildavsky uses his concepts to analyze a filmic text. *Thief* is about the adventures of Frank, a diamond thief, who exemplifies the values of competitive individualism. As Wildavsky writes, "The virtue of Michael Mann's thief is that he exemplifies, understands, and acts upon pure principles of competitive individualism."

These principles, Wildavsky tells us, involve individuals who operate in free markets under conditions of perfect competition in which freedom of contract prevails and individuals are free to engage in transactions if they wish. Failures are blamed on bad luck or doing a bad job, but not the system itself. What we have here is the competitive individualist version of the American Dream. The hero of this film, Frank, believes strongly in the American Dream and strives to make it come true for him.

He finds himself involved with the mob, "hierarchical collectivists with a monopoly to maintain," just as competitive individualists often find themselves at odds with hierarchical elements of society. The mob arranges for him to adopt a baby (a baby his wife wanted) and, in return, Frank agrees to do a job for them. Like all good hierarchical collectivists, however, they believe that he "belongs to them," setting the stage for a battle that ends in the destruction of several members of the mob.

The dilemma of competitive individualism is that it is inadequate on its own. Wildavsky explains:

> From the risks he chooses to take, comes opportunity. But without order to support sanctity of contract, he will not be allowed to compete. The hierarchy he rejects, and rightly so when it changes the rules by force, turns out to be indispensable. Without a modicum of order, there can be no spontaneity. The very hierarchy that crushes Frank's way of life is also, in lesser but still vital degree, necessary to its achievement.

Frank's dilemma is one which is found played out in all democratic societies, where competitive individualists find it necessary to function in a society in which hierarchical elites, their antitheses in many respects, are needed to make it possible for the individualists to function.

Thief is an important film, Wildavsky suggests, because Frank is a superb embodiment of a constellation of cultural values and the film, "far from being about an outsider, gives us a glimpse of one American dream."

Up Against The Wall: The Vietnam Veterans Memorial

This essay deals with a very significant work of architecture, the Vietnam Veterans Memorial in Washington DC. The author, Carol Wilder, considers a number of important questions relative to this work:

1. How do we account for the incredible influence of this work?
2. How do we explain the power this work has?
3. How does the pain of remembrance generated by the work affect the matters of healing and reconciliation?

The essay starts with a discussion of how the idea of making a memorial to the Vietnam veterans got started, in March, 1979, by a Vietnam veteran named Jan Scruggs. The political and financial problems in creating this memorial—such as raising money and getting a site—were formidable but Scruggs was, as Wilder put it, "blessed with the innocence of those who are unaware of the impossibility of the task they are undertaking."

She pays considerable attention to the rhetoric in the statement of purpose for the monument design competition and to the ideas of the person who won, a twenty-one-year-old Yale undergraduate, Maya Lin, an "apolitical young Asian-American female." The design committee was unanimous in choosing her design, and although Scruggs had some initial reservations, he later accepted the choice of the committee.

Wilder next deals with the memorial itself; the remarkable ways in which it communicates, and the way people behave when they visit it: some cry, many leave flowers and other mementos, "tokens of grieving, of greeting and of letting go." She points out that the ambiguity of the memorial has led scholars to varying ways of interpreting it. One writer, Sonja K. Foss, sees it as an effective anti-war statement while another, Harry W. Haines, see it as something "vulnerable to political manipulation . . . linked to the power strategies of future wars." Wilder deals with these two varying interpretations in considerable detail.

The essay concludes with some speculations about how the memorial communicates to people. Wilder suggests that it is the "enthymemic structure that invites the viewer to participate in making meaning" that is central to understanding the power of the monument. It can also be seen, she adds, as what Umberto Eco has called "an open text," that is one that can be thought of as, in a sense, incomplete and demanding something from the spectators.

The Politics of Culture: Feminism and the Media

Muriel Cantor, the author of this essay, writes not only from the perspective of a theorist but also from that of a participant observer. Thus, this essay focuses upon two topics. First, it deals with the problems women have faced in dealing with the radio and television broadcasting industry, and second, it considers a particular event, the challenge by the National Organization of Women of a renewal application by WRC-TV (Washington, DC) in which Cantor played an important role.

The essay mentions, in passing, stereotypes of women in the media and the problems women employed by the media have faced in furthering their careers. The real focus of the essay is on the challenges by NOW to the various television stations. She writes:

> ... because of my personal involvement with the WRC-TV challenge, I know that none of the women were so naive as to expect that an NBC-owned and-operated station could actually lose its license ... However, the NOW representatives also believed that forcing station owners to respond to the challenge would itself require them to review and perhaps alter their policies on hiring and programming practices.

Cantor questions whether this tactic was responsible for the many changes that have taken place in the broadcasting industry and suggests that it may have furthered the careers of those involved in the protests rather than leading to general changes.

One of the problems that women faced in trying to deal with the media was that, as Cantor puts it, "women and other minorities were not considered topics worthy of serious research" by media scholars because most research was done by male scholars and was "male-centered and-oriented." This has changed in recent years as more and more women have become media researchers and have focused their attention on feminist issues.

Cantor suggests that 1963 marked the "rebirth" or "second wave" of the feminist movement in the United States; that was the year the Equal Pay Act was passed and Betty Friedan's the *Feminine Mystique* was published. There were numerous station challenges, none of which led to the stations losing their licenses. So the question arises—did the challenges have a lasting effect on the industry?

There are, Cantor points out, major changes that have taken place in the broadcasting industry as far as the roles played by women and minorities. But were these changes generated by the women's reform movement? Cantor suggests that more likely it was the "major demographic, economic and political shifts which occurred over the past decade(s)" that were responsible for the changes, and not the women's movement. And even with these changes, Cantor adds, many studies show that women in the broadcasting industry still lag far behind women in other industries.

Cantor suggests that probably the most important effect of the women's movement was "that it contributed a new focus" for researchers. The importance of this, she suggests, cannot be over-emphasized. Feminists learned that it was possible to use research for "political as well as for both informational and educational purposes."

Welcome to my Nightmare: Graffiti of Homeless Youth

This essay deals with the graffiti drawn by homeless youth in Los Angeles, San Francisco, and Seattle. C. Cajetan Luna quotes Herbert Kohl who argues, in a 1969 essay from *Urban Review* that:

> ... graffiti does not represent attempts to deface walls. Nor is it a simple way of showing off. There are too many regularities in the forms in which graffiti manifests itself not to suspect that one is dealing with a complex cultural phenomenon.

Whether Kohl is correct is a matter about which there is considerable controversy. What is not controversial, however, is the fact that the homeless youth who create these graffiti live under terrible circumstances and have to deal constantly with violence and exploitation. They leave home, generally, because they "flee turbulent households racked by conflict, violence, indifference, and, in a large number of cases, sexual abuse."

These children, Luna tells us, have enormous medical and psychological problems and engage in a variety of self-destructive behaviors. The graffiti these street youths create reflects their terrible anger and alienation. Luna explains, "The graffiti of street life present an unobstrusive glimpse of street life. Their meanings are associative, the graffiti capture the essence of the runaway, castaway, homeless youth experience." He provides some examples which read: "Welcome to My Nigthmare" (sic); "Don't You Know Yo're already ded?;" "We Sold Our Love Here;" "The Urban Jungle;" "Kirk Dies Slowly." These are cries of anguish from souls that seem lost and without hope.

These graffiti are, perhaps, the only means of public expression available to these young people and offer us insights into the motivations and lives of some graffiti writers. It is wrong to romanticize graffiti writers, as some people have done, as new kinds of urban artists whose lawlessness is of no importance. But it is also wrong to pay no heed to the anguish and desperation reflected in some of the graffiti.

"1984": The Commercial

This essay is an extended microanalysis of the celebrated Macintosh commercial created by Ridley Scott and broadcast during the 1984 SuperBowl. The commercial was broadcast only once, but it attracted a great deal of attention because of its gripping images. It called to mind the Orwellian nightmare society depicted in his novel *1984* and portrayed a "total" society of prisoners, with their heads shaved, dominated by a "big brother" figure who spouted ideological gobbledygook to them over television.

The only "free" person in the society was a beautiful blonde woman clutching a sledgehammer, who was shown racing through the corridors of the institution pursued by guards. She enters a huge auditorium where an indoctrination/brainwashing session is going on and hurls her sledgehammer at the gigantic television screen at the front of the room. The sledgehammer crashes into the screen and generates a huge explosion that, one surmises, may wake the hypnotized prisoners to action. After the explosion, a message from Apple Computers appears: "On January 24th, Apple Computers will introduce Macintosh and you will see why 1984 won't be like *1984*."

There are a number of different perspectives brought to bear on this short text. First, the heroine is dealt with as a "mythic" figure, whose exploits call to mind both the primal Adam and Eve story (in which apples played an important role) and David fighting Goliath. Apple Computers, it is suggested, casts itself as the David figure fighting against the giant IBM corporation.

It is also suggested that the blonde woman is an ego figure who helps establish a balance between the overpowering Big Brother superego figure and the weakened and perverted id elements in the prisoners. If we expand these concepts to the realm of society and politics, she mediates between a dehumanized and alienated group of proles and a dominating, dehumanizing, and heartless ruler. In this respect, the blonde woman's actions have revolutionary significance.

There are two readings which make sense of the events in this commercial. In the first, the entire story involves IBM, which is known for the way it regiments its workers. In the second, and the preferred reading, the episode involves a war between IBM, "the big blue," and Apple:

> The battle, then, is between the beautiful blonde heroine fighting against the monolithic monster bureaucratic corporation full of faceless nobodies mindlessly following rules and regulations, enslaving the multitudes.

The Macintosh, it is suggested, is so user-friendly that it will liberate the masses by making computing available to all. The commercial followed a brilliant strategy. It showed the dangers inherent in *not* using a Macintosh and focused on the avoidance of something horrible, a subtle form of conditioning.

Conclusion

The essays in this book cover varying aspects of political culture and public opinion. This introduction is meant to give you a taste of the topics discussed in the book—and to whet your appetite. Now, the essays themselves await you. I would hope that after you have read them you will have a better understanding of political culture and public opinion and of the role they play in our societies and our lives.

References

Berger, Arthur Asa. 1980. *Television as an Instrument of Terror*. New Brunswick, NJ: Transaction Books.
Berger, Arthur Asa (ed.). 1988. *Media USA*. New York: Longman Books.
Bogart, Leo. 1987. *Polls and the Awareness of Public Opinion*. New Brunswick, NJ: Transaction Books.
Douglas, Mary. 1975. *Implicit Meanings*. London: RKP.
Kottak, Conrad. 1987. *Cultural Anthropology* (4th Edition). New York: Random House.
Pye, Lucian W. 1962. *Politics, Personality and Nation Building*. New Haven, CT: Yale University Press.
Tylor, Edward. 1873. *Primitive Culture*. London: John Murry (also reprint, 1958 by Harper & Row).
Wildavsky, Aaron. *The Nursing Father: Moses as a Political Leader*. Huntsville, AL: University of Alabama Press.

Part I
A Theoretical Overview

1

Choosing Preferences by Constructing Institutions: A Cultural Theory of Preference Formation

Aaron Wildavsky

> *The question of where political ideas come from is not only highly deserving of study, but also within the competence of our contemporary research techniques. I join Bill Riker in commending it to you as one of the truly exciting and significant areas of investigation in our field.*—Herbert Simon

> *Agreement on political fundamentals cries for an explanation. Why, how, through which mechanisms do people come to think alike about political fundamentals?*—Charles E. Lindblom

Preferences come from the most ubiquitous human activity: living with other people. Support for and opposition to different ways of life, the shared values legitimating social relations (here called cultures) are the generators of diverse preferences. After discussing why it is not helpful to conceive of interests as preferences or to dismiss preference formation as external to organized social life, I will explain how people are able to develop many preferences from few clues by using their social relations to interrogate their environment. The social filter is the source of preferences. I will then argue that culture is a more powerful construct than conceptual rivals: heuristics, schemas, ideologies. Two initial applications—to the ideology of the left-right distinctions and to perceptions of danger—test the claim that this theory of how individuals use political cultures to develop their preferences outperforms the alternatives.

22   A Theoretical Overview

The formation of political preferences ought to be one of the major subjects of political science. Although it is eminently reasonable to study—as most of us, including myself, have throughout our professional lifetimes—how people try to get what they want through political activity, it is also *unreasonable* to neglect the study of why people want what they want. To omit or slight the most important reason all of us have for studying politics, namely, educating our preferences, is a particularly unfortunate lapse for scholars.

I am making a double argument: first, on behalf of the usefulness of a cultural approach in general (rooting explanation in social life), and, second, on behalf of a particular cultural theory (cultures characterized by boundedness and prescription). Readers might find the first more persuasive than the second. There may be better formulations. My brief for the cultural theory that follows is based upon the usual criteria of parsimony and power, that is, getting the most explanatory and predictive capacity from the fewest variables. Challenges and improvements are welcome.

Interests As Preferences

Ask political scientists where preferences come from and if they don't just stop the conservation with "haven't a clue" or refer disparagingly to the muddle over ideology, you are likely to hear that ubiquitous catch-all term "interests." Preferences presumably come from the interests people have. Indeed, a sweeping review of the literature done by Michael Thompson and Michiel Schwarz (1985) tells us what we already suspect: politics of interests is the mainstay of political science.[1] Yet, if preferences come from interests, how do people figure out what their interests are (presumably, these do not come with a birth certificate or social security card) so they will know what they prefer? For if interests and preferences are synonymous, we still are no wiser about how people come to have them.

In the beginning, apparently, there were interests—lumpy, fully formed psychological facts, self-evident and self-explanatory. How any one of us would come to know what our interests are need not matter if they are derived from immediate sense perception. Individuals, presumably, size up the situation, distinguish opposing interests, separate the interests of others from self-interest, and choose (or choose not to choose) the self. Instead of this phenomenological understanding—interests are self-evident, chiseled in stone on objects that force themselves as they are upon human perception—I would rely on the convergence of certain strands of work in social science, according to which meanings are shared; they are conferred on objects or events through social interaction.

If the interests that we consider ours are indeed the products of social relations, then the origins of our preferences may be found in the deepest desires of all: how we wish to live with other people and how we wish others to live with us. "The real moment of choosing," as Mary Douglas maintains, "is ... choice of comrades and their way of life" (1983, p. 45). But that fateful choice, while broad, is not unlimited.

The first choice—the available combinations of values and practices—is made *for* us. Human beings do not choose what they want, like ordering a la carte, any more than they (so far) select their body parts in any size or shape they want, regardless of the configuration into which these have to fit. Preference formation is much more like ordering prix fixe from a number of set dinners or voting a party ticket. Only those combinations that are socially viable, that can cohere because people are able to give them their allegiance, to share their meanings, may be lived. Some things—accepting authority while rejecting it—just can't be done. Only second-level choices (which of the available ways of life do I prefer?) and third-level choices (which policies do I believe are efficacious in supporting my preferred way?) are potentially available to choice. If preferences are formed through the organization of social relations, however, these preferences must come from inside, not from outside, our ways of life—from institutional arrangements.

Preferences Are Endogenous, Not Exogenous

Ask an economist where preferences come from and you will be told that they are exogenous, external to the system being considered.[2] The motive force for participation in markets, the desire to do better through living a life of bidding and bargaining by competing for resources, is ruled out as a noneconomic question! Worse still, preferences are referred to as "tastes," for which, as the saying goes, there is no accounting, thus rendering them not merely noneconomic but nonanalyzable.

The difficulty for economics conceived as rational choice is stated cogently by R. T. Michael and G.S. Becker (1976):

> For economists to rest a large part of their theory of choice on differences in tastes is disturbing since they admittedly have no useful theory of the formation of tastes, nor can they rely on a well-developed theory of tastes from any other discipline in the social sciences, since none exists.... The weakness in the received theory of choice, then, is the extent to which it relies on differences in tastes to "explain" behavior when it can neither explain how tastes are formed nor predict their effects. (in Burt 1982, pp. 347-48)

Nevertheless, Becker goes on to state that "all human behavior can be viewed as involving participants who maximize their utility from a stable set of preferences" (p. 348). If preferences are fixed and outside the process of choice, then we cannot inquire into how preferences are formed. The least interesting behavior, instrumental actions, may be explained by preferences; but about the most interesting, preferences themselves, nothing at all can be said. Lindblom is right: "We have impoverished our thought by imprisoning it in an unsatisfactory model of preferences taken as given" (1982, p. 335).

Cultural theory, by contrast, is based on the premise that preferences are endogenous—internal to organizations—so that they emerge from social interaction in defending or opposing different ways of life. When individuals make important decisions, these choices are simultaneously choices of culture—shared values legitimating different patterns of social practices. Always, in cultural theory, shared values and social relations go together: there are no disembodied values apart from the social relations they rationalize, and there are no social relations in which people do not give reasons for or otherwise attempt to justify their behavior. When choices are not completely controlled by conditions (cultural theory holds), people discover their preferences by evaluating how their past choices have strengthened or weakened (and their future choices might strengthen or weaken) their way of life. Put plainly, people decide for or against exisiting authority. They construct their culture in the process of decision making. Their continuing reinforcement, modification, and rejection of existing power relationships teaches them what to prefer.

"If political preferences are molded through political experiences, or by political institutions," James March and Johan Olsen (1984) state, "it is awkward to have a theory that presumes preferences are exogenous to the political process" (1984). Cultural theory, by contrast, gives preferences an endogenous political explanation: preferences are formed through opposing and supporting institutions.

Rejecting a social science that begins at the end by assuming interests, I wish to make *what people want*—their desires, preferences, values, ideals—into the central subject of our inquiry. By classifying people, their strategies, and their social contexts into the cultural biases that form their preferences, cultural theory attempts to explain and predict recurrent regularities and transitions in their behavior. Preferences in regard to political objects are not external to political life; on the contrary, they constitute the very internal essence, the quintessence of politics: the construction and reconstruction of our lives together.

Deriving Preferences from Cultures: Four Ways of Life

Cultural theory is based on the axiom that what matters most to people is their relationships with other people and other people's relationships with them. It follows that the major choice made by people (or, if they are subject to coercion, made for them) is the form of culture—shared values legitimating social practices—they adopt. An act is culturally rational, therefore, if it supports one's way of life.

A basic proposition of this cultural theory (which cannot be demonstrated here) is an impossibility theorem: there are only a limited number of cultures that between them categorize most human relations.[3] Though we can imagine an infinite number of political cultures, only a relatively small number (here I shall work with four) are filled with human activity; the rest are deserted. What makes order possible is that only a few conjunctions of shared values and their corresponding social relations are viable in that they are socially livable.

The dimensions of cultural theory are based on answers to two questions: Who am I? and What shall I do? The question of identity may be answered by saying that individuals belong to a strong group, a collective, that makes decisions binding on all members or that their ties to others are weak in that their choices bind only themselves. The question of action is answered by responding that the individual is subject to many or few prescriptions, a free spirit or a spirit tightly constrained. The strength or weakness of group boundaries and the numerous or few, varied or similar, prescriptions binding or freeing individuals are the components of their culture.

Strong groups with numerous prescriptions that vary with social roles combine to form hierarchical collectivism. Strong groups whose members follow few prescriptions form an egalitarian culture, a shared life of voluntary consent without coercion or inequality. Competitive individualism joins few prescriptions with weak group boundaries, thereby encouraging ever new combinations. When groups are weak and prescriptions strong—so that decisions are made for them by people on the outside—the controlled culture is fatalistic (See Figure 1.1).

The social ideal of individualistic cultures is self-regulation. They favor bidding and bargaining in order to reduce the need for authority. They support equal opportunity to compete in order to facilitate arrangements between consenting adults with a minimum of external interference. They seek opportunity to be different, not the chance to be the same, for diminishing social differences would require a central, redistributive authority.

Hierarchy is institutionalized authority. It justifies inequality on grounds that specialization and division of labor enable people to live together with greater harmony and effectiveness than do alternative arrangements. Hence, hierarchies are rationalized by a sacrificial ethic: the parts are supposed to sacrifice for the whole.

FIGURE 1.1
Models of Four Cultures

Number and Variety of Prescriptions	Strength of Group Boundaries	
	Weak	Strong
Numerous and varied	Apathy (Fatalism)	Hierarchy (Collectivism)
Few and similar	Competition (Individualism)	Equality (Egalitarianism)

Source: Adapted from Douglas 1970; 1982.

Committed to a life of purely voluntary association, those from egalitarian cultures reject authority. They can live a life without coercion or authority only by greater equality of condition. Thus egalitarians may be expected to prefer reduction of differences—between races, or income levels, or men and women, parents and children, teachers and students, authorities and citizens.

An apathetic culture arises when people cannot control what happens to them. Because their boundaries are porous but the prescriptions imposed on them are severe, they develop fatalistic feelings: what will be, will be.[4] There is no point in their having preferences on public policy because what they prefer would not, in any event, matter.

But none of these modes of organizing social life is viable on its own. A competitive culture needs something—the laws of contract—to be above negotiating; hierarchies need something—anarchic individualists, authority-less egalitarians, apathetic fatalists—to sit on top of; egalitarians need something—unfair competition, inequitable hierarchy, nonparticipant fatalists—to criticize; fatalists require an external source of control to tell them what to do. "What a wonderful place the world would be," say the adherents of each culture, "if only everyone were like us," conveniently ignoring that it is only the presence in the world of people who are not like them that enables them to be the way they are. Hence, cultural theory may be distinguished by a necessity theorem: conflict among cultures is a precondition of cultural identity. It is the differences and distances from others that define one's own cultural identity.

Alone, no one has power over anyone. Power is a social phenomenon; power, therefore, is constituted by culture. But the form and extent of manipulation vary. Apathetic cultures are manipulated; fatalists live by rules others make and impose upon them. Manipulation is built into hierarchies; orders come down and obedience presumably flows up. The evocative language of New Guinea anthropology (the "big men" versus the "rubbish men") expresses the growth of manipulation in market cultures as some people cease to possess the resources to regulate their own lives. Egalitarians try to manipulate the other cultures by incessant criticism; they coerce one another by attributing inequalities to corruption and duplicity.[5]

To identify with, to become part of a culture, signifies exactly that: the unviable void of formlessness—where everything and therefore nothing is possible—is replaced by social constraint. Even so, individuals keep testing the constraints, reinforcing them if they prove satisfactory in practice, modifying or rejecting them, when possible, if unsatisfactory. It is individuals as social creatures, not only being molded by but actively molding their social context—shaping the maze as well as running it—that are the focus of cultural theory.

Suppose a new development occurs. Without knowing much about it, those who identify with each particular way of life can guess whether its effect is to increase or decrease social distinctions, impose, avoid, or reject authority—guesses made more definitive by observing what like-minded individuals do.[6] Of course, people may be, and often are, mistaken. To seek is not necessarily to find a culturally rational course of action. Gramsci's would-be capitalists may try to establish hegemony over others, but they are often mistaken about which ideas and actions will in fact support their way of life. They may, for instance, use governmental regulation to institute a pattern of cumulative inequalities that convert market arrangements into state capitalism, leading to their ultimate subordination. To be culturally rational by bolstering one's way of life is the intention, not necessarily the accomplishment.

If social life is the midwife of political preferences, how do people get from culture to preferences? Perhaps politics is too complicated to allow many people to figure out what they prefer.

"Preferences Need No Inferences"

An obstacle to the development of a theory of political preference formation is the view, dominant in psychology until recently, that cognition must precede affect. For if "preferences are formed and expressed only after and only as a result of considerable cognitive activity" (Zajonc, 1980, p. 154), then it would indeed be difficult to explain how most people, including many who engage only in minimal cognitive activity, at least in regard to politics, come to have so many preferences. If, however, one goes along with Zajonc and the considerable literature he cites "that to arouse affect, objects need to be cognized very little—in fact minimally" (p. 154), more promising theoretical avenues open up. Preferences, Zajonc continues, "must be constituted of interactions between some gross object features and internal states of the individual" (p. 159). But how, we may ask, do preferences get from object features to internal states?

The cultural hypothesis is that individuals exert control over each other by institutionalizing the moral judgments justifying their interpersonal relationships so they can be acted upon and accounted for. The prevailing view is that the interrelatedness among attitudes in the mass public is low, that is, people are inconsistent. Now, criteria of consistency expressing what ought to be related to what are not found in nature but, like the categories of culture I am expounding, are imposed in an effort to make sense out of people's political behavior. If these criteria are incorrectly or insufficiently specified, they will make people's opinions unrelated where another set of criteria would make them more consistent. When there is a question as to whether it is the people who do not understand what they are doing or we social scientists who do not understand the people, I am inclined to think that *we* have fallen down. All of us in social science are looking for bedrock, for the most basic value and factual premises that we can hypothesize as lying behind specific political and policy preferences. My claim is that this foundation lies in social relationships, roughly as categorized by political cultures.

How does the social filter enable people who possess only inches of facts to generate miles of preferences? What is it about cultures that makes them the kind of theories that ordinary folk can use to figure out their preferences? The ability of people to know what they prefer without knowing much else lies at the crux of understanding preference formation. Culture codes can be unlocked, I maintain, because its keys are social. By figuring out their master preferences, as it were—who they are and are not, to what groups they do and do not belong—they can readily figure out the rest. A basic reason people are able to develop so many preferences is that they actually do not have to work all that hard. A few positive and negative associations go a long way.

It is no more necessary for a person to verbalize about culture than it is necessary to know the rules of grammar in order to speak. The stock phrases "one of us" versus "one of them" goes a long way. Preferences might come from insight into general principles, but, because meanings have to be shared, ideologues and theorists often discover that their views are rejected or modified by others. Preferences can and do come sideways, from identifications, experiences, and conversations. What matters is not how preferences are first proposed (many are called but few are chosen) but how they are ultimately disposed through the presence or absence of social validation. It is not the lone individual, after all, who creates what is called *ideological constraint* ("one thing entailing another") among preferences but social interaction among adherents of a particular culture in contrast to other cultures whose identifiers have different preferences.

Heuristics

Brady and Sniderman, in pursuing a closely related question, "How . . . can citizens make sense of groups—that is, know which is relevant too which issue and which stands for what—without having to know a great deal about them?" (1985, p. 1073),

> focus on the operation of an affective calculus, or, as we call it, a *likability heuristic*. This calculus is organized around people's feelings toward groups such as liberals and conservatives. Clearly, many in the mass public lack a firm understanding of political abstractions. All the same, many know whom they like, and, equally important, they also know whom they dislike. If coherent, these likes and dislikes can supply people with an affective calculus to figure out the issue positions of strategic groups. We suggest that in this way many in the mass public can figure out who wants what politically without necessarily knowing a lot about politics. (pp. 1061-62)

The more people are able to choose sides—ours versus theirs—"the more they appreciate the differences between the issue positions of the two sides. What counts, then, is not how people feel toward groups, one by one; rather it is how they feel toward *pairs* of opposing groups" (p. 1075). It is precisely this pairing or, more accurately, this triangulation of rival cultures, I believe, that enables people to position themselves in political life.

Preferences may be rationalized from the top down, specific applications being deduced from general principles. But complexity of the causal chains invoked leaves people who lack a capacity for abstract thought unable to form preferences. Reasoning in steps is also slow. Without social validation at each step, moreover—which is difficult to achieve—the chain of reasoning may snap. Fortunately, faster methods are available. People can know what they believe or whom they trust without knowing how the belief is derived. Sniderman, Hagen, Tetlock, and Brady (1986) agree that such bottom-up processes operate on white attitudes toward blacks. In their view

> It may be nearer the mark to say that citizens, so far as their reasoning about policy is affect-driven, start at the beginning of the chain, taking account of their feelings toward blacks. Then, rather than working their way along the chain hierarchically, from general to specific, they skip over the intermediate links of the chain and go straight to its end. Having reached the end of the

chain, they work their way backwards and fill in the missing links. That is to say, not only do they reason forwards, from general to specific; they also reason backwards, from specific to general. And, because they can reason both forwards and backwards, with affect guiding them, they can indeed figure out what they think about questions, such as the reasons for racial inequality, they may not ordinarily think about. (Sniderman, et al., 1986, p. 33).

Mediating their perceptions through their cultures, people can grab on to any social handle to choose their preferences. All they need are aids to calculation.

"How," Paul Sniderman and his colleagues ask, "do people figure out what they think about political issues, given how little they commonly know about them?" (Sniderman et al., 1986, p. 2). They state that "three heuristics are of particular importance: affect (likes and dislikes); ideology (liberalism/conservatism); and attributions of responsibility (the so-called desert heuristic)" (p. 2). The desert heuristic is a version of system versus individual blame through which adherents of political cultures seek to hold others accountable for their behaviors. "Liberal" versus "conservative" stands as a surrogate for equality of condition versus equality of opportunity, that is, for the rivalry of egalitarian and market cultures. (When "liberal" meant "laissez-faire," its cultural associations were different.) The two heuristics—desert and ideology—are related: market forces blame individuals (they are undeserving); egalitarians blame the system (it is oppressive). Liberals dislike conservatives because they "blame the victims;" while conservatives dislike liberals because they encourage irresponsible behavior. All these aids to calculation are ideological (or, to use the anthropological term, cosmological) in the sense of rationalizations for preferred social relationships.

I agree entirely that

> it would be . . . a mistake merely to enumerate various heuristics; a mistake partly because they are likely to proliferate endlessly; a mistake more fundamentally because it is necessary to understand how these aids to judgment are themselves interrelated. It is, that is to say, necessary, to understand how people work their way, step by step, through a chain of reasoning. And to understand how they manage this, one must establish what they do first, then second, then third. (Sniderman et al. 1986, p. 47)

Cultural theory attempts to unify heuristics by suggesting that these chains have but one link: the internalization of external social relations.

Schemas

Another entry for understanding the formation of political preferences has now appeared—schema theory. According to Pamela Conover and

Stanley Feldman (1984), this theory views "people as 'cognitive misers' who have a limited capacity for dealing with information, and thus must use cues and previously stored knowledge to reach judgments and decisions as accurately and efficiently as possible" (p. 96). Political cognition is about how different schemas, such as party identification and economic class, organize perception. How are the schemas that form our preferences formed?

Although the logic of schemas may appear similar to that of cultural theory—a small number of premises generating a large number of premises—this appearance is misleading. Cultures are not disembodied ideas; they are not merely cognitive.[7] The mental activity has a purpose: the justification of desired social practices. It is both together, shared values indissolubly connected to social practices, that make up cultural theory. Comparing cultures means just that—comparing cultures as totalities with values and practices joined, not isolated.

The concept of schemas, essentially a reinvention of our old friend "attitudes" under a new name (like "political behavior" for "political science"), falls prey to the same disability—the endless proliferation of explanatory constructs until there is an attitude or a schema for every act. I think that the notion of schemas lacks a crucial element that cultural theory offers: a systematic context from which preferences can flow. Let us try a couple of quick tests.

Two Tests of Cultural Theory: Ideology and Risk

Cultural theory is open to tests normally applied in social science: *retrodiction* (Can it explain historical puzzles? [Ellis and Wildavsky 1986]) and *prediction* (Does it account for future events better than do other theories?). The degree of incorporation into group life and the degree of prescription can be measured so as to arrive at (forgive the cumbrous expression) intersubjective coder reliability. Jonathan Gross and Steve Rayner's book, *Measuring Culture*, does just that.

One test of cultural theory is conceptual-historical; I contend that the cultural categories described here fit far better in accounting for political preferences than the usual left-right, liberal-conservative dimensions. A second test is both contemporary and future-oriented; I claim that perception of danger and disposition toward risk—from technology and from acquired immune deficiency syndrome—are better explained and predicted by cultural theory than by competing theories.

A Confusion of Cultures: Competitive Individualism versus Egalitarian Collectivism

The single worst misunderstanding about U.S. politics, in my opinion, is the joining together as a single entity, called "individualism," two separate and distinct political cultures with opposing preferences for policies and institutions—competitive individualism and egalitarian collectivism. Between equality of opportunity (enabling individuals to accentuate their differences) and equality of results (enabling them to diminish their differences), there is a vast gulf.[8] To say that equal opportunity is empty without more equal results is to say that the latter is more important than the former.

Individualistic cultures prefer minimum authority, just enough to maintain rules for transactions, but they do not reject all authority; if it leaves them alone, they will leave it alone. While egalitarians also like to live a life of minimal prescription, they are part and parcel of collectives in which, so long as they remain members, individuals are bound by group decisions. This critical distinction in group-boundedness, the freedom to transact for yourself with any consenting adult vis-à-vis the requirement of agreement with group decisions, makes for a radical difference in the formation of political preferences.

The confusion to which I am objecting manifests itself more generally in the use of dichotomous instead of triangular designations of political cultures. The most infamous of these is left versus right. Left, or liberal, presumably designates a tendency toward greater use of central government for policy purposes, including an inclination to welfare state measures designed to be at least somewhat redistributive. Presumably, right, or conservative, signifies a disposition against central governmental intervention in the economy but of greater respect for collective authority. As political shorthand, these terms have their uses. But for purposes of political analysis, they obfuscate more than they clarify. The preference for greater use of government may stem from a hierarchical culture in which the individual is subordinated to the group. Yet the very same preference for central governmental action may be rooted in a desire to reduce all social distinction, including those on which hierarchies are based. Hierarchies and egalitarian collectives may, in certain historical contexts, ally themselves in favor of redistributive measures, yet they may also, at the same time, be bitter opponents in regard to respect for authority. For equalization of statuses would destroy hierarchy. It is not easy, as the Catholic Church is learning, to say that all forms of inequality are bad but that popes and bishops are good (Wildavsky, 1985a).

The left-right distinction is beset with contradictions. Hierarchical cultures favor social conservatism, giving government the right to intervene in matters of personal morality. Thus egalitarians may support intervention in the economy to reduce economic differences but not intervention in social life to maintain inequality. Libertarians, who are competitive individualists, oppose both social and economic intervention.

A division of the world into left and right that is equally inapplicable to the past and to the present deserves to be discarded. Efforts to read back the left-right distinction into U.S. history, for instance, succeed only in making a hash of it. In the early days of the republic, egalitarians pursued their objectives through severe restrictions on central government because they then regarded the center as monarchical, that is, hierarchical. Nowadays, after decades of dispute and struggle, they regard the federal government as a potential source for increasing equality. Their egalitarian objectives remain constant, but their beliefs about what will be efficacious instruments of policy vary according to the conditions of the times (cf. Banning, 1978).

Without knowledge of the historical context, and therefore, without being privy to the internal discussions through which shared meanings are worked out, it is impossible to explain why a given culture prefers certain institutional arrangements and instruments of policy at one time and different ones on other occasions. How, nowadays, make sense of the Republican alliance of economic free markets and social conservatism or the Democratic combination of statism with distrust of authority? Is it the "left" that supports the authority of central government and the "right" that opposes it, or is it the "right" that respects authority and the "left" that denigrates it?

The division of the political universe into liberals and conservatives, when based on innate tendencies toward change, is bound to be misleading because historical context alters whatever the various political cultures wish to preserve. Given the current extent to which most proposals for government action involve redistribution of income or regulation of business, it is not surprising that people who are opposed to these policies have learned to dislike change. So, when asked, they reply that most change is for the worse. People who prefer these programs respond that they like change. Were the tables turned, so that most legislation was in favor of maintaining social and economic differences, say anti-abortion and anti-inheritance taxes, contemporary liberals would learn that most change is bad and their conservative opponents that change is by and large good.

In a rich analysis of differences and similarities among left- and right-wing activists, McCloskey and Chong conclude that "thus, paradoxically, despite its patriotic fervour, spokesmen of the radical right are profoundly

34   A Theoretical Overview

antagonistic to the status quo" (1985, pp. 346-47). It is paradoxical if conservatism is identified with resistance to change but not if desire for change depends on perceived distance from desired behavior. Those who look at life from the conservative perspective "continually lash out against what they consider to be the government's conciliatory stance towards Communism, its support for welfare programmes, (which, in their view, rewards laziness and lack of initiative), its encouragement of moral depravity (sexual license, tolerance of abortion, homosexuality, etc.), and its lenient treatment of criminals" (pp. 346-47). If readers believe that, they might also want big changes. What kind of changes we want depends not nearly so much on our predispositions toward change per se, as if the destination did not matter, but on the gap between desired and actual power relationships.[9]

The further the distance between the real and the ideal, the greater the desire for rapid and radical change. If this proposition is correct, it should follow that "left" or "progressive" forces, when they consider existing power relationships more desirable than proposals for change, should cling to the status quo with as much passion as any reactionary who prefers the last century to the present. Wandering in the void between the Articles of Confederation (interpeted as minimal central authority) and the Constitutional Convention (which, by comparison, elevated central power), the antifederalists preferred the past to the future. Worrying about the return of monarchy or, just as bad, monarchical principles, the individualist Jacksonians (who believed that equality of opportunity, rigorously enforced, would lead to relative equality of condition), fought a rearguard action against commercial capitalism.[10] Similarly, the Federalist party (a hierarchy coalescing with market forces to form an establishment) fought to achieve and maintain the relative centralization of the Constitution—a radical change from the immediate past.

An advantage of cultural theory is that it handles both economic and social issues without strain. Conover and Feldman wrote that

> traditionally, it was assumed that the meaning of ideological labels and self-identifications could be easily summarized in terms of a single dimension: the liberal/conservative continuum. In recent years, however, this viewpoint has undergone some modification. The decade of the 1970s ushered in a variety of "social" issues—abortion, marijuana use, the Equal Rights Amendment—which did not fit easily into the traditional liberal/conservative spectrum. Because of this, many researchers now posit that the meaning of ideological labels and self-identification must be interpreted within the context of two liberal/conservative dimensions: one economic and one social. (Conover and Feldman, 1981, p. 168)

Using cultural concepts, however, makes such ad hoc category massage unnecessary. Individualists, being nonprescriptive and anticollectivist, prefer minimal economic and social regulation. Egalitarians, combining nonprescription with collective decision, prefer strong economic but weak social regulation. And adherents of hierarchy, joining hard group boundaries to heavy prescription, desire strong social and economic regulation. Presumably, students of cultural theory would not be surprised at a U.S. president who (combining market individualism with social hierarchy, like his party) urges compulsory urine tests to detect drug users.

Culture and Risk

Comparing perceptions of danger is especially useful as a test of cultural theory. The subject abounds with anomalies; it is fiercely contested; rival theories are already in place; and, best of all, readers can check out the performance of cultural theory vis-à-vis its competitors by reading their daily newspapers.

"Ideology," Samuel Barnes reminds us, "is one of the most frequently cited and inadequately understood subjects of empirical inquiry" (1966, p. 513).[11] In an effort to improve the situation, a number of anthropologists (Claude Levi-Strauss, Clifford Geertz, David Schreider, Ward Goodenough) have brought up the concept of cultures as "ideational codes" (Elkins and Simeon 1979). For Geertz, "culture is best seen not as complexes of concrete behavior patterns—customs, usages, traditions, habit clusters ... but as a set of control mechanisms—plans, recipes, rules, instructions (what computer engineers call 'programs')—for the governing of behavior" (Elkins and Simeon, 1979, p. 129). In order to give greater precision to this research program, Elkins and Simeon list a number of questions (regarding people's assumptions about causality, human nature, the "orderliness of the universe") that would get at who is controlling whom or what controlling which. Let us take one of their most explicit questions— "Should one try to maximize gains, or to minimize losses? In other words, what assumptions are made about the relative payoffs of optimistic or pessimistic strategies?" (p. 132)—and compare the kind of answers given by cultural theory with the kind given by other theories of risk-taking and risk-aversion.

In discussions of technological danger, one theory is that people are reacting to the actual dangers; they are risk-averse because the risks are rising. Another theory is psychological; there are risk-taking and risk-averse personalities. Still another theory concerns an intuitive sense of justice: people are willing to accept dangers that are voluntarily undertaken, but they reject risks that are imposed on them. In *Risk and Culture* (1982), Mary Douglas and I argue that perception of danger is a function of political culture, risk acceptance going along with approval of individualistic and hierarchical cultures and risk aversion with egalitarian opposition to these other cultures on the grounds they are coercive and domineering. Put briefly, we contend that the debate over risk stemming from technology is a referendum on the acceptability of U.S. institutions. The more trust in them, the more risk acceptance; the less trust, the more risk rejection.[12]

Consider, in this context of competing explanations, a variety of survey findings. The first, a survey of the feelings of a variety of elites about the safety of nuclear power plants shows, among other things, an immense gap (far greater than survey research usually produces) between nuclear energy experts (98.7%) and the military (86.0%) saying "safe" compared to relatively tiny proportions of leaders of public interest groups (6.4%), movie producers and directors (14.3%) and elite journalists (29.4%). The difference between people expected to support and to oppose authority is very great (Rothman and Lichter, 1985).

A second poll compares the general public to executives of small and large corporations and environmentalists on a variety of preferences related to politics and public policy. Whereas around two-thirds of the general public and executives favor a strong defense, only a quarter of environmentalists give it a high priority. Maintaining order in the nation gets around 80 percent or more from everyone else but just 47 percent from environmentalists. On an egalitarian issue, such as having more say at work, the situation is reversed. Two-thirds of environmentalists and the general public give it a high priority but only a quarter of executives in large companies and two-fifths in small ones do the same (Bloomgarden, 1983). Polarization of elites is evident.

A third study surveys business and ecology activists vis-à-vis the general public in West Germany in regard to their political positions on a left-right basis. It is obvious that ecologists and business elites are divided (twice as sharply as the general public) on ideological grounds. Similarly, in a study of voters in the United States Senate, Kalt and Zupan (1984) report, "It turns out that politicians consistently package liberalism and environmentalism together—the correlation between the LCV [League of Conservation Voters]'s and the ADA [Americans for Democratic Action]'s rating scales is 0.94." But why are the two found together?

Nuclear war may well be the greatest contemporary risk of all. Glenn Sussman (1986) has conducted a survey of U.S. and British anti-nuclear weapons activists in which he asked them to rate four goals: fighting rising prices, giving the people more say in important governmental decisions, maintaining order in the nation, and protecting freedom of speech. A priori there is no reason to believe that these activists have anything else on their minds except opposition to nuclear war. Yet approximately two-thirds valued more say in government as their first priority while maintaining order got less than 5 percent.[13] If one posits a cultural connection between this "anti" activism and opposition to existing authority as inegalitarian, the low ranking of "order" makes more sense. Viewing environmentalists as protestors against inegalitarian institutions (recall their concern about "endangered species" and corporations that cause cancer) helps us understand their political alliances. Because Berkeley constitutes a kind of political-medical museum for this purpose, we can observe a member of the city council, accused of spending too much time on foreign affairs instead of local concerns, respond, "You can't explain one without the other. If the money was not going to Central America, we would have the money to fix the sewers."[14]

Why, if we are dealing with a reasonable adaptation to emerging knowledge, do attitudes to political authority distinguish so well positions on nuclear power? Why, if there are major personality differences, do ecologists and environmentalists and businessmen divide so neatly on general ideological grounds? (See Table 1.1). Why, if it is the voluntary/involuntary distinction that matters, are there such strong and similar differences on public order and defense? Rooting explanation in adherence to several different ways of life rather than the usual left-right dichotomy, I think, makes more sense out of the data.

A striking contemporary example connecting culture and risk comes from perceptions of acquired immune deficiency syndrome. The more hierarchical the group, I hypothesize, following cultural theory, the more it minimizes technological danger as the price of progress while maximizing fear of casual contact with people who have AIDS. For, in its view, when people violate divine commandments, the Lord brings plague. Conversely, egalitarians tend to grossly overestimate the dangers from technology (on grounds that the social and economic relationships they dislike are bad for your health) while minimizng the dangers from casual contact with carriers of AIDS. Gays are good in the egalitarian view because they are anti-

TABLE 1.1
The Double Polarization in West Germany, 1980:
Left Versus Right

Respondents	(n)	Strong Left	Middle Left	Center	Middle Right	Strong Right	No Position
Ecology activists	(98)	9%	27%	29%	15%	3%	14%
General public	(1,088)	3	16	39	23	6	12
Business leaders	(130)	1	8	30	49	8	3

Source: Milbrath 1981a, 1981b; Lauber 1983.

38   A Theoretical Overview

establishment and because they reduce differences among people. Only cultural theory explains why, when we know a group's general ideology, we can tell how much danger they will impute to technology versus AIDS.

Now this conclusion, which is sure to be contested, depends on a substantial scholarly apparatus. How can laymen, that is, most of us most of the time, figure out what our preferences ought to be?

The Calculation of Preferences

How do people make so much, derive so many preferences, from so few clues? We know that most people are not interested in or knowledgeable about most issues most of the time. Consequently, the clues must be exceedingly simple. Even the highly educated and interested cannot know much about most matters of politics and policy, yet they are able to generate and express preferences when necessary. Indeed, the educated may well be getting more than their due from social scientists. Though they do know more about a few major issues than the less educated, people with high levels of formal education have many more preferences than they can know much, if anything, about. It is likely, therefore, that the highly educated have many more unfounded preferences than do those who have far fewer preferences about subject matter of which they know little.

Rational people, I have argued, support their way of life. By answering two questions, they are able to discover their cultural identity: Who am I? (free to negotiate or bound by a group?) and What should I do? (follow detailed prescriptions that vary with role or decide for myself?). Knowing who they are and are not—the cultures to which they do and do not belong—helps them to begin sorting their preferences. Cultural identity enables individuals to answer for themselves the crucial quantitative and qualitative questions about preferences: How many are they expected to have? What kind should these be? Fatalists know that they do not need to know anything (it won't matter) except what others tell them to do. They are prescribed to, not prescribing. Members of hierarchies can rule in whatever goes with their station and rule out whatever does not. By relying on others whose duty is to take care of whatever they neglect and by positive reinforcement of this nonparticipation—it is normative not to act above (or, for that matter, below) your station—both groups come to learn how much of what kind of preferences they are expected to have and how much they can leave to the authorities. Individualists are expected to figure out for themselves whether and to what extent participation is worthwhile. There is no onus on nonparticipation.[15]

Overall, it cannot be too difficult to arrive at preferences on most matters, because everyone does it. Just as we consider our connections with those who advocate petitions as a quick way of determining whether we would feel comfortable in signing, so do people in general learn how to know what they ought to prefer without knowing much about it. People who do not pay much attention to politics or public policy can nevertheless develop preferences by getting them from Berelson, Lazarsfeld, and McPhee's (1954) well-known ("But," as James Stimson [1986] reminds us, "we keep forgetting it") two-step flow of communication from activists to less attentive citizens. Stimson (1986) shows that "mass perceptions track activist positions." His thesis is that this social connection "accounts for the riddle of inattentive electorates who seem to know much of what they need to know to make policy informed choices." Wholly in the spirit of cultural analysis, Stimson concludes "that many of the things that matter in political life ... have very little to do with individual psychological processes. They are macro behaviors, such as mediated cognitions, that require for understanding a focus on 'between' rather than 'within' individual effects" (pp. 4, 19, 20). All I would add is that "between ... individual effects" *become* "within individual effects."

"System" or "person" blame are dead giveaways. The slightest clue as to whether the authorities and the institutions vis-à-vis individuals are at fault helps people know whether they want to go along with egalitarian or hierarchical or market policies. Anyone who thinks that attribution of blame to "the system" or to individuals is not diagnostic should consult Table 2 from Verba and Orren, in which they address that very question to a variety of elites. The differences could hardly be greater (Wildavsky, 1985b).

If it were necessary to go back to the cultural source each time a new preference is involved, building back up to the actual preference through some sort of chain of inference, many people could not manage the complexity; hence there would be far fewer preferences. Consequently, con-

TABLE 1.2
Poverty in the United States

Group	Fault of Poor	Fault of System
Business	57%	9%
Labor	15	56
Farm	52	19
Intellectuals	23	44
Media	21	50
Republicans	55	13
Democrats	5	68
Blacks	5	86
Feminists	9	76
Youth	16	61

Source: Verba and Orren 1985, p. 74.

certed political action would be a rarity. Near universal preference formation requires that preferences be inferred from all possible directions. Culture is the India rubber man of politics, for it permits preferences to be formed from the slimmest clue. By knowing who or what is involved, the arena or institution of involvement, the subject or object of involvement, people know whether they are supposed to have preferences and what these preferences ought to be.

What is it that enables everyone to come up with reliable solutions to the problem of preference formation whenever it arises? The one source all human beings know something about is their social relations.

Cultures Constitute Our Political Selves

> *Even when I carry out* scientific *work—an activity which I seldom conduct in association with other men—I perform a* social, *because* human act. *It is not only the material of my activity—like language itself which the thinker uses—which is given to me as a social product.* My own existence *is a social activity.*—Karl Marx

The view of human life as suffused in social relations makes the study of institutions central to political science. To use Elkin's apt expression, "Values are thus 'in' politics, not above or outside it. Hannah Arendt makes the point when she comments that in political activity 'the end (telos) is not pursued but lies in the activity itself'" (1985, pp. 17-18). Michael Oakeshott's (1962) insistence on good form and better manners, his "idioms of conduct," is based on the understanding that the purposes institutions create are expressed in their practices (Elkin, 1985, pp. 17-18). Elkin goes on to say that "the institutions are a way in which citizens experience each other and for different institutions the form of experience is different.... Political institutions constitute the citizenry in the sense of ... giving it an organized existence" (pp. 16-17). Wolin defines democracy as I would a political culture: "Democracy involves more than participation in a political process. It is a way of constituting power" (1986, p. 2). Similarly, Connell and Goot explain that "politics must be invoked not merely as the outcome of political socialization but a cause thereof as well" (Cook, 1985).

On the level of ideas, a research program on political culture would seek to increase our understanding of how opposed visions of the good life are selected, sustained, altered, and rejected. As social scientists following Robert Merton and knowing, therefore, that unanticipated consequences are a staple of social life, we want to understand what else we choose when we choose our political cultures. The Great Depression was a market phenomenon. The great holocaust was perpetrated by a hierarchy (the Nazi party) that tolerated no rivals. The second greatest holocaust was perpetrated by egalitarians (the Cambodian Khmer Rouge) (Jackson n.d.). Deadly visions as well as virtues are also rooted in our public lives. Appraising the consequences of living lives of hierarchical subordination or of the purely voluntary association of egalitarian liberation or of the self-regulation of individualistic cultures, at different times, on different continents, with different technologies, languages, and customs would be a remarkably productive research program. So would comparing cultures rather than countries or, put precisely, comparing countries by contrasting their combinations of cultures. Such a research program would enable us to test the general hypothesis that how people organize their institutions has a more powerful effect on their preferences than any rival explanation—wealth, technology, class, self-interest, tradition, you name it. The field of preference formation is open to all comers.

Notes

This essay is the presidential address presented on August 28, 1986 at the 82nd annual meeting of the American Political Science Association.

1. "Interest explanations are reason explanations. That is, when we explain an action by pointing to the interest that prompted, produced, or motivated it, we allude not to a human cause but to a *reason* or *ground* for acting" (Ball, 1979, p. 199). Reasons justify our behavior to others.
2. See a perceptive paper by James March for a list of the "the properties of tastes as they appear in standard prescriptive theories of choice." His list includes two properties of special interest: "Tastes are *relevant*. Normative theories of choice require that action be taken in terms of tastes." Yet, "tastes are *exogenous*. Normative theories of choice presume that tastes, by whatever process they may be created, are not themselves affected by the choices they control." As March observes, "each of these features of tastes seem inconsistent with observations of choice behavior among individuals and social institutions" (1978). Keith Hartley's paper "Exogenous Factors in Economic Theory" explains the general perspective, "Utility or preference functions are central to neoclassical economics and are assumed to be given" (1985, p. 470).
3. Michael Thompson and I are working on a book, *The Foundations of Cultural Theory*, that will attempt to demonstrate this proposition.
4. "Fatalistic attitudes are discernible in many Romanian literary creations, indeed even in folklore. The most famous Romanian folk ballad is 'Miorita,' or 'The Lamb.' It is the moving, beautiful story of a Moldavian shepherd whose fellow shepherds plot to kill him and steal his flock. Learning of the plan from his 'wonder lamb,' the young shepherd makes no move to keep it from being carried out. He serenely accepts his fate, comforted by the thought that he will be reunited with nature" (Shafir, 1983, p. 405).
5. Michael Thompson argues in favor of the viability of his hermit category, a marketlike people who, however, seek subsistance rather than domination, to

escape (a) from manipulating others and (b) from being manipulated themselves. I wish them luck (see Thompson, 1982).
6. A test of cultural consistency is provided by what March and Harrison call "Postdecision Surprise." When things go badly, the excuses should fit the culture. The market-oriented should accept more personal responsibility than the members of a hierarchy; egalitarians should blame "the system" (see Harrison and March, 1984).
7. Many more cultures can be conceived than can be lived in. As Robert Lane says, "Although for every act there is an implicit or explicit belief to justify the act, the reverse is not true; not every thought, fantasy, image, or argument is reflected in behavior, especially since thoughts often rehearse alternative lines of behavior. The world of behavior, therefore, is smaller than the world of thought; the two worlds are not isomorphic" (Lane, 1973, p. 97).
8. Another common confusion is mixing up egalitarianism with exclusive hierarchies because they are both passionate and moralistic in defending their strong group boundaries. The fervor of the exclusive hierarchy comes from its simplicity: only a small number of prescriptions are applicable to the vast diversity of life forms. Deviance (and, hence, deviants) are excoriated. The difference is that whereas egalitarians find society at fault because the distances between people are too large, members of hierarchies believe that the moral spaces are too small. The lack of complexity in small hierarchies means that they are left without sufficient variety for the objects they wish to control. Therefore, they get rid of people who do not fit either by labeling them as deviants or treating them as moral trash, thus removing them from those who deserve to be taken into account in making decisions. The alternative is to co-opt more people by creating moral, and hence social, compartments for them. Using variety to cope with complexity (as in Ashby's "Law of Requisite Variety"), however, greatly increases the size (the number and diversity of subunits) of the hierarchy. Once hierarchy is complex, as almost any but the most rudimentary government must be, its fervor declines because of the necessity of accommodating a broad range of values and adjusting relationships among more diverse life-styles.
9. For the reasons given, I disagree with the view that liberals are pro- and conservatives anti-change (see McCloskey and Chong, 1985; and Robinson, 1980).
10. The widespread belief among those who theorized about Jacksonian democracy in his time, a belief apparently shared by their supporters in the citizenry as well, was the equality of opportunity, meticulously followed, would lead to an approximation of equality of result. The operation of economic markets, unimpeded by the federal government, would eventually approximate real equality of condition as closely as innate differences in human ability permitted. At the very least, central government would not add artificial to natural inequality, thereby preserving representative government. Individuals would be allowed, indeed encouraged, to keep all gain that resulted from the unfettered use of their own talents. But everything artificial and unnatural, everything government imposed on man in his free state, such as charters, franchises, banks, and other monopolies, became anathema. It is this belief—not in equality undefined nor in just one kind of equality but in the *mutual reinforcement of opportunity and result*—that I think made the United States truly exceptional. Another way to describe U.S. exceptionalism is to say that liberty (i.e., individualism) is held to be compatible with equality (egalitarianism). Just as suppor-

ters of hierarchy understand that their organizations are likely to be rigid and egalitarians recognize that perfect equality is unattainable, so adherents of U.S. individualism understand that liberty can conflict with equality and vice versa. What they deny is that this conflict is immutable, and what they affirm is that their two cherished passions, liberty and equality, can reinforce one another (see Wildavsky, 1986).
11. The impasse comes through in these two comments: 1) "There is mounting evidence that mass publics do not react in ideological terms. It seems equally true that much contemporary political conflict has an ideological dimension" (Barnes, 1966, p. 513). "Although the conceptual and methodological problems with ideological belief systems are serious enough for Bennett to have called for a moratorium on empirical research pending the development of better concepts and measures, a 'cottage industry' of comments and rebuttals continues to fill the journals with challenges to each and every piece of research" (Hamill, Lodge, and Blake 1985, p. 850).
12. Often distinctions are made between active and passive risk (active risk being more voluntary and controllable by the individual and passive risk less voluntary and perhaps uncontrollable) in order to justify why certain risks are more and other risks less acceptable. But the distinction is misleading. One might imagine a static social system whose values, including its rules of accountability, were petrified. The people who conferred meaning on objects must have lived long ago, no one having come along since with any changes to make. Classifications are clearly labeled and immobile. Then, and only then, might one allocate dangers according to those that are active and voluntary and, therefore, properly subject to governmental regulation or prohibition. Once social change enters the picture, however, the active-passive distinction is constantly redrawn. We now see that egalitarians consider the dangers stemming from technology (nuclear power or chemical carcinogens) as a passive risk, while they perceive the dangers stemming from casual contact with sufferers from acquired immune deficiency syndrome as an active risk. At the very same time, adherents of hierarchy view the dangers of technology as actively chosen. To say a danger is voluntary is tantamount to saying it is acceptable; involuntary dangers imposed on passive people, by contrast, are unacceptable. Classification and decision are one and the same. If the anger against institutions were comprehensive enough, suicides would be owed redress by the implacable institutions that drive them to their undeserved and involuntary end. Just as "we the people" are the ones who confer meaning on these distinctions, so we are also the ones who change these meanings.
13. The actual figures are 1) more say: U.S. citizens 64.5 percent, British 68.6 percent; 2) order: U.S. citizens 4.3 percent, British 2.1 percent; 3) freedom of speech scored a little over 25 percent; 4) rising prices were 4 percent or below.
14. *Oakland Tribune*, 10 August 1986.
15. This discussion of the conception of apathy as a part of cultural bias is congruent with Carole Pateman's view that "there is more than one way to *interpret* the norm of political efficacy and the other norms and values traditionally associated with democracy; there is more than one view on what 'really' constitutes responsiveness of leaders and so on, and these differences in interpretation also encompass divergent notions of what form[s] of democratic institutions actually embody, or give practical expression to those norms and values" (1971, p. 304).

References

Ball, Terrence. 1979. "Interest Explanations." *Polity* 12(2):187-201.
Banning, Lance. 1978. *The Jefferson Persuasion*. Ithaca, NY: Cornell University Press.
Barnes, Samuel H. 1966. "Ideology and the Organization of Conflict: On the Relationship Between Political Thought and Behavior." *Journal of Politics* 28:513-30.
Berelson, Bernard R., Paul R. Lazarsfeld, and William N.McPhee. 1954. *Voting: A Study of Opinion Formation in a Presidential Campaign*. Chicago: University of Chicago Press.
Bloomgarden, Kathy. 1983. "Managing the Environment: The Public's View." *Public Opinion* 6: 47-51.
Brady, Henry, and Paul Sniderman. 1985. "Attitude Attribution: A Group Basis for Political Reasoning." *American Political Science Review* 79: 1061-78.
Burt, Ronald S. 1982. *Toward a Structural Theory of Action*, New York: Academic Press.
Conover, Pamela Johnson, and Stanley Feldman. 1981. "The Origins and Meaning of Liberal/Conservative Self-Identifications." *American Journal of Political Science* 25:617-45.
Conover, Pamela Johnson, and Stanley Feldman. 1984. "How People Organize the Political World." *American Journal of Political Science* 28:93-126.
Cook, Timothy E. 1985. "The Bear Market in Political Socialization and the Costs of Misunderstood Psychological Theories." *American Political Science Review* 79:1079-93.
Cotgrove, Stephen, and Andrew Duff. 1980. "Environmentalism, Middle-Class Radicalism, and Politics." *The Sociological Review* 28: 333-50.
Douglas, Mary. 1970. *Natural Symbols*. Harmondsworth: Penguin.
Douglas, Mary. 1982. *In the Active Voice*. London: Routledge & Kegan Paul.
Douglas, Mary. 1983. *Identity: Personal and Socio-Cultural*, Uppsala Studies in Cultural Anthropology, vol. 5, ed. Anita Jacobson-Widding, 35-46.
Douglas, Mary, and Aaron Wildavsky. 1982. *Risk and Culture*. Berkeley: University of California Press.
Elkin, Stephen. 1985. "Economic and Political Rationality." University of Maryland, College Park. Typescript.
Elkins, David J., and Richard E. B. Simeon. 1979. "A Cause in Search of Its Effect; or, What Does Political Culture Explain?" *Comparative Politics* 11:127-45.
Ellis, Richard, and Aaron Wildavsky. 1986. "A Cultural Analysis of the Role of Abolitionists in the Coming of the Civil War." University of California, Berkeley. Typescript.
Gross, Jonathan L., and Steve Rayner. 1985. *Measuring Culture*. New York: Columbia University Press.
Hamill, Ruth, Milton Lodge, and Frederick Blake. 1985. "The Breadth, Depth, and Utility of Class, Partisan and Ideological Schemata." *American Journal of Political Science* 29:850-68.
Harrison, J. Richard, and James G. March. 1984. "Decision Making and Postdecision Surprise." *Administrative Science Quarterly* 29:26-42.
Hartley, Keith. 1985. "Exogenous Factors in Economic Theory: Neo-Classical Economics." *Social Science Information* 24(3):470.
Jackson, Karl. N.d. *Rendezvous With Death: Democratic Kampuchea, 1975-1978*. Princeton, NJ: Princeton University Press. Forthcoming.

Kalt, Joseph P., and Mark A. Zupan. 1984. "Further Evidence on Capture and Ideology in the Economic Theory of Politics." *American Economic Review* 74:279-300.

Lane, Robert E. 1973. *Handbook of Political Psychology.* San Francisco: Jossey-Bass.

Lauber, Volkmar. 1983. "From Growth Consensus to Fragmentation in Western Europe: Political Polarization over Redistribution and Ecology." *Comparative Politics* 15:329-50.

Lindblom, Charles E. 1982. "The Market as Prison." *The Journal of Politics* 44:324-36.

March, James G. 1978. "Bounded Rationality, Ambiguity, and the Engineering of Choice." *Bell Journal of Economics* 9(2):587-608.

March, James G., and Johan P. Olsen. 1984. "The New Institutionalism: Organizational Factors in Political Life." *American Political Science Review* 78:734-49.

McCloskey, Herbert, and Dennis Chong. 1985. "Similarities and Differences between Left-Wing and Right-Wing Radicals." *British Journal of Political Science* 15:329-63.

Michael, R. T., and G. S. Becker. 1976." On the New Theory of Consumer Behavior." In *The Economic Approach to Human Behavior*, ed. G. S. Becker. Chicago: University of Chicago Press.

Milbrath, Lester W. 1981a. "Beliefs about Our Social Paradigm: Are We Moving to a New Paradigm?" Paper presented at the twenty-second annual conference of the International Studies Association, Philadelphia.

Milbrath, Lester W. 1981b. "The Relationship of Environmental Beliefs and Values to Politics and Government." Paper presented at the fourth annual conference of the International Society for Political Psychology, Mannheim, Germany.

Pateman, Carole. 1971. "Political Culture, Political Structure, Political Change." *British Journal of Political Science* 1:291-305.

Robinson, John, and John Holm. 1980. "Ideological Voting Is Alive and Well." *Public Opinion* 3:52-58.

Rothman, Stanley, and S. Robert Lichter. 1985. "Elites in Conflict: Nuclear Energy, Ideology, and the Perception of Risk." *Journal of Contemporary Studies* 8:23-44.

Shafir, Michael. 1983. "Political Culture, Intellectual Dissent, and Intellectual Consent: The Case of Romania." *Orbis* 27(1):393-401.

Sniderman, Paul M., Michael G. Hagen, Philip E. Tetlock, and Henry E. Brady. 1986. "Reasoning Chains: Causal Models of Policy Reasoning in Mass Publics." Stanford. Typescript.

Stimson, James A. 1986. "The Process of Perception of Party Issue Position: A Longitudinal and Regional Perspective." Paper presented at the annual meeting of the Midwest Political Science Association, Chicago.

Sussman, Glenn. 1986. "Postindustrialism and Anti-nuclear Weapons Activism." Paper presented at meetings of the Western Political Science Association, Eugene, Oregon.

Thompson, Michael. 1982. "The Role of the Centre." In *Essays in the Sociology of Perception*, ed. Mary Douglas. London: Routledge and Kegan Paul.

Thompson, Michael, and Michiel Schwarz. 1985. "Beyond the Politics of Interest." Paper presented at the thirteenth world congress of the International Political Science Association, Paris, France.

Verba, Sidney, and Gary R. Orren. 1985. *Equality in America: The View From the Top.* Cambridge, MA: Harvard University Press.

46   A Theoretical Overview

Wildavsky, Aaron. 1985a. "Idolatry and 'The Poor.'" *Catholicism in Crisis* 3:42-44.
Wildavsky, Aaron. 1985b. "A World of Difference: The Public Philosophies and Political Behaviors of Rival American Cultures." University of California, Berkeley. Typescript.
Wildavsky, Aaron. 1986. "Industrial Politics in American Political Cultures." In *The Politics of Industrial Policy*, ed. Claude E. Barfield and William A. Schambra, 15-32. Washington, DC: American Enterprise Institute.
Wolin, Sheldon S. 1986. "Democracy and the Welfare State: Staatsrason and Wohlfahrtsstaatsrason." University of Wisconsin, Madison. Typescript.
Zajonc, R. B. 1980. "Feeling and Thinking: Preferences Need No Inferences." *American Psychologist* 35:151-75.

Part II
Hierarchical Collectivism

Introduction

Hierarchical collectivism is characterized by many prescriptions and strong boundaries. Describing the basic features of this political culture in his essay "The Three Cultures: Explaining Anomalies in the American Welfare State," Wildavsky points out that it strives:

> to impose order centrally through a division of labor. Inequality is deemed necessary to safeguard the collective, each element being taught to sacrifice for the whole. Envy is controlled by teaching people their places, by reserving ostentation for collective bodies (such as the state or church) and by examples of sacrificial behavior by the elite.

This perspective along with that of competitive individualism make up what constitutes "the modern social establishment." It, in turn, is opposed by the egalitarians (Wildavsky used to call them "egalitarian sectarians" but dropped the term "sectarian" to avoid certain confusions which stem from that term).

Other characteristics of hierarchical collectivism are:

1. Risks are undertaken for the gain of the group, not of individuals.
2. Leadership is a function of hierarchical relations.
3. Blame is assigned to "deviants" who cause problems because they have been improperly socialized.
4. Inequality is seen as natural and it imposes responsibilities on those on the top of the scale. All are deemed equal before the law, however.
5. Fairness involves being treated correctly according to one's station in life.
6. Wealth is created by collective sacrifice for group gain.
7. Scarce resources are allocated by bureaucratic means.
8. Loyalty is generated by results, which places the survival of the whole ahead of danger to any of its parts.
9. Uncertainty is reduced by intervening in the economy, to generate desirable results, and by clarifying and reducing ambiguities as far as roles are concerned.

Why might people be attracted to collectivist hierarchies? They seem, at first sight, antithetical to such basic American values as individualism (and the "achievement" orientation) and egalitarianism. Wildavsky offers several suggestions. First, by creating values which affirm the notion that to achieve some desired goal such as glory or prestige, the sacrifice of individualism is worth it. Second, people may be put off by the stresses and strains generated by competitive individualism. And finally, the structure of hierarchies may offer people the promise of support and finding "meaning" in their lives.

I have categorized the essays by Bogart, on public opinion, and Dutton, on new technologies and politics, as hierarchical collectivist because they both deal with elites and entities which have attributes closest to hierarchical collectivism, as described by Wildavsky. The fit may not be perfect, but it is a pretty good approximation.

2

Mass Communication and World Opinion

Leo Bogart

"World opinion" is a term that persistently recurs in international polemics, a kind of updated version of "*Gott mit Uns*" invoked to enhance national self-righteousness while it presumably saps the will of the opponent. Yet there is little support for the notion that world opinion exists in objective reality.[1] This essay examines the forces that promote the flow of ideas across international boundaries and the restrictions on that flow. It discusses the growth of international polling, the limits on the comparability of polls conducted in different information environments and the distinction between transient opinions and values deeply rooted in culture. It reflects on the relationship between information and opinion, and on the role of the mass media as vehicles of current political information across national lines. This brings up the subject of imbalance in the movement of information through the world's media systems, a subject closely linked to the theme of economic development. In conclusion, two major research projects are proposed.

Opinions and Frontiers

Public opinion requires a public definable in terms that are understood by its members and accepted by outsiders. The concept of a public simply cannot apply to the whole of humanity, divided as it is by geographic barriers, by political boundaries, and by formidable cleavages of language, culture, and interests that make most people largely oblivious to events beyond their immediate ken.

The concept of public opinion has permeated political thought for centuries, but the notion of a world public opinion is of very recent origin. Not very long ago the world was conventionally divided between its "civilized" parts and those that were considered to be sunk in barbarism. As long as much of it was under colonial rule and without even the fiction of self-government, it was impossible to conceive of public opinion on a global scale. Only with the ending of the colonial system in the aftermath of World War II did it become plausible to think of mankind generally as a comprehensive assemblage of national polities.

The creation of the United Nations was attended by a prodigious output of manifestoes and proclamations whose grandiose vocabulary was adapted from the language of the American and French revolutions. This made it possible for the first time to think of a world system paying lip-service at least to the tenets of democracy. The Soviet Union, which had learned the utility of democratic terminology during the Popular Front days of the 1930s, adopted it in the Newspeak of the "People's Republics" it set up to consolidate its wartime conquests.

Both the theory and the practice of a democratic society require the recognition of public opinion as a political force, while non-democratic governments may choose either to acknowledge it or to ignore it. One must search hard to find benighted autocracies like Saudi Arabia, which can still get along without constitutional formalities that suggest, if only in theory, acceptance of the principle that rulers should be responsive to the popular will. The jargon of the international organizations has given that principle the appearance of universality.

Even the report of UNESCO's International Commission for the Study of Communications Problems, chaired by Sean MacBride, raises the question of whether world public opinion, "this cosmopolitan community of national publics," exists.

> If it exists, it must be admitted that it is still in the process of formation, and thus is fragile, heterogeneous, easily abused and still unable to be considered as an authentic power ... World public opinion is being gradually formed either around national problems common to a large number of countries (under-development, hunger and malnutrition, social inequalities, the energy crisis, youth problems) or around questions of international scope (cooperation for development, general disarmament, the establishment of a new economic order, decolonization, etc.) If "world public opinion" is still at its initial stage, it is possible all the same to identify certain issues around which it is taking concrete shape. World public opinion desires the preservation of peace through international agreement ... is opposed to torture and inhuman treatment ... is opposed to privilege on the basis of race or colour ... wishes to see action taken more urgently to remedy the conditions of poverty, hunger and backwardness[2]

This report, despite its earlier hesitation, flatly concludes that "world public opinion is gradually becoming a reality" and invokes it to support the position that the function of media is to change the world rather than to report on it: "Concerning all of these problems, the media have a moral and political responsibility to take account of public attitudes and opinions."

The very notion of a world public opinion conjures up the appealing, if utopian dream of a world community, a "global village" in Marshall McLuhan's felicitous though inappropriate term, with all its inhabitants linked in a sense of kinship, shared responsibilies, and common fate. It is logical, therefore, that the idea of a New World Information Order has been linked to the idea of a worldwide economic community in which the wealthier nations would share their good fortune with the impoverished ones, moved by the same generous sentiments that operate within an extended family. But the altruism that the wealthy nations manifest on occasions of disaster in remote parts of the world is not normally sustained on a continuing basis, when calamity is so persistent that it is no longer newsworthy. Major programs of international economic assistance are in many (though not in all) cases conducted for reasons of strategic national self-interest rather than out of a genuine desire to share the wealth.[3]

Even on what may be regarded as an unambiguous conflict between good and evil, it is impossible to find a unanimity of response across international lines. During World War II, it was comforting for the Allies to think of the Axis powers as acting in defiance of world opinion. In the United States, at least, it was easily assumed that they were hated, not only by their embattled enemies, but in occupied countries and in neutral ones, as well. Yet in retrospect it is quite apparent that no such universal sentiment really existed. In some neutral areas like Latin America there was general apathy, while the elite were divided in their allegiance; in such countries as France, Yugoslavia, and Indonesia important blocs of the population cooperated with the occupying power. The Nazi collaborator Subhas Chandra Bose is honored as a hero in today's India.

More recently, the shooting down of Korean airliner Flight 007 by the Soviets in 1983 was perceived in the United States as an act that had aroused worldwide indignation. In fact, from the outset Soviet disinformation tactics deflected the blame onto the victims, thus creating uncertainty rather than revulsion.

Subjected to scrutiny, world opinion quickly breaks down into bloc opinions, and even bloc opinions turn out to be far from monolithic. Around the world, certain values are, indeed, shared almost universally, like the yearning of most people for peace and a better life. But even these "universal" values must be reinterpreted for Shiite Moslems who extol the glory of death in Holy War, or for Hindus who accept the ordained fate of earthly existence and the inevitability of future incarnations. Even when there is agreement on fundamental values, there are sharp differences on the tactics for achieving them and often in diagnosing the obstacles that stand in the way.

It is not surprising that in spite of their cultural kinship, the inhabitants of the United States and the Soviet Union, or for that matter, France and Bulgaria, generally support their respective governments on international issues. Their differing opinions reflect the political, social, and information systems in which they live. It is hardly surprising that such differences should be all the more profound between inhabitants of Benin and of New Guinea, whose cultural common ground is to be found only in the multiple heritage of European influence.

Even when countries resemble each other, like Canada and the United States, Belgium and Holland, Colombia and Venezuela, their outlook on important political issues is often profoundly different. Striking differences in opinion emerge quite rapidly in nations that have been artificially split into separate states, as in the cases of West and East Germany, South and North Korea, or (for certain tribal groups like the Fulani) Nigeria and the Cameroons.

For years in the corridors of international organizations, nations have been assigned to the first or industrially developed capitalist world, the second or "socialist" world, or to the third "less-developed" world. Such designations are commonly made without the use of quotation marks, as though the classification made evident sense. Yet just as there is no world opinion, there is no first, second, or third world opinion.

The only sense of community shared by the people of third world countries derives from their common sense of disadvantage and isolation. This may be sufficient as a basis for temporary voting alliances in international bodies, but it cannot serve to create a constituency of opinion. The expressed opinions of the governing elites in these countries tend to agree only in their reflex response to key verbal symbols ("neocolonialism," "transnational corporations"), or with respect to significant ideological trigger points like South Africa and Israel. In international political forums the spokesmen for less developed countries are often given to making statements that appear to coincide in their premises and orientation, but these diplomatic utterances seem to have little relationship to any informed public opinion at home.

The very notion of public opinion is in itself utterly inconsistent with the political systems that prevail in most of the less developed countries. An informed public opinion can take shape only on the foundation of mass literacy, access to a variety of sources of information, and widespread discussion of public issues. These conditions are conspicuously lacking in countries that are impoverished, both in material wealth and in access to information and that are, moreover, characteristically under dictatorial rule.

In 1985 the number of countries with full political freedoms represented about one-third of the total number of sovereign states. But this does not mean that public opinion exists only in those countries. In some nations where freedoms are restricted, like Chile, Taiwan, Indonesia, and South Africa, opinion is allowed free rein with respect to issues on which the government has not defined a policy. People are even permitted to speak their minds freely on issues that are peripheral to government policy and on which dissent from the official line can be tolerated. In Communist countries, differences of opinion are permitted, or even encouraged, on a considerable variety of subjects, and public opinion polling has recently achieved a legitimacy it formerly lacked.

What Polls Measure and Don't

It is easy to confound the results of polls with public opinion, which existed long before polls were invented. Public opinion may be found in the changing climate of discussion and debate rather than in the sum total of individual answers to pollsters' questions. In the West, most questions that pollsters ask deal with matters that have nothing to do with politics, or at least with politics that carry a strong emotional charge. So it is not surprising that pollsters go about their business even under dictatorships, inquiring about marketing and consumer behavior, media exposure and content preferences, attitudes toward work, hobbies, interests, sporting and cultural events, and all the other topics of conversation beyond politics, with which people are accustomed to pass the time.

It is by now commonplace for cross-national polls to be conducted in which identical (or at least similar) questions are asked of people in societies with rather different political systems. If membership in the World Association for Public Opinion Research or the International Association for Mass Communication Research may be taken as a criterion, public opinion surveys of one kind or another are currently being conducted in seventy-seven countries. Sometimes these polls are done collaboratively by different research organizations for a single commercial client; sometimes they are done through a network of associated polling organizations, like Gallup or International Research Associates. Sometimes they are done by a number of cooperating academic research organizations.

Such polls assume that there is a common base of cultural values that makes the same questions meaningful in countries with different languages, life styles, and institutions. It is possible both in the West and in the Soviet bloc to ask a question like, "Is it a good idea or not such a good idea for mothers of children below school age to hold a job?" We can anticipate that the answers will vary widely, not only within countries but among countries, depending on the standard of living, the percentage of women actually in the work force, the unemployment rate, the family structure, the system of social services, and the strength of tradition. But it would be meaningless to ask such a question in Africa or Asia in societies where women work as a matter of course, regardless of what age their children are, and where their work is done within the framework of the household economy rather than through outside employment.

For an international opinion to exist would require some interaction among the opinion-holding publics of separate nations. This would presume that these publics share both a common fund of information and the sense that a particular subject is salient. They must also employ the same structure of thought to accommodate debate and form opinions. Without such a common structure, similar-sounding slogans may still be mouthed, but they will convey different meanings in different national contexts.

One question that makes sense in any country that follows the Western calendar would be along the lines asked by Gallup International in six countries (the United States, Mexico, Brazil, Great Britain, Japan, and West Germany) in 1980: "So far as you are concerned, do you think that 1981 will be better or worse than 1980?" (The proportions saying "worse" ranged from 10% in Mexico to 48% in Britain, presumably reflecting local economic conditions at the time, though national character may also have influenced the results.)

Similarly, opinion surveys conducted by Radio Free Europe among travelers from the Eastern European countries show that they by no means represent a uniform set of views. The percentage saying (in 1984) that life had changed for the better "in the past twenty years or so" ranged from 3 percent of the Romanians to 62 percent of the Hungarians. (The proportions were 5% for the Poles, 12% for the Czechoslovaks and 23% for the Bulgarians.) Their attitudes toward their own governments and toward the Soviet Union and the United States varied considerably. These variations reflect the individual countries' different characteristics and developmental stages, their political and social histories, and the separate evolution of their own economic systems under the rule of Communism. (To some degree they probably also reflect differences in the proportions of their residents who are permitted to travel and to be interviewed in such surveys.)

A 1982 Gallup International poll for *Newsweek* asked people in five Western European countries, "How much confidence do you have in NATO's ability to defend Western Europe against an attack?" The proportion saying they had a "great deal" or a "fair amount" of confidence ranged from 61 percent in West Germany to 39 percent in France. This is quite a range, but it occurs within a common universe of information and discourse; we can be reasonably sure that the question carried the same meaning wherever it was asked.

The emergence of the European Economic Community provides a unique example of multinational political activity, in which distinct national constituencies have been forced to weigh their individual selfish interests against the mutual good, with a common voting timetable and debating structure. Still, a study of elections to the European Parliament found considerable variation among nine country polls in the level of interest they aroused and in approval of the time devoted to them on television.[4]

On less newsworthy, less widely discussed subjects, opinions are held only by members of informed elites, but this is true, after all, for domestic issues as well as those that excite international interest. No country is without an opinion-holding elite, but its size (proportionate to the whole population) and the informedness of its members vary considerably.

An issue that is a matter of broad public opinion in one country often evokes opinions from only a small interested majority in other countries. How widely held must such opinions be in order to qualify, in effect, as manifestations of international public opinion?

A great many opinions measured in surveys simply reflect agreement or disagreement with positions that are attributed to authorities in whom different sectors of the public have varying degrees of confidence. When people are polled on complex questions of public policy, many of them tend to respond along the lines that they associate with a particular leader, party, or faction. But they do so because they have accepted these authorities (as a result of self-interest, family loyalty, local tradition, personal admiration, empathy, or some other non-principled cause). They don't answer as they do because they have themselves thought through the particular problem, familiarized themselves with the facts, and come to a reasoned conclusion as to what the best policy should be.[5] They are generally predisposed to support their own national leaders and national policies, especially when these face challenges from other nations.

Opinions can only be taken seriously when those who hold them have a sense of responsibility and power—a sense that their opinion "counts." When questions are asked about issues on which opinions are polarized and emotionally intense, they tend to be answered in terms of "us" and "them." We distinguish the opinions appropriate to our own group from those we consider appropriate for another, and those who fail to share these conventional views may be pilloried as renegades.

However, our opinions are hardly limited to such keenly felt "gut issues." If asked, most of us are willing to express opinions about subjects in which our own interests or group identities are not clearly evident.

In almost every country where political polling is a common practice, the public is periodically asked which side it favors in international disputes or wars, because such conflicts generate news coverage, attention, and discussion in which opinions are formed. As outsiders, we are ready to take sides in a tribal conflict in Zimbabwe or in a border dispute between Venezuela and Guyana.

The definition of one's own self-interest is critical to the formation of opinion about an external event. Before Pearl Harbor, many Americans preferred to regard the war in Europe as one between rival imperialisms. They chose to reject the probable scenarios that would result, and the consequences in their own lives, if Hitler won rather than the Allies.

While it is possible to be emotionally disengaged from the subjects on which we voice opinions, that disengagement gives the opinions less weight than they might carry when we acknowledge that our own interests are involved. For this reason, the opinions of the Japanese about American policy in Central America must be read differently than the opinions of Americans on the same subject. Americans, whether or not they disagree with their government's policy, know that it will have direct consequences for them. For the Japanese the consequences are much more remote, and perhaps cannot be traced at all. Though the Japanese may not feel responsible for what the American government does, their opinions on the subject are known to their own government, which may exert its own limited influence through diplomatic channels or in the course of international meetings. Thus even the opinions of outsiders may have an effect in certain situations. (Clearly what the Japanese think about Soviet policy in Central America would be of largely academic interest.)

The 1984 election campaign in the United States received extensive worldwide news coverage. Given the importance of the United States to Western Europe, this may have suggested that Western Europeans should have been able to form opinions of the candidates' personalities and policies comparable to those of the American public, which was faced with the actual task of voting. It was surprising therefore to find in an international Gallup Poll held a week before the American election that half the West Germans and French, and one-third of the British public said they did not care who won.[6] Among those who were not indifferent, the French preferred Reagan by a wide margin, while in West Germany and Britain, support for Reagan and Mondale was virtually identical.

While the opinions of Europeans could translate themselves into actions at a much more attenuated level than those of American voters, these actions must not be considered to be without significance. Since the foreign policies of these countries are conducted within the bounds of what their own voters will tolerate, the reaction of those voters to an American president obviously has consequences in international political alignments. (Greek Prime Minister George Papandreou, for example, edged his country to the margin of NATO in the mid-1980s with a keen awareness of what the domestic polls showed.) But if, in democracies, a national public opinion may have a bearing on international issues, that does not in itself give public opinion an international scope.

Opinion and Information

Polls constantly remind us that people who are informed on a subject have different views than those who are unfamiliar with the facts. Opinion Research Corporation, in a regional survey, asked "Which of these groups do you think should own and operate the electric light and power company?" Those respondents (about one-third) who knew that the local utility was privately owned but government-regulated favored private ownership 82 percent to 16 percent, but among those who were unaware of this, only 12 percent favored private ownership and 57 percent favored government ownership.[7] A CBS News study conducted after the October 1973 war asked respondents about their knowledge of U.S. dependence on Arab oil and of Israeli territorial gains since 1948. Of those who were familiar with the facts, 41 percent thought that Arab intentions were to destroy Israel and 45 percent that they were to regain land lost in 1967. Among those who answered both factual questions incorrectly, only 15 percent thought Arab intentions were to destroy Israel and 59 percent said they were to regain the land.

To hold opinions presupposes prior information. The information may be factual, it may be interpretative, or it may consist of an overriding structure of belief into which facts can be assimilated. Moreover, the information cannot be idiosyncratic or private; it must be shared. Opinions are found even in primitive societies where information is passed along in conversation or observed and acquired through patterns of non-verbal behavior. Our own extended society utilizes a complex communications technology to diffuse information. Public opinion exists within a country when the entire population has access to the same knowledge. Where only a limited part of the population has access to it, as in peasant societies with a small educated class, it makes more sense to speak of elite opinions than of public opinion per se.

On extremely complicated matters where expert or technical knowledge is involved (for example, on specific questions of fiscal policy or of nuclear defense and disarmament) people's opinions are likely to reflect their alignment with the groups or spokesmen whom they associate with one position or another in a continuing debate. In an advanced society, most people probably assume that they could acquire the information necessary to make better informed judgments *if* they wanted to go to the necessary trouble. But their investigation of the cosmic issues is inevitably postponed as they pursue the more immediate problems on their personal horizons. In the meantime they put their trust in those who wield authority or those with whom they feel most congenial and comfortable, on the assumption that they must surely know what is best.

In an open, media-rich society like the United States, the amount of information potentially available is staggering, and considerable effort is required to sift through it for items pertinent to any judgment that an individual may be asked to render. Needless to say, what is accessible with effort is not the same as what is routinely exposed to the average person. The differences between advanced and undeveloped societies in actual exposure to mass media are not nearly as dramatic as they are in the range of choice.

The population generally (though not in every country) has greater access to information about its own domestic affairs than is available in other countries. However, people in other countries may have enough information about those affairs to form an opinion about them, (as I indicated earlier in referring to European preferences for American presidential candidates). A particular individual in Country X who has access to good information about a policy question being discussed in Country Y (and who has the means to overcome any language barrier) may very well form opinions on that question, while the general public in his own country may be totally oblivious to it.

Communications that are accessible to masses of people in some countries are accessible only to a minority in others. Information that is accessible in depth from a variety of viewpoints and sources in some countries is available elsewhere only in truncated, unambiguous form: as bulletins without interpretations.

Literacy must be considered a prerequisite for an informed public opinion, but it is hardly essential to the formation of opinions as such. Only between half and two-thirds of the world's adults are classified as literate, at least by the varying standards set by the statistical bureaus of their respective countries. Surely the rest of the world's people have opinions that are no different in nature or intensity. Many of them, through radio and television, have direct access to news that covers broad horizons, not just the kind that is limited to word of mouth. While a handful of shy, isolated tribal peoples still pursue an autonomous existence in obscure patches of tropical rain forest, the masses of the world's peasants are today aware that there are connections between their own lives and those of other more distant people and powers. However vague, crude, or inaccurate their perception may be of their own national identity or that of others, they still define the larger forces around them as good or bad; they differentiate among alternative paths along which the future might carry them. Thus they have political opinions, whose consequences have been felt in every peasant revolution from ancient times to the present day.

Yet the density and complexity of an individual's opinions, the range of subjects on which they are held, obviously are determined by the amount of information to which he has access, and the amount of thought and discussion that information has generated. An illiterate mountain villager in Bolivia may never have heard of Sri Lanka and certainly cannot have an opinion on the ethnic strife there. An illiterate workman in La Paz may have heard a news bulletin on the radio or caught a film clip on the TV news, but this may barely have brought the subject to his awareness. An educated resident of the city, with access to more complete and varied reports in print, would be more likely to have formed an opinion, if only by analogy to situations with which he is more familiar.

Pollsters can query people on any silly subject they like, but opinions can be held only on matters of knowledge, and public opinion presupposes matters of common knowledge. An important function of public opinion research is to explore the degree of public ignorance or apathy on subjects that may objectively be of great importance, and which the public really should know about. In 1983 a CBS–New York Times poll found that only one American in four knew that national policy was to support the government of El Salvador and only one in eight knew that it was to support the rebels in Nicaragua. People ignore information that is within their reach on matters that they do not consider significant or meaningful. Their very ignorance may therefore be regarded as an expression of their opinion that the subject is not important. But this is true only to the degree that they do have access to information about it and choose to pay no attention. It cannot be said to apply to those situations in which information is inaccessible to them because of their isolation, their economic or social handicaps, or the imposition of political controls on what they can learn. The public's unfamiliarity with particular facts or issues can only be interpreted if we know what pertinent information is actually available to it.

Opinion and Cultural Values

The idea of a world public opinion is at odds with the notion of a *Weltanschauung*, a distinctive and comprehensive outlook on the world that makes sense only if it is contrasted with alternative outlooks, characterizing other cultures and other periods.

When opinions are elicited on questions that have nothing to do with politics ("What is your favorite dessert?" "Who is the greatest person who ever lived?"), the answers are likely to be expressions of national character and reflections of national cultures and value systems. Opinions are themselves a part of the culture, controlling the direction and pace of change. For example, American culture in all its aspects has been transformed by the changed technology of birth control, by the entry of women into the work force, by the subsequent changes in sex roles and family structure. All of these profound changes are mirrored in changes of attitude as well as of behavior. They are reflected at the level of opinion in the trends shown by the Gallup Poll's periodic inquiries about the acceptability of premarital sex.

Since Roman times it has been possible to speak of a European culture whose geographic boundaries have shifted over the centuries but in which people have shared certain systems of behavior, thought, ritual, and technology. Countries like the United States and New Zealand, geographically separate from the contiguous core culture of Europe, are nonetheless firmly part of it, though each contains a distinctive minority subculture. The cultures of countries like Russia and the mestizo nations of South America have reflected a blending of different traditions, while Japan and Thailand have been culturally homogeneous and free-standing.

Even within a society like that of Japan, there are subcultures, which reflect the variety of environments, roles, and relationships of the society's individual members. There are varying opinions, not only among these groups of the population, but within each of them. The lack of unanimity is much more striking when we look at more complex and culturally heterogeneous societies like those of the United States or the Soviet Union.

But if culture does not determine opinions, it shapes them. Just as subcultures exist within cultures, so culture groupings transcend national borders and shade into each other. In transitional zones, the features of two different culture areas often coexist. They may be represented by different ethnic elements (castes) or social classes within the same society; they may even appear in different roles or aspects of the lives of the same individuals. These differences are inevitably reflected at the level of opinion.

Communication within culture areas, in spite of national rivalries and animosities, has always been facilitated by the existence of shared values, which lead to a renewal of ties even after the most brutal wars. (We can see this in the postwar relationships of France and Germany, of China and Japan.)

The contagion of ideas spread the revolutions of 1787 and of 1848 throughout Europe. These revolutions stopped at the outer limits of their cultural communities and had no significant repercussions on other continents. In no way could they be termed a movement of world opinion.

Opinions are volatile; cultures outwardly change but do not change easily in their innermost aspects. It is not surprising that the traumatic reestablishment of what Lenin once described as "infantile communism" in China was labeled a "Cultural Revolution" and that the principal objects of its attack were ancient philosophy and art. Icons were also smashed during the Bolshevik Revolution and the Protestant Reformation. But subsequent events have shown how difficult it is to change long-rooted values that are embodied in family structure and in traditional forms of intimate social intercourse.

The fundamental lineaments of a culture remain intact, even when, as in Japan, significant adaptations are made to incorporate imported customs and techniques. Twenty-eight years after the departure of the Dalai Lama from Tibet, and the attempted extirpation of the monastic system, visitors to that country encounter a widespread loyalty to traditional religious institutions, openly manifested after the relaxation of Chinese Communist repression in the era of Deng Xiao Ping.

This does not mean that institutions imposed by force can not become acceptable as they become familiar, and as new generations find any alternatives to be unthinkable. Opinion surveys on politically sensitive subjects are either not permitted under dictatorships, or else produce results of dubious validity. But a unique opportunity to conduct unfettered research occurred under the short-lived Dubcek regime in Czechoslovakia, during the "Prague Spring" of 1968. An opinion poll found that only 5 percent of the people wanted to return to capitalism. After only twenty years of the alternative, few wanted to endure another stressful transformation. (However 86% approved of a vote by the National Assembly to abolish censorship, and 91% approved of rehabiliation for the victims of purges in the Stalinist era. Political values had remained steadfast, even if the old economic system had lost acceptance.)

Political institutions are cultural creations, and in turn shape the culture, but cultural phenomena have far wider currency than political ideas. When there are common cultural heroes and interests, or a shared familiarity with the same universal symbols of consumption, this hardly means that there are also common political values. The names of Coca-Cola, Shell, Mickey Mouse, and Luciano Pavarotti resonate with identical meanings for people in widely separated societies, but this has little bearing on public opinion.

Ideas and artifacts have been diffused since the beginning of human history. In their travels, as they become familiar, their origins are forgotten and they are accepted as indigenous. In the days when there was indirect trade between Rome and China, this process went on at a languorous pace, and so it continued for centuries.

Human interactions on an international scale have steadily intensified, with a profound effect on the transmission of culture. The invention of the jet airplane facilitates firsthand exposure to the experience of objects or ideas in use in an environment that has already accepted them. Along with improvements in transportation technology, the rising level of real income in Western countries has made possible the movement of people in massive numbers for touristic, business, and professional purposes.

World trade outside the Soviet bloc went from $57 billion in 1950 to nearly $2 trillion in 1980, far outstripping the rate of inflation (which was 242% in the United States for those years). Companies with international affiliates and subsidiaries account for a growing proportion of this trade. During the 1970s the number of passengers carried on scheduled airlines more than doubled. Between 1960 and 1983, the number of international journeys multiplied more than four times. In that same period, faciliated by the introduction of world-wide direct dialing in the 1970s, the number of overseas telephone calls made from the United States alone multiplied by nearly 100 times, and the number of telephones in the world increased by nearly four times.[8]

The breadth of international political linkages has expanded since the end of World War II, with the creation of the United Nations and a variety of affiliated specialized bodies. Groupings like NATO, the Warsaw Pact, ASEAN, the Arab League, OPEC, the Pan African Congress, and the European Economic Community have involved far more nations than were linked together in the alliances of the past. Private membership organizations like Friends of the Earth, Earthwatch, and Amnesty International operate on an international scale. Thus in the political realm, as within occupational and professional organizations, direct interpersonal contacts have multiplied among nationals of different countries.

The growing ease of contact has facilitated the creation of international groups that share common interests and are eager to exchange ideas not only through written communication but face to face. Chemical engineers, neurosurgeons, urban sociologists, newspaper editors, orchid growers, department store owners, and innumerable other professional, business, and avocational groups maintain international connections and share a common body of information about which opinions may arise.

The enormous increase in international personal contacts has its counterpart in a vast increase in contacts through the mass media. The printing press made it possible to transmit information in great quantities; steam transportation meant that it could arrive across great distances while it was still relatively fresh.[10] When electricity was harnessed through the telegraph, the telephone and radio, it became possible to communicate instantaneously across the continents.

In contrast to the face to face contacts of trade and travel; mediated communications require a translation system more often than not. Foreign newspapers have been copied and translated ever since the very origins of the periodical press, and travelers' letters were published long before newspapers began to send forth their own correspondents. The rapidity of cultural diffusion has been immeasurably accelerated by the technology of transmitting pictorial images as well as the words that require translation. The picture media—photography, motion pictures, and television—permit direct communication to people of different nationalities at levels of empathy and involvement for which there are no direct counterparts in verbal form.

Television audiences watch the same broadcast of "Dallas" in South Africa, Singapore, Poland, Spain, and Brazil. The evolving technology of communication and transportation has multiplied such occasions for common cultural experience on an international scale. Of course a film or television program requires dubbing or subtitles in order to be fully comprehensible to a foreign audience. Yet, powerful communication arises from the density of information that is packed into visual experience, along with the nuances of vocal inflection and the subtleties of facial expressions and gesture. Shared experience also characterizes live audiences of young people attending rock concerts given by performers who jet from one country to another, crowds of the faithful gathered to greet the Pope in the Cathedral plazas of different nations, or proletarians demonstrating in a worldwide series of rallies orchestrated by the Communist party.

Cultural phenomena are, in themselves, the subjects of opinions. People have differing tastes and preferences, are willing to express or rationalize them, and are able to differentiate their own from those of others. Culture itself is shaped by political decisions, for example, decisions to support the State Opera and deny support to Minimalist artists, to provide the press with newsprint subsidies or free postage and to restrict the hours of the broadcast day. Political decisions permit the appearance in public of certain performers, restrict the publication of some types of books or the public display of some types of art. Italian Fascism did not dictate changes in personal dress, though Mao's Communism did.

Contemporary totalitarian ideologies have stressed the idea that culture is a political weapon and have tried to maintain a cultural climate in harmony with the political system. Since time immemorial, autocratic regimes have sought to channel or control the thoughts of their subjects by rewriting history and obliterating the past. Edward Ploman reminds us that Hitler had ancient precedents:

66   Hierarchical Collectivism

> In 213 B.C., the Chief Minister Li Su petitioned the first Qin Emperor: 'May it please Your Majesty to determine right from wrong, to prescribe all unorthodox opinions, to destroy all historical records except those of the Xin . . .' His Majesty must have been pleased: the books were burned and, subsequently, 460 of the greatest scholars who were suspected of knowing the books so thoroughly that they could teach from memory were buried alive.[11]

A society that is open to cultural innovation and experimentation is obviously more likely to be open to political freedom as well. The values of a society are embedded not only in its customs, tools, and tastes but also in its view of the world, which is inseparable from its political ideas. Even if there were a universal culture, there would be no universal public opinion.

International Mass Media

If the idea of a world public opinion is unacceptable, it is partly because there is no worldwide media system as a foundation for it. Although a great deal of mass media output crosses country borders, most of its content is substantially shaped by the local institutions through which it reaches different national publics.

A communality of opinion presupposes the sharing of common communications on a specific subject. Different national publics are often reached by the same book, magazine, or film, by the same news wire service report or video news clip. But these communications are perceived with different meanings attributed to them in information environments that differ—whether the differences are as small as those between Australia and New Zealand or as great as those between Senegal and Nepal.

Opinions arise from two-way communication. Powerful as the media are, their ability to disseminate and change ideas rests on the willingness of the audience to feed back the information it receives, in reflection and conversation, to rehearse and review alternative versions of what it has been told, and thus to assimilate its acquired vision of reality. The domain in which a particular assortment of media are disseminated and discussed may be said to represent an opinion constituency. When the domain is defined in geographic terms, it is likely to coincide with a political constituency of some kind. But some media distributed to particular social classes or interest groups cut across geographic and governmental boundaries.

No two mass media systems are identical, even in adjacent countries that share a common language, like Austria and West Germany. In two neighboring American towns with separate radio stations, people in each tend to listen to the station that originates in their own community because its broadcasts are more likely to contain reference points in their own experience: commercials for the local department store, play-by-play accounts of the local high school's basketball games. For the same reasons, on an international scale, people always gravitate toward the mass media that originate within their own society in preference to those that come from outside, even when the latter are totally intelligible. East Berliners tune to Western television to keep in touch with the world beyond the Wall, because they want objective news and like the entertainment. But they do not avoid the East German programs, simply because these are the voices of the society in which they find themselves, however inadvertently.

Since the beginning of World War II, a substantial continuing propaganda effort has been conducted by a number of nations and addressed to the nationals of other countries. The purpose may be ordinary public relations, as performed by the press attaché of a minor embassy. It may have a cultural objective, like that of a Goethe Haus in Madrid or a French Film Festival in Los Angeles. It may take the form of a sustained effort to penetrate official barriers, like Voice of America broadcasts to the Soviet Union. It may seek to demoralize an enemy, as in the form of Iraqi leaflets scattered in Teheran. By all indications, such direct propaganda activity accounts for an infinitesimal share of the world's total media outputs and a minor proportion of the part that crosses national boundaries.

Ownership and control of the mass media are generally in local hands. Within the vast and full range of media voices, the number of international empires is rather small. First among them is the *Readers Digest*, whose local editions in different countries sold an average of 12.1 million copies a month in 1984, compared with 17.9 million for the U.S. edition. The Hearst and Newhouse organizations publish several European editions of such magazines as *Good Housekeeping, Harper's Bazaar, Vogue, Scientific American, Playboy, Popular Mechanics*, and a handful of technical publications publish translated and adapted editions. *Time* and *Newsweek* have, respectively, 18 percent and 15 percent of their total circulations in international editions in English. American and British newspapers have published editions in Paris for nearly a century, but these may be considered analogous to the foreign language press in North America. The *Wall Street Journal* prints by satellite in Europe and Asia, *USA Today* in Europe, but in each case the circulation is a tiny fraction of the total. The *Economist* of London now has 29 percent of its circulation in the United Kingdom; 34 percent in the United States.

In recent years, foreign publishers with capital to invest and a limited opportunity for growth in their own markets have investigated the possibility of acquiring American properties, but with the notable exception of the Australian, Rupert Murdoch, they have not tried to manage them with their own nationals.[12] In 1988, Murdoch's News Limited owned publications in Australia, New Zealand, Hong Kong, Papua, New Guinea, the

United Kingdom, and the United States. The International Thomson organization, one of two dominant Canadian newspaper chains, owned 112 daily newspapers in the United States and others in England. Conrad Black, another Canadian, owned 45 American dailies. The German publisher, Bertelsmann, was the owner of *Parents'* Magazine. Another German company, Holtzbrinck, owned *Scientific American*. Other American magazines were owned by British (Reed, Maxwell, United Newspapers), French (Hachette), and Dutch (VNU) companies.

This is an impressive list, but what is most interesting about it is the very small proportion that foreign ownership represents of the total number of media vehicles in any of the countries affected. There are exceptions, to be sure. *Time* was forced to abandon most of its Canadian readers when especially introduced legislation in 1976 would have forced it to produce a virtually new product rather to "Canadianize" its basic U.S. edition.

Newspapers in such countries as India and Morocco were once owned by citizens of the colonial powers, but only a few ex-colonies (like Singapore) are relaxed enough to permit foreign ownership today. The press is so closely linked to political power that foreign control of even a small part is widely considered inadmissible. The media are generally regarded as main channels of the national culture, whose integrity and purity must be carefully preserved from the corruption of external influence. Quite apart from actual restrictions, or the potential threat of their imposition, is the fact that entrepreneurial skills are not easily translated from one society to another in the domain of popular taste.

Aside from the question of ownership, what is the international component in media content? Entertainment (including sports) is dominant, and in large countries with their own production resources, this entertainment is overwhelmingly of local origin. Smaller countries, both in Europe and in the less developed world, are to a considerable degree dependent upon imported films and television programs, and make proportionately greater use of books and periodicals brought in from abroad.

International communications today no longer requires imports; it can take place through the direct transmission of the same messages to individuals in different countries. For this reason, the development of satellite communications links is of increasing importance.[13] When the same television program is being viewed simultaneously, or even after a short delay, by people in different countries, the same *experience* is being shared. This is quite different from the sharing of *information* that takes place when the same wire service bulletins are transmitted through the press or on the radio.

The demand for films and other programming material has expanded as a result of the development of cable television in a number of countries, the opening up of additional conventional television channels, and the advent of video cassette recorders. The growing appetite for material to occupy the tube has provided a strong impetus to the international export of films and television programs. Video cassettes open up the range of viewing choices far beyond those offered by national television networks, and make it possible to gain access to a wide range of entertainment, dubbed into the viewers' own language.

Advertising accounts for a very substantial part of all media content in much of the world. The growth of large international corporations has been accompanied by a growth of international advertising agencies and affiliated agency networks. In 1988, the three longest advertising organizations in the world were Dentsu (Japanese), Saatchi (British), and WPP (also British). Increasingly, the same advertisements appear across national boundaries, with changes in the sound track and minor adaptations in the video component. Since advertising transmits values and is a great cultural force, the increasing internationalization of advertising may be regarded as a significant component of a growing worldwide cultural commonality.

The weight of advertising by international companies varies considerably from country to country, depending on local regulations and media practices, and on the total volume of advertising itself. For example, Sweden, Denmark, and Norway had no television advertising at all in 1985. In the remaining countries of Western Europe, the amount of television advertising ranged from nine minutes a day on one of the Finnish channels to ninety minutes a day on ITV in the United Kingdom.

Over half the world's advertising investments are made in the United States, and much of the remainder has inevitably followed the American pattern. In fact, American media content occupies a prominent part of the content of media throughout the world—in films, television programming, and newspaper comic strips. In part this is because its formulas, techniques, and symbolism are inherently attractive; in part because there is so much of it available. As I have already emphasized, the mass media are inexhaustible in their appetite for material. The fact that American media produce such a large proportion of the world's total means that they always have something available to meet the need. The American film and television industries can draw on an enormous pool of talent and resources. Their production standards are therefore higher, on average, than they can be in a society with more limited means.[14]

The international, and especially the American, components of media content have aroused charges that "cultural imperialism" has eroded national cultural distinctiveness.[15] Such concerns relate directly to my earlier observation that political opinions arise from underying cultural values. However, the formation of opinions most directly reflects the handling of the *news*, and here the issue of national sovereignty has become especially acute.

Since different countries have different media systems, their residents at any time are always exposed to different sets of information, each of which reflects its own society, culture, and political system. These differences are particularly striking in the realm of politically relevant information, which is embedded in the news. The news of any given day is managed and interpreted in different places according to different philosophies and to the requirements of different degrees of political freedom. And news is heavily slanted toward the polity in which it is disseminated or finds its principal audience.

Within any given country, both in newspapers and broadcast bulletins, local and regional news stories change the total mix of the day's news from place to place. The shifting of priorities is much more marked when news media are compared cross-nationally. Only an extraordinary news event, like the end of World War II, is likely to receive the same prominent treatment everywhere. (Even the first moon landing was given low-keyed treatment in the Soviet press, and ignored in China.) Partly this is because the notion of what is newsworthy varies from place to place. (Accidents, disasters, crime, sex, and scandal are not worth the serious attention of Communist journalists.) Apart from that, the notion of what is newsworthy everywhere concerns those matters that are closest to home and with which the news-reading or-viewing public can make a direct personal connection.

International sportscasts, especially for international soccer matches in Europe, are among the most widely shared media events. But although such broadcasts represent a common experience for viewers in different countries, the passions they arouse seem to polarize national loyalties rather than to submerge them in a sense of greater affinity.

In any community, the inhabitants possess information that is local in character and holds little interest for anyone else. Accordingly, the divisions of opinion on local issues and personalities have no meaning for outsiders unless they can find parallels for them in their own experience or perceive them as illustrations or expressions of controversies with a wider significance. For this reason, except in societies where the press is centrally controlled, the newspapers of different communities abound with the chronicles of happenings that have no particular interest anywhere else. The stories of more universal concern, within the country or internationally, receive widely varying coverage and positioning, depending on what priorities are assigned to the highly variable component of local news.

The inconsistency in the treatment of major world news stories by the press of different nations derives directly from the practice of viewing news priorities from a localized perspective. Just as elite opinion often differs from public opinion at large, the elite press throughout the world is distinguished by its cosmopolitan outlook, its ability to transcend the immediate and the transitory. Popular newspapers, by contrast, focus on the stories that are close to home, on familiar personages, on vivid human dramas that are closest to the readers' own experience.

By contrast with the press, radio news began with limited newsgathering resources of its own and has thus been generally dependent on wire services that serve a wider constituency. Television newscasting began as a cross between radio bulletins and the movie newsreel. It discovered at an early stage that it required video footage to hold its audience. Thus it developed a dependence on national network news facilities and on international news video services, which have become even more important with the advent of satellite transmission. The highly developed local TV newscasts of the United States have few counterparts in other countries, where local transmitters are usually used merely as relays for the national network. The American viewer sees mostly local newscasts dominated by scenes of fires, accidents, and crime, with occasional excursions into local politics, strikes, demonstrations, and oddities of behavior. The viewer in other countries is more likely to watch national news broadcasts in which world news is a generous component.

In spite of the difference of priority or prominence that the same events assume in different places, there is a common thread of content that runs through current information in a variety of countries at the same time. This common thread is provided by the great international news wire services, editorial syndicates, and video news services. Some of these services (AFP, for example) tend to have most of their clients in countries that are similar in culture, language, or political system to those of the originating country. Others (AP, Reuters) tend to be more universal in scope. In a number of cases (Tass, Prensa Latina) the services are linked to particular governments.

Over a more recent eight-year period, UNESCO's International Program for the Development of Communication spent about $2 million a year in grants primarily to strengthen government-controlled press services and other media operations. UNESCO and UNDP have sponsored the establishment of the Caribbean News Agency, and for information ministers of the Organization of African Unity sponsored the Pan African News Agencies (PANA) in Africa. (Their radio news service allocates a daily five minutes to each member nation, regardless of the presence or absence of real news from each place.)

Even when a news agency cannot be considered official by any stretch of the imagination, it is likely to embody the outlook and perspective of the country where its headquarters are located. When that country is itself a major actor on the stage of world politics and news, as is the United States, the news service's clients elsewhere are inevitably concerned about its evenhandedness, its ability to serve the many national constituencies to which it provides information.

The New World Information Order

The idea of a world public opinion presupposes, I have argued, a common base of information, presumably unhindered and diverse. From a Western perspective, the establishment of such a common base is impeded by the political barriers imposed by undemocratic governments and by the economic obstacles that poor countries face in purchasing information they may want. But from the viewpoint of the governing and academic elites in much of the world, access to information is constrained by a monopolistic Western news processing structure that is firmly in place and that imposes its biases upon them against their will. This view was embodied in the blueprint for a New World (or International) Information Order which originated at the 1973 Summit Conference of the Non-Aligned Movement in Algiers, and was embodied in the already mentioned report of the International Commission for the Study of Communications Problems, chaired by Sean MacBride. While the report referred only to the possibility of establishing an "international code of journalistic ethics," a violent controversy arose over other subsequent proposals that journalists actually be licensed by the countries on which they report. The licensing of journalists was eventually opposed by the 1981 Declaration of Talloires, adopted at the initiative of the World Press Freedom Committee. However, the idea continued to send off reverberations that were ultimately felt in the American withdrawal from UNESCO in 1984.

The proposal originated, of course, in a grievance—in the notion that foreign journalists bring a critical perspective to bear on the internal affairs of impoverished countries and that the reports that they feed back to the rest of the world are distorted and negative.

The United Nations Development Program's Narinder Aggarwala characterizes "development news" as "the reporting of development processes rather than events," and suggest that Western reporters have a penchant to report spot news (which is apt to deal with conflict or disaster) rather than the ongoing undramatic story of gradual progress in the fight for a better life. But this is a meaningless distinction when applied only to the less developed world, since news media are generally preocccupied with the events that are fresh on a particular day, rather than with the continuing stories for which an arresting headline is inapplicable. Such evolving stories are the stuff of books, films and documentaries, articles in elite magazines, and occasional features in newspapers; they rarely make the front pages of the Western press, or the radio and television bulletins anywhere. That this is so probably reflects the economics of the marketplace, though it also arises from the established conventions of Western journalistic practice. By contrast, Marxist journalism has a didactic mission, and regards spot news as largely incidental to the registration of larger social and political messages.

This ideology is reflected in some of the more strident exhortations in the MacBride Commission report: "If Pan African consciousness has not developed as expected, have media really done enough to stimulate solidarity throughout the continent? And if many Western industrialized nations pay scant attention to developing world concerns, is not this due to some extent to the media?"[17] The report also points out that

> the press and media in many countries have already played a notable part in mobilizing world opinion against apartheid.... The media can play a significant part in promoting and accelerating ... changes in attitude. Sympathetic and truthful reporting can portray the courage and self-sacrifice in struggles for racial equality, and explain why these struggles are justified.

Referring to "monopolistic and oligopolistic trends," the MacBride report dismisses the doctrine of "free flow of information" by pointing out that "under its present guise, some governments, transnationals, media, and organized pressure groups have on occasion tried to undermine international stability in other countries, violating their sovereignty and disturbing national development. Evenhandedly, the report remarks, "Still, there are also instances where national sovereignty has been invoked to justify restrictions on news collection and dissemination." "In order to be really free, information flows have to be two-way, not simply in one direction.... The news flows are neither free nor balanced. This solid base of criticism is the foundation of the present call for a new world communication order."[19] Since "free flow" was nothing more than "one-way flow," the MacBride report argued that the principle on which it was based should be restated so as to guarantee "free and balanced flow:"

> The criticisms ... start from the observation that certain powerful and technologically advanced States exploit their advantages to exercise a form of cultural and ideological domination which jeopardizes the national identity of other countries.... It has been frequently stated, in particular, that due to the fact that the content of information is largely produced by the main developed countries, the image of the developing countries is frequently false and distorted. More serious still, according to some vigorous critics, it is this

false image, harmful to their inner balance, which is presented to the developing countries themselves.[20]

A Nigerian official has carried the accusations to an even more remarkable extreme, blaming Western mass communications specialists for the failure of "developing" nations to develop:

> Research—particularly American social science research— ... has spread dubious theories of the 'passing of traditional societies,' of urbanization leading to modernization, of westernization leading to civilization, of metropolitanism leading to the development and adoption of innovations, of high correlations of radio sets, television sets, copies of newspapers, and cinema, seats with certain population units leading to economic and social progress in society. Such research, theories and concepts succeeded in selling costly equipment, 'expertise' and more propaganda but resulted in revolutions of rising frustrations and a trend to socioeconomic deterioration in Africa and many other Third World countries, with neither development nor modernization in sight."[21]

The New World Information Order, it was proposed, would provide direct news service links among underdeveloped countries so that each could report through its news media on the cheerful and good things happening in the others by a direct exchange of government handouts rather than by an independent and therefore presumably hostile view.[23] However, the news media in the underdeveloped countries do not ignore each other's affairs because of the judgments exercised by the news managers or gatekeepers in international news organizations. They ignore each other as part of the almost universal concentration of their news media on the internal affairs of their own countries. In many parts of the world, information about external affairs is limited to an occasional broadcast news bulletin or a paragraph or two in the local papers. Members of the elite who wish to stay properly informed are inevitably dependent upon shortwave radio broadcasts or upon flown-in (but still delayed) copies of foreign publications. There is simply no way in which the average individual in Burma or Mali can have more than an inkling of what is going on in the wider world. For that matter, except for the elite press, most newspapers in the United States and Western Europe provide their readers with remarkably little detailed news coverage of events in other countries, unless these involve political confrontations, wars, or disasters of a magnitude that simply cannot be ignored.

Citizens of Western countries are generally poorly informed about major public issues in their own countries. Is it surprising that they are even more oblivious to developments elsewhere? The generally low level of information represents an important reason why it is difficult to find a common basis for international opinion.

Two Modest Proposals

This essay has belabored a point that may be self-evident: World public opinion, frequently invoked and occasionally prayed for, does not exist. It is not likely to come about in the foreseeable future, in a world separated by national sovereignties, language barriers, ideological differences, and enormous disparities in culture and wealth. Common values are shared only to a limited degree, and opinions are formed everywhere on the basis of information that is limited in scope and never exactly resembles the information available in other places. The resulting absence of consensus is visible in a world that is splintered, filled with ignorance, acrimony, and injustice.

But this conclusion reflects my subjective assessments rather than the hard and comprehensive data that a proper study of the subject requires. Two specific research projects could provide much needed evidence on 1. the degree of commonalty in mass media experience and in exposure to news of current events, and 2. the degree of commonality around the world in values and beliefs. Each of these studies would require a very large effort, both to secure the necessary cooperation from governments and to secure the necessary funding.

1. A systematic world-wide comparison of media output, with an emphasis on news media. A number of cross-national analyses have been made of the content of a limited number of publications of a similar type. (It can be assumed that elite media would resemble each other more than a cross-section of the media.) However, there has never been a true international cross-section of the news media compared at the same point in time. Where circulation or audience figures are available, this analysis should be done with proper attention to audience size (relative to the total population) in each case.

The primary purpose of such an exercise would be to see how much common content there actually is, and particularly to check the use of international news sources and services. The study would document for each country the variations in the total volume of news, and in the news share of total media consumption. Comparisons could be made of the degree of prominence, and the interpretation, given to the same news stories. In short, this study would tell us, for the first time, what the actual flow of international information is.

2. A study to investigate whether there are common human values and whether any common areas of discourse and information exist on a world-

wide scale. "Motherhood" is often cited to exemplify a totally non-controversial and universal value, but even this simple biological function is imbued with very different meanings in different cultures.

Questions should be asked about fundamental values: principal daily preoccupations, belief in the afterlife, relationships of parents and children, responsibility to the aged, definitions of sex roles, attitudes toward work and leisure. Another series of questions might be asked about knowledge of major current events of international or presumably worldwide interest. Still others, localized to each country, would deal with universal aspects of government, like the activities of the head of state. Others would ask about sources of current news and information.[22]

It may be a vain hope for such a study to be done in every single country. However, the proposed research would offer a substantial start in the direction of doing a truly multinational opinion survey in enough countries to permit comparisons based on different rates of literacy, living standards, and mass communications systems. (While, as already mentioned, it is quite common practice for surveys to be conducted on an international scale by governments, corporations, polling organizations, or cooperating scholars, in normal practice only a handful of countries are involved.)

In many countries, polling has never been extended seriously beyond the urban elite, as it should be to provide a series of true national cross-sections. These in turn would require multiple language versions of questionnaires, even within individual countries where a number of languages or dialects are in use. (The problem of making translated questionnaires truly comparable has been a standing obstacle in cross-national research.)

A cross-national survey would certainly document the persistence of highly distinctive value systems in small, out of the way societies. Perhaps it would show that certain standards of conduct and belief and certain aspirations (more limited in scope than those cited by the MacBride Commission) are virtually universal. These common values would not constitute a world public opinion, but they would represent a preliminary sketch of the outer limits within which opinions might be formed on an international scale.

Notes

This chapter written on the initiative of Frederick T. C. Yu and with support from the East-West Center at the University of Hawaii.

1. I first addressed this subject in a paper, "Is there a World Public Opinion?" (*Polls*, Spring 1966 v.1, No.3, pp. 1-9), which is incorporated in my book "*Polls and the Awareness of Public Opinion*, New Brunswick, N.J.: Transaction Books, 1985.

2. Sean MacBride *et al.*, *Many Voices, One World: Communication and Society Today and Tomorrow*, New York: Unipub, 1980, pp. 198-9.
3. The sense of community is not always manifest even within the same country. The energy crisis of 1973 resulted in emergency measures throughout the United States, but in Salt Lake City the city commissioners insisted that the holiday lights be left on downtown, noting that there was no local threat of an electrical shortage. One commissioner, James Barker, said that leaving the lights off would be like asking the people of Salt Lake City to fast one day a week because of famine in India.
4. Jay G. Blumler, "Broadcasting and the European Elections," *Intermedia*, v. 7, No. 5 (September 1979) pp. 30-33. Even in this instance, the nature of the election campaign differed from country to country. In some cases, broadcasts were primarily organized by the political parties, with varying levels of effort; elsewhere, the broadcasters took the initiative.
5. An opinion poll taken in Holland soon after the Soviet invasion of Afghanistan and the suppression of Solidarity in Poland found that a large proportion of the Dutch felt they had no moral right to criticize the Soviets "as long as housing conditions in Amsterdam fail to meet the highest standards of modern comfort, as long as women remain exploited, and the legal rights of heterosexual married couples are denied to homosexual couples." *Business Week*, December 31, 1984, p. 10.
6. *New York Times*, October 31, 1984.
7. Michael Rappeport, "The Distinction the Pollsters Don't Make," *The Washington Monthly*, March, 1974, pp. 13-15.
8. The attractions of immediate contact by voice brought an effect on more traditional communications: the number of pieces of international mail sent from the United States remained static between 1970 and 1984, and in the last five years the trend was actually downwards.
9. As with international media, there are typically great disparities in the rates of participation in international meetings between those from rich, advanced countries and those from poor ones. This imbalance has stimulated international organizations to lend support to the exchange of persons, especially in the form of travel grants.

    In practice, divisions of opinion within international congresses tend to reflect the larger political differences that separate the participating nations. Debates that may begin as professional, technical, or scientific become politicized as they are subsumed by rival ideologies, accommodated to fit more comprehensive world views, or attached to irrelevant topical issues. This is particularly true insofar as Marxist philosophy pretends to be all-embracing and incorporates theories of science and culture into its economic and political schema.
10. In 1820, half a dozen years after the first steam engine was harnessed to a printing press, the British statesman George Canning compared the power of public opinion to that of steam.
11. Edward Ploman, "The Communications Revolution," *Inter Media*, 9, September 1981, p. 9.
12. American publishers have not been inhibited from importing British and Canadian talent and the Latin American press has always been hospitable to exiled journalists from sister republics.
13. This has been recognized by the Soviets in their steadfast opposition to international direct broadcasting by satellite.

78   Hierarchical Collectivism

14. The advent of satellite signal transmission and linked international computer networks has added a new dimension to the long-standing concern about American dominance. The United States has about half the world's computers. Russell Pipe notes that of some 700 strategic games used in 1976 to train French military and business leaders, only twenty had originated outside the United States. As Jean-Michel Treille points out, "This imposes ways of reasoning on Europeans and takes away part of their ability to formulate independent strategies." The dependence on foreign data bases not only creates dependence; it produces threats to privacy and national sovereignty. Pipe comments, "National laws are limited to the geographical confines of the country; which means that national requirements (e.g. data protection), and the legal power to control the use of country-related information, largely evaporate when data and information leave the home territory." Russell Pipe, "Transnational Data Flows," *Inter Media*, 7 November 1979, 12.
15. Cf. Jeremy Tunstall, *The Media are American*, New York: Columbia University Press, 1977.
16. Sean MacBride *et al., op. cit.*, p. 58.
17. *Ibid*, p. 189.
18. *Ibid*, p. 199.
19. *Ibid*, p. 142.
20. *Ibid*, p. 37.
21. Frank Ugboajah, "The U.S. Decision to Withdraw from UNESCO," *Journal of Communication*, 34(3), Autumn 1984, p. 106.
22. Such questions incur a certain risk. A Bedouin, interviewed in a survey for the Voice of America in the early 1950s, was asked the biggest news he had recently heard. "My brother's third wife died," was the answer. "So that was bad news," commented the interviewer, anticipating the next question in the sequence. "No, good news," said the Bedouin. "She was a bad woman." This incident merely reminds us that what people consider newsworthy, and what they communicate to each other, does not always fit the model of an international mass media system.
23. The momentum on behalf of this notion continued unabated. In mid-1988, the IPDC had drafted a new World Communication Report, again documenting the paucity of media in poor countries as opposed to rich ones. For contradictory views of the subject cf. Colleen Roach, "The U.S. Position on the New World Information and Communication Order," *Journal of Communication* 37, No. 4 (Autumn 1987), pp. 36–51, and Robert L. Stevenson, *Communication, Development, and the Third World* (New York: Longman, 1988).

3

Looking Beyond Teledemocracy: The Politics of Communications and Information Technology

William H. Dutton

Technological advances in computing and telecommunications always generate an ample amount of utopian and dystopian imagery of the future of democratic institutions. The same technologies have been depicted as potentially able to inform or manipulate a society, to empower or enslave the public, and to decentralize or centralize political control. Most often, however, discussions of the political consequences of the new communication technologies are limited to their impact on public opinion polls, political campaigns, and elections. In this context, debate usually centers on whether futurist images of teledemocracy—various schemes for electronic polling and voting from the home—are desirable and feasible. But because many images of teledemocracy are rather outlandish, the political implications of the new media are easily dismissed and left unexamined.

In this article, I show how study of the politics of communications and information technology extends beyond teledemocracy to focus on the more general issues of power shifts, defined by Anthony Downs as changes in the relative decisional effectiveness of different actors in the political process. If viewed in this way, the political implications of the new media encompass several larger arenas of power, where technological change has already been extensive. While there are diametrically opposed views on the nature of power shifts, my summary of research findings supports the notion that technological change has most often reinforced the prevailing structure of power within organizations and society rather than systematically enhancing the relative decisional effectiveness of particular kinds of groups and interests. In this way, the new media will continue to be important to "who gets what, when, and how" in several major political arenas, even if, in the short to mid-term, they are not revolutionary in their consequences.

Perspectives on the Politics of Information Technology

The new media of any age can contribute to change or stability in political institutions and processes. Historians have linked the rise of print media to such developments as the expanse of empires and have tied the rise of electronic media to major changes in political campaigning. Since the 1970s scholars have grappled with the implications of newer media taking shape through advances in computing and telecommunications, accelerated by developments in microelectronics, microwave radio relays, satellites, and fibre optics—what I will broadly refer to as *the new media*. In doing so, they have addressed classic political questions: Who controls these media? Whose interests are served by changing technologies?

Who Controls?

Control is a central issue because communications technology is likely to serve the interests of those who control its use. Control is also problematic given that the new media are complex systems of people, equipment, and technique, what might be called *high technology*. Discussions of control reveal at least four competing views (Table 3.1).

The first is of a *democratic* marketplace view adopted by those who see technology ultimately controlled by public (consumer) needs and preferences, operating through normal marketplace processes within the context of liberal democratic institutions. The scholars most optimistic about the impact of technological change often take this perspective. If the new media diffuse within organizations and among the public, it is, according to these observers, because they meets the needs and interests of the users.

A second view is a more *technocratic* perspective and is characteristic of critics of the new media. They argue that information and communication technologies are driven more by military and industrial applications than

TABLE 3.1
Competing Perspectives on the Politics of New Media

Who Controls?	Whose Interests are Served?
• Democratic Marketplace	• Neutral or conflicting
• Technocratic Perspective	• Elitist bias
• Pluralist	• Democratic, pluralist bias
• Reinforcement Politics	• Reinforcement

by public communication needs, that public preferences are controlled through marketing techniques, and that the new media increase the likelihood that communications will be controlled by a technological elite, experts who know and understand the technology and who are primarily responsive and accountable to the economic elite of a society.

A third perspective is decidedly more *pluralist* in its orientation, viewing control over communications and information technology as but one political resource and, like others, access and control over it is shaped by the pulling and hauling of competing groups of elites. The new media are thus controlled by a pluralistic process of conflict and cooperation among a variety of actors with different resources and stakes in the political process. Pluralists view technocrats as among the influential actors but consider public officials, economic elites, and the public to be important actors as well.

A fourth perspective, *reinforcement* politics, views communication technologies as malleable political resources that are most often controlled by the dominant coalition of interests within an organization or society. Information technologies are, therefore, used in ways that enhance the power of already powerful groups and thereby reinforce the prevailing power structure of a political system rather than affecting any particular configuration of power, whether pluralist or elitist.

Whose Interests are Served?

Are the new technologies neutral, or are they inherently biased toward serving certain groups and interests, and therefore holding a potential for creating power shifts? Again, four competing perspectives have emerged, variously viewing the technological changes as neutral or conflicting, democratic, elitist or reinforcing in their political effects (also shown in Table 3.1).

A prevalent view is that the media are politically *neutral*, if not apolitical. Many in the television industry, for example, have argued that the nature of the content, not the technology, shapes the effects of this mediium. In contrast, most scholars maintain that media exert a bias in political communications that is independent of their content. Comparing oral and written traditions, Harold Innis argued that the political organization of modern societies is dominated by a written tradition because written communications, particularly in printed forms, can be more permanent, less constrained by distance, and more centrally controlled. Others, following Innis, have pointed to the potential disruptive influences of radio and television, as well as newer information technologies, that differentiate them from print media in being less permanent, even less constrained by distance, less compatible with centralized political arrangements.

A similar view is that the implications of communication technologies are inherently counter-veiling if not often contradictory. Ithiel Pool developed such a "dual effects" theme in discussing the social implications of the telephone, but examples can be found in discussions of a variety of new technologies. The telephone, Pool and others found, can erode as well as provide privacy; it can strengthen or circumvent an organizational hierarchy, and it can facilitate centralization and decentralization simultaneously. One problem with both the neutral and conflicting influence perspective is that they focus more often on potential impacts than the actual consequences of how technologies are used in specific social contexts, which are less often neutral or dual in their effects. They also ignore the degree to which neutral or contradictory effects suggest that the technology is politically malleable, as opposed to neutral, in being capable of facilitating the accomplishments of diverse groups and interests.

The most dominant perspective within the communications field is that the new media will have a *democratic* impact. Perhaps the telephone is most often viewed from this perspective. Jacques Attali and Yves Stourdze argued that the telephone introduced an inherently more democratic bias into the French political landscape by replacing the visual telegraph, which was designed to insure centralized control over telecommunications. They claimed that the telephone facilitated dialogues between center and periphery and communication among political interest groups rather than simply a monologue from the center to the periphery. In the case of newer information technologies, a democratic view finds frequent expression. According to Edwin Parker, the newer media provide the public with more information packaged in more ways, less controlled in content and timing, with more processing capacity and improved feedback. Harlan Cleveland has echoed this thesis, claiming not only that the new electronic media can spread information far and wide but that they will inevitably do so and thus accelerate the erosion of hierarchies and power monopolies while promoting the development of more open, less secret, and more participatory decision making. Ithiel de Sola Pool, referring especially to the development of interactive media, labelled them "technologies of freedom," leading to more varied choice for the public. Others have offered images of the new media breaking down communication barriers between nations and classes, as in Marshall McLuhan's "global village."

Another line of speculation argues that the media exert a non-democratic, *elitist* bias in political communication by creating bottlenecks, with powerful entities in a gatekeeper role in communication systems. Elitists argue that the complexity of high technology further distances elites from a public that is increasingly not involved and uninformed about the decisions of large public and private institutions in society. They have pointed to the expense and complexity of high technology as a factor that exacerbates knowledge gaps among individuals and organizations, which in turn accentuate economic and political inequalties. Kenneth Laudon has noted that the interactivity of such new media as opinion polling and two-way cable systems masks the degree to which they are designed in ways that erect more efficient vertical communication networks between elites and masses rather than creating horizontal networks among the public and groups. He argues that these vertical communication systems are more likely to facilitate manipulation of the public than greater democratic participation.

Each of these competing views on the interests served by technological change suggest that there are features of information technology that exert a systematic bias on the distribution of power. Technologies that are more complex and that facilitate vertical communications, such as centralized data processing facilities, for example, are said to have an elitist bias. Technologies that appear less complex and supportive of horizontal communications, such as telephones and personal computing, are said to have a democratic bias (Hiltz and Turoff, 1978). Langdon Winner put it quite well in suggesting that different technologies are more compatible with some social and political arrangements than with others. A data processing facility is more compatible with centralized management, while the use of personal computing is less so. Or the telephone networks of today might be more compatible with decentralized control than was the technology of past decades.

A common criticism of each of these perspectives on the bias of technologies is that they ignore the degree to which all technologies are essentially social constructions. People design, develop, manage, and use them for particular purposes. The very idea of technology as something apart from society is therefore misleading. Those who pursue the logic of this argument often trace the driving forces behind the development and diffusion of particular technologies as a means to establishing their social origins. Of course, many useful analytical constructs simplify. I think it is possible to accept the merit of this line of inquiry and still argue that it is often useful, analytically, to draw a distinction between technology and society and argue that technological innovations at any point in time, driven by whatever set of factors, present societies (organizations, households, individuals) with a range of problems and opportunities to which they must respond, if only to do nothing. Just as public policy is a useful construct for discussing the products and consequences of a political system's responses to a problem, technology is a useful construct for analyzing

84   Hierarchical Collectivism

the development and implications of a particular organization of people, equipment, and technique used for such purposes as communications.

Critics of various forms of technological determinism rightly point out, however, that the implications of media derive only in part from their various technical features. They are more or less malleable technologies. All are designed by people. People in authority choose to use or reject them for particular purposes. In this sense, as Steve Woolgar and others have argued, all information and communication technologies are socially constructed. And in this respect, their implications are never independent of who controls their design and use. However, one need not be a technological determinist to argue that any given time, the current technological landscape constrains or facilitates different forms of political and social control of information technology. That is, the political consequences of technological change are an outcome of the interaction between who controls the technology in specific settings as well as features of the technology.

Arenas of Power: Political Uses of Information Technology

Since the 1960s, empirical research has focused on how different actors and groups shape the purposes for which the new media are employed. Wide speculation as well as empirical research addressed such questions, with an ample amount of both utopian and dystopian conclusions. While discussions of the political implications of the new media have been almost exclusively tied to political campaigns and elections, there are at least four broad institutional settings in which the political implications of communications and information technologies have been the focus of both empirical and speculative inquiries: 1. political campaigns, 2. governmental communications, 3. public telecommunications, and 4. international communications.

Political Campaigns and Elections

New technology has increased the sophistication and use of direct mail in campaigns by permitting a greater volume of more personalized and targeted correspondence. Computer-assisted telephone dialing and interviewing systems, interactive cable and videotex applications, and other developments in opinion polling have increased the potential speed and sophistication of the candidate poll in ways that can dramatically enhance the effectiveness of a political campaign. Computing also extends the potential for matching data in different mailing lists, public opinion polls, voter registration records, housing data, census, and other data bases to compile more detailed data banks about the individuals who compose the voting public. Techniques of profiling can be used in conjunction with these data banks to predict the likely supporters of a candidate or cause so that mailings and other contacts can be more precisely targeted. Video conferencing has permitted candidates to develop their own closed-circuit television campaigns, independent of the broadcast networks. Together new media offer channels of communication between candidates and voters that can do more than complement the mass media. They can provide a different set of messages from those conveyed over the mass media, yielding different agendas and different affects on public opinion and voting behavior.

New technologies have been used extensively in campaign planning and administration. Desktop computers have brought budgeting, accounting, and payroll applications along with specially designed campaign management software within the reach of even modestly financed campaign organizations. Electronic mail and conferencing systems have also been used in managing communications among campaign personnel and coordinating the work of geographically dispersed speech writers, media consultants, and field staff.

This increasing centrality of computing and telecommunications raises several issues. These new media bring new skills and actors into the political fray, bolstering the role of new kinds of campaign consultants. Their rise may undercut the value of other consultants, but also diminish the role of unskilled volunteers, whose jobs (e.g., distributing leaflets) can be increasingly taken over by the new media specialists.

The application of the new media to campaigns and elections may have dual effects, both centralizing and decentralizing. On the one hand, the electronic media permit candidates to bypass the traditional mediating institutions of parties and interest groups, as well as journalists, and reach their audience directly via mailings and teleconferences. In this respect the media might weaken parties, facilitate the development of more single-issue interest groups, and lessen the influence of media gatekeepers, thereby decentralizing control over campaigns. On the other hand, greater reliance on electronic communications media may lessen the role of distance and travel on interest group formation and decision making. Such an outcome could erode local political organizations and enhance regional and national organizations. Furthermore, by permitting groups to appeal to a national audience, the new media might centralize control of the campaign in national organizations, parties, and interest groups that can marshal the economies of scale, resources, and specialists necessary to conduct a high-technology campaign.

The utilization of newer media may also have redistributive effects, altering the relative influence of different socio-economic groups in society.

Differential access to electronic media by various socio-economic groups could reinforce disparities in access to other political resources. More affluent members of the public have greater access to computing resources such as electronic bulletin boards, word processing, high-speed printers, and campaign management software. The use of this technology was recently evident when the Federal Communications Commission discussed the imposition of access charges for those who use the telephone network for computing services. The FCC was the subject of one of the heaviest direct mail campaigns it had seen. Thus the new media may increase inequities rather than level the influence of groups. The implications are also likely to be redistributive in reinforcing the influence of campaigners as opposed to the general public and other subjects of political campaigns. There is little doubt that the new media permit campaigns to reach more of the public, more frequently and in more effective and personalized ways.

Governmental Institutions and Processes

Here the focus is on the values of computing and telecommunications for achieving more effective and responsible government. Modern reformers and futurists have often viewed new communications and information technology as a path to more democratic participation in government and greater governmental responsiveness to public opinion. They have seen its potential as a "citizen technology." But critics rightly argue that this same technology can be used for manipulating public opinion—a dual effects thesis. Whether the media will ultimately erode or enhance democratic institutions and processes is an issue that has received increasing attention since the 1970s. Three issues are most central to the debate.

The first is whether technological change will further communication between citizens and government. Proponents of the idea argue that the new media eliminate the major physical barriers to more direct democratic participation in government. They see interactive communication systems such as cable and electronic mail providing means for the public to be better informed and more frequently polled on public issues. Some fear the establishment of improved linkages between citizens and their public officials on the same grounds that others have feared the power of unrestrained majorities, preferring instead a more republican form of government. Political scientists commonly question the degree to which the public is as informed or interested in public affairs as the designers of these new linkages imagine them to be. So images of a family listening to a public affairs program, discussing the policy options among themselves and registering their opinion on their interactive cable system (as was done during the trail of the Qube system in Columbus, Ohio) are countered by images of people pausing at a commercial break in "Miami Vice" to vote on the strategic defense initiative. Beyond the wisdom of electronic participation, critics point out that such schemes have been proposed since the 1950s, but government applications of computing and telecommunications have yet to involve the public in ways that even remotely approach images of "citizen technology." For the most part computing has been used to automate administrative functions and the routine processing of large-volume record-keeping and record-searching operations. And cable television utilization by governments at various levels has been limited to efforts at enhancing traditional public information activities, such as cablecasts of local council meetings and national legislative proceedings or distributing local government annual reports in video format.

Nevertheless, more recent advances in the application of teleconferencing, videotex, and personal computing have resurrected images of citizen technology. Like the telephone, the proponents of the new media argue that these technologies could facilitate horizontal communication among citizens and thereby enhance the development of groups within a pluralist society. While the new media have rarely been effectively applied to such purposes, there are some innovative attempts (at early stages of their development) that suggest the possibility. For example, the City of Santa Monica, California has a mini-computer based electronic mail system for use by the city's personnel. Members of the city council already use laptop computers over the electronic mail network on a routine basis to support their work and to communicate with each other, the city manager, and staff. Since a citizen raised the possibility of gaining access to the network in order to read staff reports—sent to the council over the electronic mail network—the City has been considering the possibility of expanding access so that residents could use publicly accessible terminals as well as personal computers or terminals in their homes to accomplish many activities in this virtual city hall that they might otherwise do in person. Santa Monica is an interesting case because it is an application that has evolved incrementally from ongoing developments (it is not another teledemocracy experiment) and because it is not an isolated example. A variety of educational, health, and voluntary organizations have been developing what some have called public access computing networks, echoing the earlier notion of public access to cable television. So it is too early to dismiss the potential for citizen technology.

A second issue is whether communications and information technology might facilitate more democratic and otherwise "better" decision making. Studies relating to the role of information technology in decision making, have likewise led to mixed conclusions. The computer revolution generated proposals for so-called *information utilities*, large computerized databanks accessible through telecommunications networks, to provide both the public and decision makers with essential information at all levels of government, so that decisions could be based more solidly on the merits of each case. It also generated efforts to apply modeling and other management science techniques to the decision-making process, since computing has facilitated their diffusion and application. Empirical studies of the use of energy and economic models have tempered these expectations, finding computer-based information systems used more often to legitimate decisions made on grounds other than the merits of the case. Nevertheless, the existence of numerous decision support systems can play a positive, albeit political, role in the policy process.

In the case of computer-based models of urban fiscal impacts, for example, this author found that the process of modeling performed a positive and unanticipated role in facilitating negotiation and bargaining among contestants in local development and land-use decision making. At the same time, the use of modeling tended to further distance the participants in the decision making from members of the lay public, who were left out of the modeling process. With the diffusion of personal computing and associated software, which enable end users to develop models with spreadsheet and other programs, many more computer-based models will be brought to bear on public decision making. Likewise, as research and development efforts proceed with the application of communications and information technology to ever more sophisticated group decision support systems in the public and corporate world, which use information systems to faciliate group communication and decision making, the use of more conventional decision support tools is likely to become more common if not routine.

A third issue concerns the application of new technology to the routine functioning of bureaucracies. While the impact of new communications and information technologies is as controversial in this area as nearly any other, there is more evidence to indicate that this has been where the major payoffs of the technology have been. Studies of local government computing, for example, demonstrate that where the technology is well managed, computing has improved the performance of most routine information processing tasks, such as record-keeping, record-searching and calculating-printing. It is in this area that new technologies have been most intensively applied and where the political implications of their use, for example, on the relative power of individuals in relation to large bureaucracies, has been least futuristic. David Burnham has argued that the migration of more information from the individual into the automated files of private and public organizations has fundamentally reinforced the influence of bureaucracies vis-à-vis the general public.

Relationships between public and private institutions, as well as among governmental institutions, may also be affected by the application of the new media in public bureaucracies. The most common hypothesis is that the accumulation of power in national agencies and bureaucracies will be enhanced by their relatively greater utilization of computing and telecommunication resources when compared to their local counterparts. National governments have adopted communication technologies earlier and more extensively than local governments. However, power shifts are not always straightforward. For example, national computing resources such as those created by law enforcement systems in the U.S. have sometimes tended to reinforce the effectiveness of state and local agencies, since these agencies can obtain access to much of the same data and information resources that are available to national agencies. Generally, computing has reinforced the role of agencies at all levels of government more than it has centralized power at the national level.

Relations among the executive, judicial, and legislative branches of government may also be affected by changing technology. The rise of television has often been cited as one factor contributing to the increasing influence of chief executives. The greater use of new communications technologies within executive agencies and bureaucracies have probably enhanced their decisional effectiveness relative to other branches of government, diminishing the ability of legislators and chief executives to monitor and lead the bureaucracy. Here again, however, there is the potentially conflicting effect of making the activities of bureaucrats more visible and accountable, as when investigators were able to recover Oliver North's electronic mail messages. Kenneth Kraemer and John King, as well as this author, have argued that there is little evidence to support claims that technological change is fundamentally altering the checks and balances of the American federal system. But it is difficult to imagine how, over time, the executive office and Congress can effectively oversee a massive federal bureaucracy without employing or becoming more like the technocrats they wish to control than the lay politicians the framers of the U.S. Constitution intended them to be.

Public Telecommunications Networks and Services

During the 1980s, nearly every advanced consumer-oriented nation introduced changes in public policies affecting telecommunications, broadcasting, cable, and satellite communications. Cable systems, particularly, have been the subject of major policy initiatives in Japan, North America, and Western Europe. But telecommunications policy changes, such as the divestiture of AT&T and the privatization of British Telecom, have been even more salient around the world. These developments lead a number of scholars to examine the driving forces and social implications of these changes, with one central question being who had the power to affect these changes?

Prominent interpretations of who controls public communications policy parallel the more general perspectives outlined previously. Some journalistic accounts offer classic democratic marketplace interpretations of these policy shifts being brought about by the drumbeat of the marketplace. Among other reasons, since many Western Europeans or Americans had little understanding of cable television or new telecommunication regulations prior to their introduction, few political scientists take this argument seriously. One democratic interpretation that has merit, in the American context, is suggested by studies of the politics of regulation in the United States. Several American researchers, such as James Q. Wilson, have put forward a public interest perspective, which aruges that moves to deregulate telecommunications have been driven by the power of ideas, particularly the persuasiveness of pro-competitive economic arguments, which have overcome the interest group regimes supporting government regulated monopolies. Pluralist interpretations have also been put forward. One argues that the changes in cable and telecommunications policy were the outcome of special interest group politics. For example, Tom Forester argued that a cable interest group regime engineered Britain's new cable policy. Dan Schiller interpreted deregulation in the U.S. as largely the outcome of pressure by large telecommunications users and AT&T competitors. Other pluralists view recent policy shifts as the outcome of partisan politics (extensions of Margaret Thatcher's or Ronald Reagan's programs into the communications sphere for example). A more elitist or technocratic perspective is offered by critical scholars, who argue that the self-interested politics of transnational economic elites is molding cable and telecommunications policy in most advanced consumer oriented societies.

My own research in Britain, France and the U.S. lead me to an interpretation of cable and telecommunications policies as outcomes of an "ecology of games," a metaphor Norton Long offered several decades ago to describe the politics of local communities. For example, the history of a number of more or less independent games shaped the evolution of British cable policy. A public service broadcasting *game* predominantly shaped the politics of cable policy into the 1980s. It was dominated by the BBC and the Post Office early on and later by the BBC and the IBA and supported by ministers and civil servants within the Home Office responsible for broadcasting. Eventually, cable operators and their lobbyists, the British Cable Television Association, pushed for the liberalization of cable programming regulations to permit them to offer pay services. To do so, they became involved with public interest groups and local organizations interested in public affairs and local programming within a community programming game. With the publication of a report from the Information Technology Advisory Panel (ITAP), cable was suddenly defined as a strategic resource—an infrastructure of an emerging information economy—leading cable system development to become a central objective within an industrial policy game, which involved new and more powerful actors in the cable and broadcasting policy arena.

But it was not only this game that shaped the outcome of the policy process. It was the outcome of a number of other games, including: a telecommunications game, which lead British Telecom to view cable as a potential area for expanding its services in light of a declining market for plain old telephone services; a privatization game in telecommunications, which lead members of the government, the telecommunications section of DTI and the newly established Oftel to view cable as instrumental to developing competitors to BT in local and long distance telecommunications; a partisan game, which lead the Conservative party to accept cable system development that was in line with its efforts to privatize public services; an intra-party game that weakened the traditional wing of the Conservative party, which had a stronger affinity to the BBC and IBA as British institutions; a tax policy game, dominated by the Chancellor of the Exchequer, the Department of the Treasury and Inland Revenue, which possibly had as critical a role in shaping private investment in cable systems as did the Cable and Broadcasting Act; and an R & D game, which also played a role in the formation and outcome of cable policy by holding out the expectation that advanced technology was close at hand.

The interests served by changing cable and telecomunications policies highlight the significant political implications of national telecommunications policy. The development of cable systems, for example, raises concerns over the consequences this industry might have on: a nation's culture, such as the maintenance of programming standards and programming that supports national cultures in the face of lowest common denominator and foreign (American) programming; social equity, such as a widening of regional and socio-economic disparities and the siphoning of major media events from over-the-air television to pay cable systems; governance, such as privacy and the impacts of cablecasting public events and partisan political broadcasts; and the national economy, including employment opportunities, international trade, and a variety of potentially affected industries, ranging from broadcasting to the new information technology industries.

Most recently, in the telecommunications area, images of wired cities have been rekindled by an emerging consensus among telecommunications experts that integrated broadband networks are becoming a financially and technically feasible development within the next decade. This is not new. In the United States during the late 1960s the electronics industry and a high-level presidential commission saw social and political opportunities in a nationwide broadband communications network to provide an "electronic highway" into every home and business to carry all kinds of information and services. A more integrated network regulated as a common carrier held the promise of providing more channels of communication, a greater diversity of programming, a more equitable distribution of services, and an opportunity for new constituencies to become involved in broadcasting.

Images of wired cities were influential in shaping public policy during the 1970s that promoted the development of cable television in the United States. But enthusiasm over wired cities faded with the growing recognition of the limitations of interactive cable, the limited market for new services, the economic problems of the cable industry, the failure of cable operators to live up their promises when awarded a franchise, and the rise of a host of newer media that competed with cable television services.

In the 1980s competition among media lead to another burst of utopian visions of marketplace competition among telephone, cable, newspaper, television, videotex, and videocassette media providing a pluralistic array of communication channels and services that would lead to more democratic patterns of public communications. But the promises of competition have been largely unfulfilled, as were the promises of cable television. Households in the U.S. have access to appreciably more television channels but not to significantly better or more diverse program offerings. Moreover, while competition has lowered long distance telephone rates, it has been associated with increasing concentration within the communications industry as a whole, driven out commercially unprofitable services, and widened the gap between the information poor and rich in societies.

It sounds as if debates over the future of public communications are an expression of differences of opinion among technical experts. But at the heart of these debates is controversy over who should own, control, and use communications networks and services and on what terms. Wired city proponents generally argue that control over communications infrastructure should be centralized to insure the efficient integration and universal provision of an infrastructure regulated as a common carrier, much as the telephone system was regulated prior to the divestiture of AT&T or as most

European PTTs have been structured. Opponents claim that centralized control is no longer practical given the nature of the new media, no longer legitimate in the U.S. context since there is no natural monopoly, or no longer desirable if competing, decentralized networks can provide services more efficiently. For example, cable operators argue that they should not be subject to common carrier regulations nor even the regulations governing broadcasters since they are electronic "publishers." In reply, the telephone companies see broadband communications, such as cable TV, as one natural area of expansion with the advent of integrated broadband networks.

The cable and telephone industries might have the most direct stakes in this issue as it will shape their respective roles in wiring the nation. But other communication industries, such as the videotex and satellite industries and computing and electronic equipment manufacturers will be affected as well. How this debate unfolds will undoubtedly affect the interests of people beyond the communication industries per se, particularly business and residential consumers, but also the competitive position of each nation in an increasingly international communications market.

International Communications

International communications concerns the array of facilities available for communications across national boundaries. Advancements in video recording systems, fibre optics, microwave relays, and satellite communications have expanded the multiplicity, capacity, and reach of worldwide telecommunications networks. The development of these systems has lessened technological limitations on international communications and correspondingly focuses attention on economic, cultural, and political factors that promote and impede communications across national borders. As with domestic public communications, issues of who controls and whose interests are served loom large.

Some students of the new media have argued that technological change has fundamentally undercut the ability of nations to control the international flow of communications. The videocassette recorder, for example, limits a nation's ability to control the importation of foreign programming through traditional means. Likewise, prospects for the widespread use of direct broadcast satellites have raised questions of whether nations will continue to be able to control the character of broadcast offerings. Others have argued that the new media can be shaped in ways that will permit nations more control over international flows of communications. One aim of the post-1981 French national cable plan, for example, was to provide a communications infrastructure that would facilitate public efforts to provide a balance of programming, ensuring access to an ample array of French as well as other foreign and more commercial programming. Likewise, even if direct broadcast satellites became economically feasible, the use of satellite broadcasting could be effectively blocked by nations through a variety of technical measures.

However, the thesis that the new media will reinforce the economic, cultural, and political interest of those actors and nations that already control international communications has been widely accepted. International communication networks are complex and costly, two features that have buttressed the dominant role of the most economically and technologically advanced nations in creating and distributing news and television programming. The new media of computing and telecommunications are also high-technology products that may allow greater choice to consumers, as a videocassette recorder or personal computer does, but they do not allow control over the production or distribution of the technological infrastructure and its basic content. The interests served by advances in international communication systems were perhaps the most controversial issue in the politics of communications during the 1980s, given their economic as well as cultural implications.

Economically, if one acknowledges the trend of most advanced industrial societies toward increasingly information-based economies, then international communication infrastructures represent nothing less than new trade routes. Nations concerned with balancing international trade, and such organizations as multinational corporations requiring extensive and efficient communication systems, are naturally affected by the availability of international networks and services. Large developed nations, which have been the major exporters of communication products and services, have tended to support the development of international communication systems, while small developing nations, which are among the major importers of these products and services, have been more ambivalent in their support.

Culturally, many nations have raised concerns over the maintenance of their traditions and values in the face of mass media institutions that threaten to homogenize the public around commercial rather than public service broadcasting and foreign rather than domestic programming. This issue has surrounded radio and television broadcasting for decades in nations such as Canada. However, the newer media of cable, satellites, and video recording systems raise this issue anew because they challenge existing instititions and mechanisms for ensuring national controls. These concerns extend beyond broadcasting to information systems more generally. For example, culturally defined standards for the handling of personal information are threatened by the ease with which personal data files could be processed in so-called data havens, that is, other nations or territories with less restrictive data protection and privacy regulations.

Politically, in the area of governance, information technology raises such critical issues as national sovereignty. With regard to computer communications, for instance, Canadians have been among those who have voiced concerns over the amount of information vital to the Canadian economy that is processed on computers in the United States. To some this places Canada in a dependent situation, leading to a national campaign for their independence from U.S. computers as a means for ensuring Canada's political sovereignty.

Innovations in communications and information technology already have profound affects on governance. One need not accept futuristic images of teledemocracy or wired cities to argue that the political implications of technological change are significant. They range widely but they largely revolve around two basic issues: Who controls technological change? and Whose interests are served by the new communication and information technologies?

One response is that communications and information technology is apolitical because it is so minimally relevant to power. While this position was prominent in the early years of computing, it is increasingly less credible since computing and telecommunications have been more obviously and frequently applied to the routine operations of governmental bureaucracies, as well as to political campaigns and the public policy process. Another response, which has gained credibility over time, is that advances in information technology systematically challenge the existing structure of power within and among liberal democratic societies. This view argues that the growing centrality of computing and telecommunications has resulted in power shifts, alterations in the relative decisional effectiveness of participants in the political process. Some scholars, such as Harlan Cleveland and Ithiel de Sola Pool, have viewed these challenges as a democratic force, as they see technological change spelling the "twilight of hierarchy." Others, such as Jacques Ellul have viewed the technology as a negative force behind increasingly hierarchical and centralized control. This author, and others, view communications and information technology as malleable political resources that are most often designed and used in ways that follow and reinforce the existing structure of power.

References

Arterton, F. Christopher. 1987. *Teledemocracy*. Beverly Hills, Ca: Sage.
Benjamin, Gerald. (ed.) 1982. *The Communications Revolution in Politics*. New York: The American Academy of Political Science.

Danziger, James N., William H. Dutton, Rob Kling, and Kenneth L. Kraemer. 1982. *Computers and Politics: High Technology in American Local Governments*. New York: Columbia University Press.

Downs, Anthony. 1967. "A Realistic Look at the Payoffs of Urban Data Systems." *Public Administration Review*. 27 (3), pp. 204-10.

Dutton, William H. and Kenneth L. Kraemer. 1985. *Modeling as Negotiating*. Norwood, NJ: Ablex.

Dutton, William H., Jay G. Blumler, and Kenneth L. Kraemer (eds.). 1987. *Wired Cities*. Boston: G. K. Hall.

Meadow, Robert. (ed.). 1985. *New Communication Technologies in Politics*. Washington, D.C.: Washington Program of the Annenberg Schools.

Part III
Competetive Individualism

Introduction

The political culture that Wildavsky describes as "competitive individualist" is obviously applicable to contemporary American society. Wildavsky describes this postion as follows:

> The culture I shall call "competitive individualism" imposes order by maintaining agreement on the basis of freedom of contract. Leaders are chosen like every other commodity, by bidding and bargaining. There is no permanent leadership, only different leaders for different purposes. Envy is mitigated by showing that everyone can have a chance, or by blaming failure on personal incapacity or bad luck. For individualists, risk is opportunity as long as winners can personally appropriate the rewards.

This individualism generates economic growth, which complements what the hierarchies provide, namely order as well as rules for competition. As Wildavsky points out in his essay-review of the film *Thief*, individualists need hierarchies to impose order on the world. There are tensions between them but they need one another.

The basic aspects of competitive individualism, as explained by Wildavsky, are:

1. Few prescriptions and weak boundaries. The one dominant prescription of individualism, freedom of contract, is worked very hard.
2. The government protects people and property.
3. A market culture in which risks are undertaken for personal gain. Risks are seen as opportunities for entrepreneurs, not anything to be avoided, and the focus is on the short-term.
4. Ostentation is permitted since all have a chance.
5. Equality of opportunity is basic.
6. Fairness involves opportunity to compete on equal terms, on the so-called "level playing field."
7. Loyalty is a function of "results" or outputs. If they are not obtained, individualists seek new combinations and arrangements that will generate the desired payoffs and consequences.
8. Uncertainty is desirable, since it creates opportunity for gain. Individualism copes with uncertainty by redundancy; it assumes that over the course of large numbers of transactions, things will work out, one way or another.

9. New knowledge is desired, since it generates new opportunities.

For this competitive individualism category I have selected an essay by Conrad Kottak, which deals with an enterprising Brazilian television network (Globo), and a review by Wildavsky of the film *Thief*, about an archetypical competitive individualist. One of the ironies of competitive individualism is that organizations are, by nature, generally hierarchical, even though their perspectives or values and activities may be best described as individualistic. "All cultures contain contradictions," Wildavsky suggests, and how they are resolved determines how political cultures maintain themselves or change.

4

Television, Culture, and the State in Brazil

Conrad Phillip Kottak

As Paul Hirsch[1] observes, American commercial television, supported by advertising rather than by government subsidies, is freer of direct government controls over its reporting of public affairs than are broadcasting media in most other countries, including the Soviet Union and many African nations. Soviet television, via 80 million sets reaching 90 percent of the citizenry, has become a nationally pervasive propaganda tool. Four channels, all emanating from Moscow, carry the same basic programs—the official news; speeches of the Supreme Soviet; lessons in geometry, grammar, and computers; and youth classes concerning one's obligations in society.[2]

The overt propaganda role of television is also obvious in Africa, according to a report[3] by the International Development Research Council, a Canadian research group, after a study of Cameroon, Congo, Gambia, Ivory Coast, Niger, Nigeria, Senegal, Zaire, Zambia, and Zimbabwe. The report found that (despite a few bright spots such as Nigeria) "television in Africa has generally become a government mouthpiece,[4] with typical content including political speeches, reports on visit of foreign dignitaries, development experts speaking over the heads of the average viewer in European languages, or dramas featuring upper-class characters dealing with typically Western problems.

There is much less competition and variety in television in these nations than in the United States, or even Brazil, the focus of this essay, where a single commercial television network, Rede Globo, dominates as none has ever done in the United States. However, this article will illustrate, with primary reference to the world's most watched commercial network (Globo), that control by gatekeepers can operate on several levels, and various degrees and types of censorship can apply to commercial as well as government-funded or -run television.

For instance, even when television is commercial, as in the United States, or Brazil—where, since late 1983, a research team under my direction[5] has been investigating TV's cultural context and impact—government officials typically allocate initial and/or continuing access to the airwaves. They also often play a role in regulating, scheduling, and content of news, documentaries, ads, propaganda, information, and entertainment programs. Several forms of censorship have affected Brazilian commercial television:

1. external/government,
2. external/public opinion,
3. external/sponsors,
4. intermediate/network executives, and
5. internal/self-censorship by creators.

Government Censorship

In 1984, as Brazil prepared for its first presidential election (albeit indirect) in a quarter century, television remained that nation's most censored medium. Brazil's foremost television critic and commentator Artur da Távola[6] contended that this was because the television industry lacked cultural power. (He was referring to elite or "high culture.") Because many intellectuals looked down on TV, they didn't make the same demands for easing television censorship as they did with theatre, film, newspapers, and books. Brazil's high culture power brokers didn't care much if popular entertainment programs were cut, and when TV writers protested censorship, they weren't taken very seriously because television still has a low value as "art".

Although television typically lacks high culture prestige, as the mass medium par excellance it can have tremendous power. Hirsch observes that

> political leaders and office-holders are generally far more alert and sensitive than social scientists and journalists to the structural characteristics which distinguish television from other news media and provide it with a *different form of power* [my emphasis].[7]

Brazil's military government (1964-1985) never doubted TV's power and was vigillant in supervising its content.

The Brazilian government has controlled television by granting access to the airwaves and by supervising content. According to a 1962 law, licenses are granted for fifteen years, but under military rule were actually revokable at any time.[8] Broadcasters therefore had precarious concessions that could be annulled arbitrarily by government decree.[9] As a result, stations had to be much more careful than in the American system, where licensing is more long-term and less arbitrary.

Brazil's electoral freedom had been terminated abruptly in 1964, when military officers ousted elected President João Goulart and instituted a period of authoritarianism and repression that began to abate only in the late 1970s, finally ending in 1985. Goulart had insulted the "honor of the military" by supporting a two-day mutiny by marines and sailors demanding improved conditions for enlisted personnel. The higher echelons of the armed forces thought that he wished to undermine military discipline and power and took over on March 31-April 1, 1964.[10]

In a 1975 speech, Brazil's Minister of Culture explicitly focused on television's huge potential influence as the reason for state control.[11] Among undesirable TV content features needing government attention, he mentioned scenes of violence, distorted presentations of reality, and foreign social and moral values and customs. According to the minister, government authorities should strive to preserve authentic Brazilian values, to protect and prepare future leaders.[12]

Government scrutiny was most intense during prime-time, from 6 to 9:30 P.M., when Brazil's most popular television programs, the Globo network's national news (8 P.M.) and its three nightly "soaps" or telenovelas, are broadcast in three time slots, 6 P.M., 7 P.M., and 8:30 P.M. Unlike American soap operas, Brazilian telenovelas end; a typical one lasts six or seven months. For each new novela rede Globo (rede means "network") had to submit a synopsis and the first fifteen chapters to a government censor for approval and modification. Even after *abertura* (political opening), which began in the late 1970s, and as military rule was ending in 1984, censorship continued and was frequently discussed in publications pertaining to television. Newspapers and TV magazines such as *Amiga*, the number one fan magazine, routinely published fans', authors', and actors' complaints about government-imposed cuts in telenovelas. One actor complained that his character had become incomprehensible because a critical personality transformation had taken place in two scenes cut by censors. The censor's scissors were routinely applied to references to politics or political figures, characters with certain tabooed occupations (*bicheiros*, or numbers racket personnel, for example), and (even slight) departures from traditional family values.

Several cases from 1984 can illustrate the kinds of content that were censored. References to the rallies for direct presidential elections that occurred in 1984 were cut from an 8 P.M. *novela*. A deranged woman's unfounded suspicion that her brother was having an affair with the mayor's wife, known as "the first lady," was excised from a 6 P.M. *novela*. From a 7 P.M. serial the censor cut a dream of light extramarital romance by an oppressed middle-aged married woman infatuated with a man other than her supermacho husband. In one 8 P.M. *novela*, which started off with two high-class professional thieves as its star protagonists, censorship forced both to shift to legitimate businesses. In a very popular 7 P.M. serial, there was doubt about whether the censors would allow the heroine, a glamourous woman in her fifties, to end up with a much younger, divorced, man, and whether the hero could marry the (reformed) villainess. (They did.)

Censorship laws stifled political reporting and debate. In 1984 São Paulo's independent TV Cultura was sued over a live broadcast of an interview in which former President Medici called Leonel Brizola, governor of Rio de Janeiro, "a bandit." Other stations cut this part when showing the tape, but TV Cultura transmitted the interview live. Note that it wasn't the slandered governor, who was no friend of the military, but the federal government that sued, because it was illegal to say "scandalous" things about government officials.

Brazilian censorship concentrated on politics and violence, paying less attention to nudity and sex than do the would-be guardians of North American morality. Brazilians still try to limit children's exposure to media violence more than Americans do. Certain television hours are still announced as "approved" for children of certain ages, and a government-imposed rating system continues to regulate movie houses, with managers paying more attention to it than American theater owners. My then thirteen-year-old son—accompanied by consenting parents—had trouble getting into such movies as *The Twilight Zone* and *Indiana Jones and the Temple of Doom* because they were considered too violent for children younger than fourteen. Managers enforce the code by asking to see a child's identity card.

Nudity and graphic romance fared better under censorship. Even primetime television, whose content was carefully monitored by the military government, showed commercials that would be considered risque in the United States. Brazilians apparently found little unusual in ads featuring ample female bodies spilling out of the same kinds of scant bikinis that could be seen by the thousands at any Rio beach. Babies' bottoms seem to be permissible (in diaper commercials) on American TV, but the genitals of male and female toddlers, which were shown in Brazilian ads, are not. One Brazilian commercial, shown in 1984 on the 7 P.M. *novela*, and seen by millions of kids, was a men's underwear ad featuring a young man clad only in bikini briefs cavorting in bed with a naked woman. A year later, following the end of military rule, I saw, in the same time slot, a commercial featuring a rooster that emerged, Woody Woodpecker fashion, from the fly of a pair of men's underpants. By 1987, female breasts and male buttocks were in vogue. Yet Brazilians still considered such imports as *The Stunt Man* and *Hill Street Blues* too violent for hours when children were watching television. If shown at all, it was after kids' bed time.

In this context, in response to the threat of government interference as well as to network controls, which are discussed below, reporters, writers, directors, and commentators have consciously and unconsciously censored themselves. Indeed, given the threat of gatekeeper veto and retaliation and the need to make a living, the "internal censor" can be the most effective and stifling, because it is a constant brake on creativity.

Consumers and Public Opinion

Measuring the Audience

The main purpose of commercial television is neither to entertain nor to enlighten, but to sell products. American and Brazilian television strive not to train proper citizens, but proper consumers. Market research, public opinion sampling, advertising, audience targeting, and other techniques designed to spur consumption and sell products are well developed in Brazil. IBOPE (The Brazilian Statistical Public Opinion Research Institute)[13] is the foremost polling organization, with a historic role equivalent to Gallup's[14] or Nielsen's in the United States. Founded in 1942, IBOPE is headquartered in Rio, with a second major agency in São Paulo, and offices in eight other cities. One indication of its prominence is that "IBOPE" has come to mean rating. A television program's success is measured by its "IBOPE," an estimate of the number of sets turned on throughout the day and the channels being watched.

IBOPE, which employs about 800 people nationwide, does 80,000 brief household interviews each day. Throughout Brazil, its pollsters gather data on number of sets in use, channel watched, and age and sex of viewers. Just as American television networks use "sample precincts" to predict elections, IBOPE (which also does political polling) maintains a group of sample areas (key neighborhoods) to permit assessment of variation in viewer habits and preferences related to socioeconomic factors, particularly class and income. Socioeconomic class is all important in sampling, because it provides the information about consumers' buying power necessary for advertising and programming strategies.

In Rio alone, IBOPE samples 192 households each half hour between 7 A.M. and midnight. This amounts to 7,300 interviews per day, 220,000 per month. IBOPE polls regularly in major cities, with occasional surveys conducted in more than 100 other cities and towns, covering the nation from extreme south, to far west, to northeast, to Amazonian rain forest. A less prominent polling organization, Audimarket, compiles television ratings using audience meters in Rio, São Paulo, and the southern city of Porto Alegre. Audimarket findings, based on 220 homes in São Paulo and the same number in Rio, confirm Globo's nightly dominance between 6 P.M. and 9:30 P.M. Audimarket and IBOPE agree that Globo telenovelas routinely get about 70 percent of the sets turned on (50-70% of all sets) in that time period. (Later in the evening there is more competition.) An indirect measure of Globo's success is utility-company monitoring of mass behavior. Each night, when a Globo novela begins, phone use drops, minute by minute, then rises during commercials. Piped water levels also drop across the nation during commercials, as hundreds of thousands of toilets are flushed. The same thing happens annually in the United States during Superbowl commercials.

Brazilian survey research is confined to cities. Neither IBOPE nor any other polling organization works in communities with recent and incomplete access to television, which is one reason why research on television's context and effects in rural areas has been needed—and was part of our research project, in six communities and five states. IBOPE's rationale for its sampling strategy is that Brazilian television is an urban phenomenon, which spreads the metropolitan patterns of Rio and São Paulo to residents of other cities and towns in a highly urban nation. Television's target is the consuming classes, who are most numerous and reachable in urban locales.

Despite constant IBOPE polling, which is professionally managed and seems to be reasonably accurate, data on the week's, month's, season's, and even year's most popular programs are publicly unavailable. In contrast to the United States, where ratings are routinely published in *Variety, TV Guide*, and newspapers, comparable information is much more restricted in Brazil. To obtain ratings data, we had to arrange personal interviews with IBOPE, Audimarket, and other market-research agency personnel, who did grant us access to ratings data during the course of our project.[15] The reason for secrecy is that these agencies make money selling their data and services. IBOPE sells its voluminous monthly statistical reports to firms that have some business use for them. A single issue of a monthly report cost about $300 in 1984. Except for subscribers, no one knows exactly what the fluctuations in program preferences are, unless one of the networks decides to publish them, usually as a marketing ploy, plugging the popularity—and hence the commercial value—of an offering. In addition to daily sampling, IBOPE (and the others) do special studies commissioned by networks, stations, and businesses. If results accord with expectations, or help the corporate image, they are publicized in newspapers and magazines. If not, they are suppressed. IBOPE gathers data but does not do detailed analyses of its results. Those who commission a study or purchase IBOPE's reports must do their own calculations of matters such as the effect of age or sex on viewing habits and preferences. My own analysis of IBOPE's monthly survey data for Rio revealed a few obvious patterns: men and women watch Globo about equally after 7 P.M. during telenovela time; slightly more men than women watch the nightly news, and men dominate viewing after 10 P.M. Overall, 41 percent of novela viewers are males.

The American market is far more competitive than Brazil's, with nothing comparable to single-network domination, and competition leads to open ratings comparisons. Nielsen results are regularly published and available for anyone to consult. American ratings are public knowledge because they are used as credentials in advertising, for example, in *Variety* and other trade journals. Ratings are used by commercial networks and stations to attract advertisers and by production companies to sell their products, including syndicated reruns, to stations. Even in Brazil, in 1984, the new-born Manchête network commissioned an IBOPE study, then gleefully publicized the results when its coverage of Rio's carnival far surpassed powerful Globo's programming, which was beaten for the first time ever in certain time slots.

IBOPE has established a useful social class scale to evaluate audience buying power. Its categories are A (upper class), B1 (upper middle), B2 (middle middle), B3 (lower middle), C (upper working), and D (lower working and people without significant incomes). The scale is based on the proportion and amount of household income remaining after certain basic expenditures have been made. These "necessities" include food, utilities (including telephone), school expenses, clothing, transportation, personal hygiene items, medical care, and domestic help. Note that IBOPE uses Brazilian cultural standards to define the basics of middle-class existence. For instance, "domestic help" (a maid and/or cook) is considered necessary by middle-class Brazilians. (The American equivalent might be the washing machine.)

The amount expended on these items is added up and deducted from gross income. The remainder is divided by total earnings to yield a percentage of gross income (disposable income) available for consumer's goods. Brazilians are grouped into IBOPE's social classes on the basis of this percentage. IBOPE also pays attention to actual gross income, recognizing that some of the poorest people manage to reduce their expenses on basics in various ways, yet still lack enough money to spend on the items hawked on television. Proportional distribution of the classes in Rio in 1983 to 1984 is shown in Table 4.1.

TABLE 4.1
IBOPE's Social Classes

CLASS	PERCENTAGE
Upper (A) and Upper-middle (B1)	6
Middle-middle (B2) and Lower-middle (B3)	34
Working (C)	34
Abject Poverty (D)	26
Total	100

Audience Targeting: Massification vs. Segmental Appeal

Television executives and sponsors make decisions based on socioeconomic characteristics of audiences. Brazil has four national networks: Globo, SBT, Manchête, and Bandeirantes. Only Globo has true mass appeal, consistently attracting large audiences in all social classes, regions, and types of community. More than Globo, the other networks target their programming at particular segments of the Brazilian population. The Manchête network, which began operations in 1983, aims many of its programs at the upper segments of the IBOPE scale, classes A and B, which comprise at least 40 percent of the viewers in Brazil's southern cities. For example, in October to November 1983, Manchête showed an attractively-produced documentary series, *The Brazilians*, written and narrated by anthropologist Roberto DaMatta. In mid-1984, to cap its Summer Olympic coverage, Manchête produced and broadcast a handsome weekly historical mini-series called *The Marquesa dos Santos*, which told the story of the love affair between nineteenth century Brazilian emperor Dom Pedro II and the title character. Well-produced musical and interview programs, a weekly magazine, and American film hits (like *Star Wars*—dubbed in Portuguese) rounded out Manchête's schedule.

Globo's popularity rests on three main program types—national news, telenovelas, and comedy-variety shows. Globo's novelas,[16] whose production standards and acting professionalism put day-time American "soaps" to shame, offer the clearest quality contrast with other networks. Other Brazilian networks have competent news programs, but Globo hooks the mass audience because six nights a week its national news broadcast is sandwiched between its two most popular telenovelas. The other networks have only managed to compete with Globo in low-and middle-brow comedy-variety programming and outside of prime time. Only on Sundays does the mass pattern of simultaneous nation-wide Globo-viewing break down somewhat. On Sunday nights Globo offers a two-hour program, a combined variety show and news magazine called *Fantástico*, which regularly ranks in the week's top ten. However, in contrast to Globo's weeknight news and telenovelas, which have a loyal national following, *Fantástico*'s audience is more segmental (as opposed to massified—appealing across-the-board, to all social groups in a nation, for examples). *Fantástico* is much more popular in small cities, towns, and rural zones than in the major cities. Availing themselves of urban recreational alternatives, middle-class *cariocas* (residents of Rio de Janeiro) and *paulistas* (residents of São Paulo) watch relatively less Sunday night television than other Brazilians.

Globo's quality is less obvious in its humor and variety programs, including *Fantástico*, which tend to have more small-town and down-scale audiences. One *Fantástico*, for example, informed viewers that extraterrestrials have been visiting Earth for 50,000 years, showing as confirmation motifs of birds purportedly unlike any found on earth in Peruvian architectural reliefs, and a supposed jaguar's head (which looked more like a rabbit's to me) at Lake Titicaca; presumably, Titicaca means jaguar.

Globo quality also suffers late Saturday afternoon, when the network offers a live variety show hosted by the clown-like "Chacrinha"—an older man who wanders around amid a supporting cast of scantily dressed disco-dancing women, professional entertainers, amateurs, and panelists who judge their acts. Punctuated by closeups of women's outrageously exposed bottoms, Chacrinha mutters to his screaming audience questions such as "Who's smarter—men or women?" For years this two-hour program has been considered a favorite of maids and cooks throughout the nation. Chacrinha also sponsors contests to determine such notables as Brazil's most beautiful maid, student, black woman, best disco dancer, and queen of the samba schools.

Trailing Globo, which has almost total national penetration, is SBT (the Brazilian Television System), owned by *paulista* impresario Sílvio Santos. Established in 1982, it took only two years for "Sílvio Santos," as the network is popularly called, to become the nation's second in scope. SBT aims at a lower segment of the IBOPE scale than does Globo or Manchête. Its most popular programs are game and variety shows, on the same level as Globo's "Chacrinha." One of them, a several-hour marathon, is hosted by Sílvio Santos himself (a Bert Parks look-alike). Through 1984 this program began Sunday at 11 A.M. and ended at 8 P.M. It has since been extended to compete face-to-face with *Fantástico*. The Sílvio Santos marathon is composed of segments, most modeled on old American game shows, such as *Name That Tune*. Most popular is the last segment, a two-hour amateur program, during which a panel of eight jurors (mostly men) judge singers, dancers, and oddball performers (a man who rubs his face in broken glass without being cut, for example). The live performances and jurors' she-

110 Competitive Individualism

nanigans are interrupted by clips from the American *Gong Show*. Occasionally a performer appears mimicking *Gong Show* acts, and often, untalented singers are gonged.

Globo's only significant competition comes on Sunday afternoon and early evening, when this Sílvio Santos game-show marathon usually at least equals Globo's audiences. Sunday, the only day without novelas, is also the day when urban middle-class Brazilians flock to clubs, beaches, and restaurants. From a commercial viewpoint, Sunday afternoon is a television disaster—a time slot that the usually dominant network can most afford to lose. Sílvio Santos's audience includes millions of class C and D viewers, people with neither automobiles nor club memberships, who cannot afford to eat in restaurants. Sunday is also the national "maid's day off," when she is allowed to be at home with her family—watching Sílvio Santos—after spending the week caring for her social superiors. Another SBT variety show, hosted by Augusto Liberato (Gugú), did so well late Saturday night that Globo had enticed Gugú to its own roster by 1987.

On week-nights, SBT airs two prime-time novelas, scheduled so as to overlap as little as possible with Globo's. One is usually a Mexican program dubbed in Portuguese. The other is Brazilian. There is a very obvious contrast in quality between SBT *novelas* and those made by Globo. Globo's are lavishly produced, with multiple outdoor scenes and location shots. Globo employs some of Brazil's finest actors and writers. The programs shown on SBT, whether Brazilian or Mexican, are inferior. They are set almost entirely indoors. Locales are less attractive and varied and well-known actors less evident; their audiences are mainly lower-class.

Like all Brazilian networks other than Globo, SBT has segmental rather than mass appeal. Brazilian elites consider SBT's most popular formats—game and variety shows—lowbrow entertainment (comparable to *The Gong Show, Gomer Pyle*, and *The Beverly Hillbillies* in the United States). SBT does compete effectively with Globo for the lower half of the IBOPE scale in certain time-slots. Viewers in Arembepe, the coastal town in Bahia I have studied since 1962, where virtually everyone is a member of the national lower class (IBOPE segments C and D), are faithful viewers of SBT shows, just as they are of Globo news and *telenovelas*. SBT does attract some class B2 and B3 viewers, who are necessary for its survival, because programs that appeal only to classes C and D, who have little extra money to invest in consumer goods, are doomed.

For example, one of Rio's most interesting programs, *The People on TV*, was taken off the air (by SBT) in 1984 because it did not appeal to the consuming classes. It was a live afternoon program, shown weekdays from 3 P.M. (later 4 P.M.) to 6 P.M. (First the length was reduced, then the program cancelled). *The People on TV* offered the closest thing I saw in

Brazil to consumer advocacy. Poor people (maids, cooks, drivers) appeared each day to report about exposed sewers, economic disputes, and incidents of victimization. Two attractive young women sat on a stage and answered viewers' phone calls, while a panel that included one congressman and one spiritualist helped host Wilton Tupinambá Franco suggest solutions. Occasionally Franco engaged in shouting matches by phone or in person with a purported villain. The program always ended with Avé Maria, as the audience filed out of the studio, stopping to pay homage to a garish statue of the Virgin Mary. Concomitantly, Wilton Franco delivered an emotional benediction.

The People on TV suffered the same fate as a series of other shows previously hosted by Wilton Franco: It was forced off the air because it appealed mainly to the poor. It never found major sponsors, or earned much of a profit. Most of its ads were for snake-oil remedies—products that the poor could afford. The fact that *The People on TV* actually had a large audience share, often beating Globo in its time-slot, shows that audience quality is more important than quantity, particularly in Brazil, where the consuming class is numerically much smaller than in the United States. In the United States, even the poorest people have more disposable income and participate more in consumerism than in Brazil.

Network Dominance

> ... some of the 'effects' commonly attributed to the television medium should be conceived instead as following from its present organizational form, in which nearly 900 separate channels are effectively reduced to being mere conduits for four centralized TV networks. It is for this reason, and the consequent lack of variation or diversity in program content to which the nation is exposed, that television now serves so well as a proxy for all of the mass media whenever questions arise over mass media effects.[17]

Paul Hirsch made those observations about American television, but they are even truer of commercial television in Brazil, where production involves the concentration of power and capital in the hands of fewer people.[18]

Globo's success, one of the foremost examples of the growth of large monopolies[19] in Brazil during the 1970s, rests on the complexity of its strategy for conquering the public and its cooperation with an authoritarian central government, in various ways.[20] For example, it has been claimed[21] that years of governmental labor repression facilitated Globo's success. With no strong unions or strike possibilities, workers had to accept the conditions the network imposed because any labor reaction could have been considered subversive.[22] Globo has been known for taking the government's side,[23] particularly from 1968 to 1974, at the height of authoritarianism and censorship. Commenting on Brazilian television in the late 1970s, one observer wrote that Globo's national news, on which people were "always beautiful and well-fed,"[24] still broadcast so many government announcements that it could have been confused with SECOM, the government press agency. Many of the criticisms that have been leveled against Brazilian television as a medium are actually directed at Globo and its political support and implications. However television executives outside of Globo also made programming decisions out of fear of, or to please, government. In 1983, for example, a government critic was dismissed by a São Paulo station in dire financial circumstances because it needed a government loan.

Brazilian broadcasters who have retained their licenses through nonoffensive popular programming and cooperation with government (and of which Rede Globo is the prime example) have been able to amass significantly more gatekeeping power than is possible in the United States, where antimonopoly laws prohibit the same individual or corporation from controlling the media by owning a newspaper and TV station in the same city. Rede Globo's success began in Rio, where a developed support industry has reinforced its dominance. The empire ruled by Globo chief Roberto Marinho encompasses production facilities and network headquarters, Rio's TV Globo channel, the city's best-selling newspaper *O Globo*, popular AM and FM radio stations, a book publisher, and a record company, which produces best-selling albums of the national and international scores of each telenovela.[25]

Monopolistic control of multiple media, marketing savvy, and federal intervention and support have combined to create in Rede Globo an empire that stands alongside, and is rivaled as a national institution only by, the Brazilian state. In recognition of the fact that Roberto Marinho is one of the most powerful men in Brazil, the 1985 presidential candidates made a point of paying him court through personal visits. Such media dominance means that Brazilians have more restricted access than Americans do to information—including anti-government views, because so many sources are controlled by a single monopolistic organization, linked to government.

Monopolistic Control over Multiple Media

Globo's popularity in Rio is helped by the fact that its programming gets extensive press support, while other channels are ignored or castigated. Each morning the newspaper *O Globo* summarizes the previous night's Globo novela happenings, ignoring the other networks. In the weekly magazine *Tevê*, distributed with Sunday's *O Globo*, Globo's offerings receive much more attention than those of other channels, which are usually mentioned only to be criticized for "low quality" and other faults. Criticisms of Globo programming in Globo publications are very rare, but each issue of *Tevê* manages to take six to ten potshots at the competition. *Tevê's* inside front page prints letters derogating non-Globo programs, columnists take up the tone. The day before the debut of one Globo *novela*, for example, a columnist lambasted the *novela* that had debuted on another channel the previous week: "Not knowing exactly what to do, TVS offered a remake of *The Right to Be Born* (an old, highly successful *novela*), with poor sets and bad acting."[26]

Globo insists on the huge gap between its style and others. In the same issue of *Tevê* (September 25, 1983), columnist Artur da Távola condescended that two Rio stations were "directed at popular programming" and called "barbarous" a variety show whose hostess sang along with a pair of guest musicians. He also criticized TV Manchête (known as a high-quality network) for too many announcements of coming programs (a failure fully as obvious any day on Globo) and for showing a music program without naming the concert pieces. Távola also made use of the "cultural imperialism" label to extol Globo's national programming over its competitors' tendency to show imported programs, such as American westerns— "exploiting the Brazilian fascination with the cowboy, which is rooted in infancy"—implying that westerns are juvenile. Távola's final insult in a single column: "There's nothing more tiresome than too much slang—as on TV Record's program 'Realce'. . . . perhaps the only good program on that channel".[27]

Generally, Brazilian television management makes it clear that not a lot good can be said about competitors. It was clear that conditions of employment permitted the insightful critic and commentator Arthur da Távola, now a federal deputy, whom some intellectuals called Brazil's Roland Barthes, as others were dismissing him as a Globo stooge, to make only occasional favorable comments about other stations. For many years, in addition to his daily column in *O Globo*, Távola also wrote for *Manchête* (a *Life* imitator) and *Amiga* (the popular TV fan magazine), both owned by Adolpho Bloch, who also owns TV Manchête and the network of that name. The same rules apply in Bloch's magazines as in *O Globo*: Praise our product, saying as little positive and as much negative as possible about the competition. Thus, on November 29, 1983, Távola, writing in Manchête's fan magazine *Amiga*, lauded the technical quality of that network's daily telejournalism (news broadcasts) and two other programs, asserting that TV Manchête had entered the realm of quality production until then present only in some Globo productions.

In addition to its treatment of the competition, Globo makes a practice of ignoring popular culture events that do not fit its schedule and plans. In 1984, for example, Globo decided to stick to its normal programming and leave Summer Olympics and Carnival coverage to the competition, chiefly Manchête. Once the decision was made to ignore Carnival, Globo's management issued memos ordering directors of musical programs not to include any of that year's newly-written Carnival samba-scores. In response, an *Amiga* columnist (employed by Manchête,[28] which at the time was hyping its own Carnival coverage), wrote that Globo was trying to deny that at Carnival time samba schools and music are the people's main interest. The columnist went on—Globo should have learned a lesson about the popular will from the 1982 gubernatorial elections, when its partisanship (misuse of poll results in favor of the government party and against the eventual winner) became obvious and affected the accuracy of its reporting. Globo's power to change the rules of the game isn't as great as its arrogance, said the columnist.

The Role of the Audience

In addition to censorship as a force in program development, networks also respond to audience preferences and reactions. In both the United States and Brazil government officials, sponsors, and network personnel routinely cite "community standards," "public opinion," and "the audience" in justifying their decisions. Globo encourages feedback from public opinion by monitoring and evaluating reactions to its novelas. Indeed, Globo is unique in Brazil in the extent to which it investigates audience reactions to characters and plot developments. In addition to consulting daily and monthly IBOPE results, Globo has its own analysis and research department, which does in-depth interviewing. While leaving no doubt that he holds ultimate power, Roberto Marinho is known to give both power and authority to the television executives under him. The supervisors of production and direction at Globo are allowed to define the basic ingredients in productions.

Távola[29] has stressed that the telenovela is a semi-open work that the audience has a role in guiding. Globo is concerned with public reaction because it wants to sell products; indeed this is one of the most important determinants of what happens to characters and plots.[30] On the basis of audience response, particular roles may be reduced or augmented. Conclusions have been changed after a writer has been deluged with letters, asking, for example, that a romantic couple slated to separate be allowed to stay together. Negative reactions to *Sinal do Alerta* (*Danger Signal*), which dealt with pollution and strikes, led Globo to avoid these subjects in later novelas. Another serial, *Os Gigantes (The Giants)*, depicted incest and euthanasia of a man attached to a life-sustaining machine. After "mothers" wrote in complaining that these were improper themes for children, that novela was shortened to eighty chapters, about half the usual length.

To take the public pulse, researchers and writers consult such information brokers as taxi drivers, hairdressers, and barbers, who are sounding boards of popular opinion. Premier telenovelist Janete Clair was known to be adept at modifying her works in progress in accordance with public wishes, and she elicited opinions in the supermarket and the street. Successful telenovelist and Clair disciple Gilberto Braga regularly consults his maid, who supposedly brings him reactions from her friends. In smaller cities and towns, researchers approach people in the central bar or luncheonette, where announcements are posted and opinion leaders congregate. The director of Globo's research department can mandate certain changes by novela directors, and authors respond in various ways when ratings fall, often reverting to proven formulas. In recompense for their popularity, successful telenovelists earn substantially more than actors, but writers with declining audiences and those who offend management are either fired or banished to 6 P.M., where, however, an aspiring writer is happy to begin a career.

Open to outside inputs, telenovelas differ from theatre and films in that actors don't have a completely predetermined character they must cling to; relationships and plots respond to external factors. Of course, production considerations also affect the development of a novela. Certain conditions, including the constraints of having to write a chapter a day, and overall budget, limit possibilities. The first fifty chapters get the most money, then Globo starts investing in its next project.

Nevertheless, Globo's attention to audience reaction (and its publicity about this attention) helps give spectators a sense of participating in the story and its development. Of course, if ordinary people are to influence a novela's course, they must know about intended developments in advance: and radio programs and fan magazines provide this information. Once segments have been filmed, some three weeks before being aired, Globo provides fan magazines with plot summaries. The TV magazine *Amiga* summarizes events for the week immediately following its issue date. It also reveals plot plans, such as murders and marriages, well into the future. Occasionally, network officials or writers divulge intended plot developments months before filming.

One interesting case of "audience participation" involved the *novela O Astro*, during whose last chapters people throughout Brazil were asking "Who killed Salomão Hayalla?" A *Globo* newspaper columnist admitted that she and the writer, Janete Clair, had combined to dupe the public about the outcome. To maintain the suspense, the columnist reported that Clair had written five endings, with different murderers, when she had really written just one. Sometimes, multiple endings actually are filmed, and *Amiga* publishes all of them—well in advance.

The 1984 Presidential Campaign

> The organizational structure of [American] television further underlies and makes possible a wide variety of 'effects' often proposed by social scientists as unique to this medium, but which also formerly characterized other mass media when they, too, were organized along the lines which television now follows. For example, the prospect of favorable television news coverage has accelerated (though did not originate) the staging of conferences, political conventions, press releases, campaign stops, and other 'pseudo-events.'[31]

President Franklin D. Roosevelt instituted the practice of going directly to the people on the radio, thereby wresting control from old boy newspaper journalists, but also paving the way for the eventual power of TV gatekeepers. Although Paul Hirsch finds that American political leaders have little control over the news judgments of broadcast journalists, there is actually a mutually reinforcing feedback between media, politicians, and government. Michael Parenti's book *Inventing Reality* (1986) argues convincingly that the American media have helped recreate a view of reality supportive of existing power relationships, with the press generally defining the news as what politicians say. Censorship works on different levels and in many ways in the United States just as it has done in Brazil. Again and again, the American news media comply with goverment disinformation campaigns, and reporters, eager to please editors, censor themselves.

In 1984 both the United States and Brazil had lengthy, but very differently organized and publicized, presidential campaigns. The American campaign was the usual media event, in which, in Paul Hirsch's words:

> Candidates for political office seeking to reach the public directly must purchase television advertising time—which has become the single largest item in campaign budgets and greatly accounts for the rising cost of seeking office and pressure to raise funds in ever-increasing amounts.[32]

In contrast, Brazilian media exposure during campaigns was regulated by a statute known as the Lei Falcão (Falcon law), according to which each candidate was allocated a specified amount of air-time of dubious value. Although Brazil had ample know-how, practice and technology to make slick political ads of the sort that have become so common in the United

States, this was prohibited. TV coverage of candidates remained in the dark ages—black and white with non-moving pictures. Candidates' television publicity consisted of typewritten lists of family, memberships, and positions, and mug-shot still photos staring out from a silent screen. Although government party candidates had to join the Falcão line-up, they also had an advantage: Whenever the President or a minister made an official visit, the welcome by incumbent local officials—often PDS candidates—was televised.

In 1984, even as the end of military rule approached and Brazil prepared for a presidential election—either indirect by an electoral college, as planned by the government, or direct, as the people wanted—there was a slowdown in the process of "opening," with censorship temporarily increasing in response to the campaign for direct presidential election. The Globo organization, in its most daring independent political act, supported direct election and the candidacy of Aureliano Chaves, then Vice President of Brazil and a popular maverick member of the government (military) party (PDS), for president. The rallies for direct election were broadcast first by Manchête, then by Globo, in its first coverage ever of anti-government protests. However, for so obviously supporting the vice president, Globo was accused of boycotting his possible opponents, including eventual PDS nominee Paulo Maluf and Rio's governor Brizola. After television gave prominent coverage to plans for rallies, and broadcast actual rallies, the government cracked down, eventually censoring all live broadcasts from Brasília during the period when the amendment permitting direct elections was being voted on (and rejected) by Congress.

Once it was determined that the presidential election would be indirect, Tancredo Nêves, a venerable member of the PMDB opposition (and the eventual winner, who died soon after taking office), became the overwhelming popular favorite. Some PDS members, including Vice-President Chaves, formed a "Liberal Front" and backed Tancredo Nêves, contributing to his eventual electoral college victory. With Chaves out of the race, the main question became who was to be the government-party candidate. The PDS nomination, contested by Paulo Maluf and Mário Andreazza, had to be won by personal cultivation of an old boy network, rather than by success in primaries and the media.[33]

By August, 1984, when the PDS held its nominating convention, some Brazilians had been following the concurrent presidential campaign in the United States, but an article in *O Jornal da Brasil*[34] reported that Brazilians didn't understand the American process of electing a president. Furthermore, after a quarter century of exclusion from presidential voting, they barely understood their own system—nor were they offered much assistance. "National-treasure" actress Fernanda Montenegro was quoted

118   Competitive Individualism

as saying she did not understand current Brazilian election procedures and political developments, and I understood why. In trying to decipher the Brazilian electoral process, I encountered an amazing amount of misinformation, which the media seemed to do as much to propagate as to resolve. So ineffective had Brazilian television been in spelling out the electoral process that my best informant in the small Bahian town of Arembepe did not realize that he would not be voting for president, that the election would be indirect—with the electoral college scheduled to make the decision on January 15, 1985. Moreover, the low level of interest in the election revealed by a Gallup poll as the PDS nomination approached was surprising given that this would be the first time since 1960 that the Brazilian president would be chosen without military intervention.

Concurrently, in the United States, it was fairly clear to anyone interested in politics who paid attention to media accounts that Walter Mondale needed 1,917 delegate votes for the Democratic nomination—at which point he would run against President Reagan. A fairly accurate delegate count was kept by the media prior to the Democrats' nominating convention. However, if anyone other than candidates and their close advisors kept tabs on delegate preferences and commitments in Brazil, the media didn't report it. The process remained a mystery, with the media speculating and the candidates making counterclaims about the outcome, up through the PDS convention, where Paulo Maluf won easily.[35]

Nor did Brazilian television seem to care much who got the nomination. Globo offered only spotty coverage of the count of the PDS convention vote in Brasília, which took place on a Saturday afternoon, although it was the only disputed presidential nomination. In the United States, this would have been one of the biggest political stories of the year, but Globo saw fit to broadcast it in occasional flashes during a Jerry Lewis movie and continuing into Chacrinha—a variety show aimed at maids.

Notes

1. Hirsch, Paul M. "The Role of Television and Popular Culture in Contemporary Society." p. 252.
2. Patt Morrison, "MTV with a Twist." *Ann Arbor News*, December 14, 1986.
3. Jerry Gray, "With a Few Exceptions, Television in Africa Fails to Educate and Enlighten." *Ann Arbor News*, December 8, 1986.
4. *Ibid.*
5. I gratefully acknowledge support from the following sources: the Wenner-Gren Foundation for Anthropological Research, for a grant to study "The Electronic Mass Media and Social Change in Brazil" (1983-84); the National Science Foundation (NSF-G-BNS 8317856-Kottak, "Social Impact of Television in Rural Brazil"), supporting field work in the states of Bahia, Para, Santa Catarina, and São Paulo (6/84-11/86); and the National Institute of Mental Health

for a grant to study "Television's Behavioral Effects in Brazil (1-R01-MH38815-01-03)," entailing field research in rural communities, as well as data entry and analysis (1/1/85-12/31/87).
6. Personal communication; see also Távola, 1984.
7. Hirsch, Paul M, "The Role of Television and Popular Culture in Contemporary Society," p. 255.
8. Maria Rita Kehl, "Um só Povo, uma só Cabeça, uma só Nação," pp. 28-29.
9. The agency Dentel was charged with applying authoritarian state regulation to Brazilian television.
10. Wagley, p. 306.
11. Miranda and Pereira, p. 26.
12. Miranda and Pereira, p. 28. Similarly, a 1986 editorial in *The Kenya Times*, owned by the government party, proclaimed that "Our youth need to be protected from corrupting foreign cultural influences that glorify violence and other attendant social vices that are slowly but effectively eroding our social values."
13. Instituto Brasileiro de Opinião Pública e Estatística.
14. Gallup has a Brazilian branch, but it is overshadowed by IBOPE.
15. The assistance of various IBOPE representatives, of Maxim Castelnau, Director of Audimarket, and of Otavio da Costa Eduardo, is gratefully acknowledged. I am especially grateful to Cid Pacheco and Lucia Ferreira Reis for many hours of conversation, enlightenment, and assistance.
16. Brazilian telenovelas are discussed at greater length in several of the author's works in progress; see also Straubhaar, 1982.
17. Hirsch, Paul M. "The Role of Television and Popular Culture in Contemporary Society," p. 249.
18. Miranda and Pereira, p. 20.
19. Kehl, p. 5.
20. Conclusion of the contributors to *Anos Televisão*, 70(7) Rio: Europa.
21. Kehl, p. 19.
22. Walter Avancini, quoted in Kehl, p. 19.
23. Elisabeth Carvalho. "Telejornalismo: A Década do Jornal da Tranquilidade," p. 37.
24. Carvalho, p. 33.
25. Herz (1987) is a recent analysis of Globo's strategy for dominance; see also Ramos, 1986.
26. *Têve*, September 25, 1983.
27. Artur da Távola, column in *Têve, O Globo*, September 25, 1983.
28. Eli Halfoun, weekly column in *Amiga*, January 20, 1984, p. 9.
29. Personal communication and in virtually all his writing.
30. Personal communication; interviews with Lucia Ferreira Reis and Paulo Alberto Monteiro de Barros (Artur da Távola).
31. Hirsch, Paul M. "The Role of Television and Popular Culture in Contemporary Society," pp. 251, 255.
32. Hirsch, p. 252.
33. An article about rival presidential candidates Paulo Maluf and Mário Andreazza in *Jornal do Brasil* on August 11, 1984, the day the PDS nominee was chosen in Brasília, shows that Maluf's career followed a classic Brazilian path, since at least the time of the "revolution" and the "economic miracle." Maluf has risen by knowing how to manipulate politics; he also knew the importance

of "personalism." An adept student, he graduated first in his engineering class; thereafter he became an impresario. He entered politics after having been appointed by the PDS to certain strategic positions in the state of São Paulo. He was elected president of various business organizations but eventually decided to buck the government party (then ARENA) leadership and run for governor against the party's official candidate. Bringing President Geisel to São Paulo to be honored, Maluf obtained Geisel's agreement that should Maluf win the convention, Geisel would support him. Maluf made a point of personally contacting, three times, all 1200 voting delegates, learning their name, as well as those of their wives and children. When it came time to vote, Maluf greeted each delegate by name, asking about family members, whereas the opposition candidate knew fewer than 5 percent of the delegates personally. The result was that Maluf won by 28 votes, a sufficient if unspectacular majority.
34. August 11, 1984.
35. Andreazza, himself educated in military schools, was supported by former military presidents Costa e Silva and Médici, but had fallen into disfavor with ex-president Geisel.

References

Carvalho, Elisabeth. 1981. "Telejournalismo: A Década do Jornal da Tranquilidade." *Anos Televisão.* 70(7), pp. 31-47. Rio: Europa.
Gray, Jerry. 1986. "With a Few Exceptions, Television in Africa Fails to Educate and Enlighten." *Ann Arbor News.* December 8.
Halfoun, Eli. 1984. *Amiga.* January 20, Rio: Bloch.
Herz, Daniel. 1987. *A História Secreta da Rede Globo.* Porto Alegre: Tchê.
Hirsch, Paul M. 1979. "The Role of Television and Popular Culture in Contemporary Society." In Horace Newcomb, ed. *Television: The Critical View.* New York: Oxford University Press, pp. 249-279.
Kehl, Maria Rita. 1981. "Um só Povo, uma só Cabeça, uma só Nação," In *Anos 70 Televisão* 70(7), pp. 5-29. Rio: Europa.
Miranda, Ricardo and Carlos Alberto M. Pereira. 1983. *Televisão: o Nacional e o Popular na Cultura Brasileira.* São Paulo: Brasiliense.
Morrison, Patt. 1986. "MTV with a Twist." *Ann Arbor News*, December 14.
Ramos, Roberto. 1986. *Grafinos na Globo.* Petrópolis: Vozes.
Straubhaar, Joseph D. 1982. "The Development of the Telenovela as the Pre-eminent Form of Popular Culture in Brazil." *Studies in Latin American Popular Culture* 1:138-150.
Távola, Artur da. 1983. *Têve.* September 25. Rio: *O Globo.*
_____. 1984. *A Liberdade do Ver: Televisão em Leitura Crítica.* Rio de Janeiro: Nova Fronteira.
Wagley, Charles. 1971. *An Introduction to Brazil*, (rev. ed.) New York: Columbia University Press.

5

Thief: At Long Last, a Good Movie about a Capitalist

Aaron Wildavsky

The cinema cannot cope with capitalism. Its portraits of capitalists are worse than caricatures: the bastards do not even want to make money. At best (Edward Arnold in *Miracle on 34th Street*), they are philanthropists in disguise, giving away their stockholders' money in yet another demonstration that profit and decency are incompatible. Their humanity (viz. Frank Capra) is measured by their bad business practice. At worse (cf. *All My Sons*), they kill their own children to build up their bank accounts or (to choose another of Arthur Miller's play-movies) see their dignity murdered by the system as Willy-the-low-man is discarded along with his shoddy merchandise. Often their behavior is so self-destructive, their personalities so twisted (they are perverts, just like the markets for which they stand), that they belong with the criminally insane. To cite an appropriately banal example, in *North Dallas Forty*, owners commit obviously illegal acts, planting dope to frame a football player who could make them a winner, because he is disobedient. Instead of being concerned with results, the hallmark of competitive individualism, these weirdo would-be capitalists take fiendish pleasure in ruining the hero's life, even though they will be worse off financially, besides being likely to land in jail. These capitalists make our skin crawl because their ambition is to make other people squirm. In *Missing*, it hardly matters whether Jack Lemmon (or his son) is murdered by the nuclear industry or the State Department. In the movies, oppression is not the unanticipated consequence of trying to make money by satisfying consumer preferences; oppression is the purpose toward which capital accumulation is merely an adjunct.

In free markets under conditions of perfect competition, each transaction is complete in and of itself. Freedom of contract prevails. Each party discharges its obligations punctiliously. When the transaction is over, each individual is free to engage in or to refuse new ones. Failures are attributed to bad luck or poor craftsmanship, but never to the principle of exchange itself. "System blame" would be appropriate only if monopolists succeeded in limiting transactions, thereby transforming markets into hierarchies. The virtue of Michael Mann's *Thief* is that he exemplifies, understands, and acts upon pure principles of competitive individualism.

From the work ethic to regulation of home life to limited liability, the *Thief* is unerring in his appreciation of capitalist mores. Extend his small scope, legalize his enterprise, and one has capitalism writ large—but without the romanticism that sometimes accompanies it. In *Thunder Bay*, directed by Anthony Mann, James Stewart played a wildcatter seeking oil off the Gulf coast of Louisiana. He is helped by a big businessman who started the same small way. He is opposed by townspeople who fear for the shrimp catch on which their livelihood depends. In the end, a gusher reveals the hidden home of the fishermen's most valuable prize—the golden shrimp. Capitalism and ecology reenforce one another. Our *Thief*, however, knows no such illusions. He does not think himself a social worker whose activities will benefit weaker elements in society. He does believe in the American Dream, which he takes to be competitive individualism until the state and the monopolists try to take it away from him.

Frank the thief, played by James Caan, emerges in his mid-thirties from eleven years in prison with a collage of the American Dream on a postcard in his pocket—wife, child, grandfather (Okla, the master thief who has taught him his craft), and suburban house. Soon owner of a used-car business, one deception fronting for another, and a string of bars and parking lots, showing himself off as the entrepreneur he is, Frank is a skillful diamond thief. He uses a diamond drill. The City of Chicago shines and glistens, its men and machinery honed to a fine point, filled with danger and promise for these hard-edged men who can make this game of chance pay off. Having paid his debt to society, so to speak, Frank is collecting his own, complete with expensive suits, an array of credit cards, and a diamond solitaire.

Diamonds may be his best friend, as Lorelei's song says, but his dream is incomplete without a wife. (The theme of Howard Hawks's *Gentlemen Prefer Blondes*, one which stands in contrast to his usual devotion to hard-boiled male professionalism, is that macho men need women.) To free himself to pursue a dangerous profession without distraction, Frank wants a stable home life. Nor is this surprising. Did not the great Scottish merchants, so swashbuckling in trade, establish strictly regulated family hierarchies at home? The domestic order not only contrasted with, but also complemented the anarchy in the outside world of bidding and bargaining. The long-standing alliance of markets and hierarchies, which we call "the establishment," provides the stability essential for maintaining the freedom of contract, without which capitalism could not long continue. Like all alliances, however, the establishment engages in a game of mixed motives: if honor and position can be bought and sold, its hierarchs may move to limit competition, gaining monopoly rents from their newly seized property. But that is hypothetical, lying as it does in the future.

In his present, Frank sets out to buy the American Dream, much as he would any other commodity. He finds a coffeehouse waitress, Jesse, played by Tuesday Weld, bruised, cynical, street-wise, wild with energy that as yet has no outlet. She has been propositioned before, no doubt, but not yet proposed to in one evening. Knowing that both sides must benefit from a bargain, Frank admits his personal life has been a mess. In return for wife and then child, just like that, he will provide the suburban house, money to go with it, protection, and, yes, affection. Quid pro quo. I cannot do justice to the earnest incongruity (Chicago glitter against diner naturalism) with which this scene at the back table is played.

Of course, there are imperfections: she wants to know what business he is really in (the marriage contract still has secret clauses), and he has to accept the fact that she cannot have children. She accepts the truth. It is demeaning for her to accept this bargain—wifely and motherly services, bought and paid for? Not according to the ethic of competitive individualism. She is getting as close to her dreams as she ever will, far closer than she could on her own.

The other difficulty is not so easily resolved. Frank is willing to adopt a child. But the adoption agency will not certify Frank's past, even though he, too, as he informs them with exasperation, has been brought up by the state. The authorities will not wipe his slate clean, allow him to be born again, able to bid for the child on equal terms with others. For the time being, the American Dream, the complete collage, is stymied.

Meanwhile, a parallel series of events has been taking place. The police observe Frank paying off (on time, as usual) one of his helpers in crime. They do not arrest him—no profit in that. They are businessmen, too, though they perform no socially useful labor. They impose their own limitation of contract by taking Frank in and beating him up. He will still not give them the percentage of his take they demand. Who else but a committed capitalist, beaten and bruised, would raise his bloody head from the station-house floor to ask the rhetorical question, which should but doesn't shame his beaters, "Don't you guys believe in working for a living?" (I quote from memory), as if they were able-bodied men on welfare, which is exactly what they are.

Enter the mob, the overlords of crime who like to think they control the action. They are hierarchical collectivists with a monopoly to maintain. How dare he, this independent entrepreneur, work for himself when he should work for them? At the start, however, having yet to get their hooks into him, they speak softly to Frank. The overlord, the company man, another character played perfectly, offers to help Frank find better set-ups and get the police off his back. In business for himself, Frank refuses. He makes the mistake, however, of mentioning his difficulty in adopting a baby. Sensing weakness, establishing a dependency, the overlord arranges the adoption in return for which Frank agrees to do a job. His need for money has increased partly because he wants to enjoy home life for a while and partly because Okla requests help in getting out of prison so he can die on the outside. Frank's objective, in line with his values, is to make enough money to stop for a while, having, in the meantime, paid off his obligations to the overlord.

Individualism is attacked by collectivism. Once Frank is obligated to the mob, they think he belongs to them, a life-time possessiveness expressed in the bureaucratese of those accustomed to keeping people in their files: the overlord says he "owns the paper" on Frank. Frank refuses on a ground that is crucial to the definition of a capitalist way of life: he owns himself. Each transaction is separate; every man is entitled to decide for himself how to dispose of his own labor. If contracts can be coerced, there is no freedom.

In order to show who is boss, hierarchy overcoming markets (as in the child's game, paper wraps rock but scissors cut paper), the overlord seeks to demonstrate that diamonds are not the hardest substance there is. He kills Frank's foremost employee and personal friend and punishes Frank himself, rubbing his nose in the blood of defeated hopes. "Grandpa" dies of natural causes almost as soon as he is sprung from jail, a conspiracy of fate prefiguring the conspiracy of collectivism against Frank's ideals.

At once, requiring no revelation, for he is as philosophically sophisticated as he is verbally inarticulate, Frank understands that his American Dream is over. Because collectivism recognizes no norms outside its own boundaries, and because it insists on subjugating everything inside to hierarchical principles, he can only fight force with force.

Having almost lost his (way of) life by answering a distress call from his friend, Frank cuts himself off from all attachments that might be used to gain leverage over him. He sends his wife and child away forever, taking care to leave them with money and with instructions on how to pay a retainer so that this man will not be tempted to act against them. He blows up his house and his used-car business: no more interdependence. He

Thief: At Long Last, a Good Movie about a Capitalist   125

invades the house of the overlord, killing him and his men. Frank is free. He has lost his American Dream but he has retained his freedom of action so that competitive individualism can live again.

The story line merely scratches the surface of this work of art. The film's effect depends on whether and how it is reinforced by outer accouterments—sights and sounds—and inner harmony—the fidelity of the acting to the plot. *Thief* is larger than itself because all its aspects reinforce each other. The film vibrates as it moves, its pulse beating ever-louder, because its various parts set off a mutual sympathy.

The clamorous disjunctions placed at the center of *Thief's* presentation of self, which allow it to grab the viewer's attention and never let go, seem just right to me. But they may merely give a headache to people who think they are watching another crime movie, albeit a superior one, or another predictable portrayal of a deviant done in by the system, or even an ersatz Sartre, showing the existential anti-hero reducing himself to nothingness by counterposing his own emptiness to the absurdity of society. Were it not so utterly false to the film's values, one might add to the spectrum, for good measure, Frank, the proletarian hero, bellowing his outrage at the unwillingness of the ruling class to let him rise, pitting his body against the eternal injustice of their enforced inequalities. But then the film would undoubtedly have an unalloyed documentary style, replete with folk melodies, rather than stylized characters dancing under the influence of the German Tangerine Dream group with its electronic, futuristic music.

The clash between the "you are there" documentary presentation and the angular characters, so sharp-edged they almost appear to be wearing masks, like the neon night glow and daytime sun glare that light up the diamond thief, is reconciled because the picture has a philosophical core to its contradictions: competitive individualism imposes a discipline so harsh (after all, one can fail) that efforts to rig the outcome by limiting transactions are ubiquitous. Without the social disorder that permits crime to flourish, our thief would have to find a different way of life, not so easy for a gruff, bluff, untutored man. From the risks he chooses to take, comes opportunity. But without order to support sanctity of contract, he will not be allowed to compete. The hierarchy he rejects, and rightly so when it changes the rules by force, turns out to be indispensable. Without a modicum of order, there can be no spontaneity. The very hierarchy that crushes Frank's way of life is also, in lesser but still vital degree, necessary to its achievement.

Thief begins with the master craftsman using a thermal lance and a diamond drill bit to penetrate a large, complex safe of cold steel. The controlled white heat reflects the barely suppressed passion with which Frank assaults society in his search for the American Dream. The account tingles. Men and machines, as city vignettes show, are in each other's grip. Tangerine Dream music pulsates with the film's theme: Is Germanic efficiency compatible with a rose-colored, futuristic dream? Is this high-stakes, high-technology caper, the viewer might ask as well, compatible with Frank's intrusive inarticulateness, which, when it is not hilarious, makes one wonder whether the thief is an anachronism, having chosen either the wrong profession or the wrong time to practice it?

Craftsmanship is culturally accommodating. It suits all ways of life, albeit in different ways. Pride and accomplishment in work go hand-in-hand with specialization and the division of labor, each element contributing its assigned mite to the whole hierarchy. Here the emphasis is on following correct forms. Under competition, the biggest payoffs go to those who combine best work with most marketing. The emphasis on results—by their works ye shall know them!—belongs to capitalist individualism. Adherents of sectarianism, the critical culture that values equality of outcomes (Frank is a believer in equality of opportunity), favor craftsmanship that supports a simple style of life. Better still, they favor crafts that help tear down established authority by unmasking its hidden corruption—the diamond drill that uncovers stolen diamonds.

Craftsmanship is the antidote to the demonic, stressing excellence in the performance of everyday activity without overreaching oneself. Just as the Israelites are happiest when crafting the Ark of the Covenant and Captain Ahab's crew demonstrate their ordered life by carving up the whale, whereas Moses sets sublime standards and Ahab worships his own fate, killing off almost an entire generation and complete crew between them, craftsmanship is a source of moderation. No one gets hurt who doesn't have to. God and evil are limited and confined. If diamonds have to be stolen, this is the way to do it; Frank's diamond "ice" cooly cuts cold steel.

As a craftsman, Frank is a man of honor. He is a straight arrow. His words are as direct as his diamond drill. If they are rough, that is because they go straight to the point. No pretense. His craftsmanship, however, whatever his distaste for society, is embedded in a social matrix. Since certain policemen can be bought, and big-crime businessmen think they can buy him, his personal integrity is not enough. Frank's ideal, his dream, is not anchored in social reality.

Frank has a philosophy, though it is not articulated. Only once does he not know what to do. So Grandpa Okla advises him to tell his future bride about his criminal activites; to do otherwise would violate the golden rule—to do unto others as a competitive individualist would like others to do unto him—open contacts openly arrived at. Otherwise, Frank acts upon his own understanding—rejecting the police's coerced cut and the overlord's effort to make him a fatalist who has to live by rules other people make—without saying why. James Caan has wisely chosen to play Frank as what he is, a man who acts on an ideal but is unable to put it into words. But he is, as a mime, nothing if not expressive. When he needs to apply his world view to new circumstances, he knows what to do. Since Frank's actions speak for him, what are we to make of his final deeds in blowing up or sending away all his connections—nihilism or idealism?

As an existential hero, Frank doesn't wash. Why not blow himself up? As a proletarian hero, he can hardly remain a loner. Where are the masses for him to mobilize? He might be more of an anarchist—echoing Proudhon's "property is theft"—except that he does not believe in redistribution. Is he, then, nothing more than a nihilist, engaging in random acts of violence?

Fredrik Barth—in his fine study of *Political Leadership Among Swat Pathans*, who are characterized by their "emphases on free choice and contract"—writes that "the only successful defense of honour is revenge, equal to or beyond the extent of the original insult, so as to re-establish parity or gain an advantage vis-à-vis one's rival." This, exactly, the thief does. By flashback, the viewer is given to understand that, while in prison, Frank's physical and moral integrity were repeatedly threatened. He learned then that by cutting himself off from all ties that make him vulnerable, and by placing nothing, not even his life, above resistance, his honor was preserved. This, I maintain, is not nothingness. This is self-defense. But that is all it is—defense of self. Emerging from prison with a way of life to defend, by contrast, Frank's final explosion takes on a broader social significance. "Nothingness" is not only losing this time but for all time. Frank remains to defend the ideal of competitive individualism. The overlord and his gunmen are no more. The message conveyed by their death is that further pressure by the mob will impose higher costs than its members may be willing to pay. The thief will not get it all (who does?), but the honor of his ideal remains alive with him.

For all its buzz-buzz, *Thief* breaks with the conventions of crime films. The usual heist film portrays the criminal as an outsider. The audience is in it for suspense and the thieves (viz. *Riffifi*) for the money, which, however, rarely brings integration into society. The best of this genre, *The Asphalt Jungle*, is about the weaknesses that afflict all men—from Sam Jaffe's professor and Louis Calhern's big shot, both of whom like little girls, to Sterling Hayden's muscleman, with his misplaced loyalties. Even Don Siegel's *The Killers*, in which the hired hoods (Lee Marvin and Clu Gulager) are treated as successful businessmen, does not point to anything larger than this sad state of affairs (unless, of course, one is referring to the appearance of Ronald Reagan, playing a criminal, doing a job while wearing a California Highway Patrol uniform). By embodying culture through a criminal, *Thief*, far from being about an outsider, gives us a glimpse of one American dream. At a time when the Academy Award that belonged to Burt Lancaster (for getting inside the skin of the left-over mobster in *Atlantic City*) was drowned in a squall of nostalgia, it is good to affirm that the American *Thief* only steals diamonds, not other people's honors.

Part IV
Egalitarianism

Introduction

The egalitarian sectarians (in later work called simply "egalitarians") function as the opposition to the establishment political cultures. As Wildavsky writes in "The Three Cultures:"

> Where competitive individualism believes in equality of opportunity, egalitarian sectarianism believes in equality of result. There is a world of difference between those who wish to reduce authority so as to promote individual differences and those who reject authority so as to reduce individual differences. While individualism encourages all transactions that maintain competition, sectarianism rejects all bargains that increase disparities among people.

What animates sectarians in the United States is a desire for "organization without authority," a rejection of all authority. What unifies them all is "criticism" of the dominant political cultures. Thus, they can agree on what they do not like even if they might not be able to agree on what they like, except on very general terms.

The basic attributes of the egalitarian political culture are:

1. Few prescriptions (since authority is not seen as valid) and strong boundaries.
2. Social organization is seen as "voluntary" so there is little coercion or use of authority.
3. Risks undertaken for the group only and benefits are distributed equally to the group.
4. Leadership generally is seen as undesirable since voluntary choice is to be optimized. Charismatic leadership arises often, especially in response to emergencies. The dilemma of egalitarian cultures is that without leadership they tend to fall apart but with it members feel that their autonomy is threatened.
5. Envy is controlled by voluntary simplicity, little show of wealth.
6. Blame is ascribed to the workings of the system under which people live—to evil institutions, which corrupt people, and conspiracies by the powerful to maintain their power and privileges.
7. Fairness is a function of equality and a recognition of the needs all people have. The equal distribution of resources is seen as primary, not economic growth and the creation of wealth.

8. An "Armageddon complex," which sees the establishment system as dangerous and unwilling to change. This helps egalitarian movements hold together, and the alleged unwillingness of the establishment to change fuels the hostile critical tone of many egalitarians. Egalitarians will neither join the system nor function as members of the "loyal opposition." Instead, they seek to separate themselves from it. It is the egalitarian ethos that is behind much of the criticism of American society and politics.

The essays by Cantor, on women and the media, and Wilder, on the Vietnam Monument, are egalitarian in nature, but they lack the harsh stridency found in some egalitarian writings.

6

Up Against the Wall: The Vietnam Veterans Memorial & the Paradox of Remembrance

Carol Wilder

Has it really been almost twenty years, I thought? In all that time I never forgot his name or our first meeting or how I felt upon hearing that he was dead.

It's funny about young people who die. They're forever frozen in time, as they were, young, never aging, and the mind brings back pictures of the past like an old family album. In Washington, D.C., at the Vietnam Veterans Memorial, I made my way to the books that held all the names of the dead. As I turned the pages I remembered him as he was and hoped somehow that his name wasn't there, but of course it was, and of course I found it. Next to the name was the information that said so little of his life: Wayne Douglas Stigen, Chicago: Panel 25 line 91. . . .

At Panel 25 I began looking for Line 91. The black granite reflected my image and clearly I saw my face, and then there he was. I stared for a moment, not at the name, but at my reflection. I had changed, my hair had some gray and the lines around my eyes showed experience and wear. I reached out to touch his name and realized my friend was the same, still eighteen, always eighteen. . . .

I touched Wayne's name and I began to cry. I cried for a long time and the granite reflected my sadness and release. I was finally able to say goodbye to my friend and I knew he would always be there at Panel 25 Line 91.[1] (CSVG REPORT, p. 4)

Michael Katakis' experience at Panel 25 Line 91 is repeated hundreds of times daily among the many thousands of people who visit the Vietnam Veterans Memorial, the most frequently visited memorial in Washington

D.C. There are few dry eyes among those who visit "The Wall," as it has come to be called, a feat of art and remembrance of such astonishing power and simplicity that it seems to work for veteran and non-veteran, hawk and dove, young and old alike.

How can we account for the immense influence of this avowedly apolitical masterpiece? What can be said about the persuasive impact of this work that purports to carry no message? And how does the pain of remembrance seem to aid the ends of healing and reconciliation?

In this chapter I will explore these questions and others first by reviewing the premises and development of the memorial, secondly by comparing several scholarly analyses of the "rhetoric of ambiguity" of the Wall which arrive at virtually opposite conclusions, and finally by examining some implications of the "paradox of remembrance" for the legacy of the Vietnam War.

From a Nightmare to a Dream

Jan Scruggs couldn't sleep. He had seen *The Deer Hunter* that night, Michael Cimino's brutal (some would say racist and inaccurate) Academy Award-winning portrayal of working-class Pennsylvania youth caught in the maelstrom of Vietnam and its homeward consequences. Scruggs had been a rifleman with the U.S. Army 199th Light Infantry Brigade—a grunt, the lowliest and most noble of all ranks.

Provoked by the film and prodded by a bottle of whiskey, in the middle of the night in the middle of his own kitchen:

> Mortar rounds hit. Twelve men were unloading an ammunition truck. An explosion. Scruggs came running. By instinct, he pulled the first-aid bandage from his trousers. Organs and pieces of bodies were scattered along the ground. They belonged to his friends. He had only one bandage. He stood and screamed for help.
>
> The flashbacks ended, but the faces continued to pile up in front of him. The names, he thought. The names. No one remembers their names.[2]

The next morning Scruggs told his wife of his idea to build a memorial to those who served in Vietnam—"It'll have the name of everyone killed." It was March 1979, and Jan Scruggs had started down a path that would change his life and the consciousness of his country forever.

Scruggs was blessed with the innocence of those who are unaware of the impossibility of the task they are undertaking. Soon Scruggs had recruited Washington attorneys Bob Doubek and Jack Wheeler to his dream. These two highly capable, committed, and well-connected men were the perfect complement to Scruggs raw enthusiasm. As Howard K. Smith put it,

> The sheer folly of the project that Scruggs and friends so boldly set for themselves makes this an adventure story with nearly as many unlikely escapes from extinction as an Indiana Jones adventure.... What unthinking Secretary of the Interior would ever agree to let cloutless amateurs have such a priceless piece of real estate for so impossible a use?[3]

The gripping story of the memorial and the Vietnam Veterans Memorial Fund that built it is well and fully told in Jan Scruggs and Joel Swerdlow's book *To Heal a Nation*, a tale of political maneuvers, hits, and near misses along the road to ultimate success. The obstacles were many: the Washington bureaucracy, the remains of the powerful antiwar movement, the radicals of the new right, even some deep divisions among Vietnam veterans themselves that were never fully resolved. Not to mention the formidable tasks of securing the right site, choosing the appropriate design, and raising $10 million dollars, all in time for dedication of the memorial on Veterans Day 1982. Symbolically, the Vietnam War was fought all over again—this time with words—as the Vietnam Veterans Memorial Fund parried attacks and resistance from all sides.

The most important rhetorical document from the early days of the process was a statement of purpose for the design competition written primarily by Bob Doubek:

> While debate and demonstrations raged at home, these servicemen and women underwent challenges equal to or greater than those faced in earlier wars. They experienced confusion, horror, bitterness, boredom, fear, exhaustion, and death.
>
> In facing these ordeals, they showed the same courage, sacrifice, and devotion to duty for which Americans traditionally have honored the nation's war veterans in the past.
>
> The unique nature of the war—with no definite fronts, with vague objectives, with unclear distinctions between ally and enemy, and with strict rules of engagement—subjected the Vietnam soldier to unimaginable pressures.
>
> Because of inequities in the draft system, the brunt of dangerous service fell upon the young, often the socially and economically disadvantaged.
>
> While experiences in combat areas were brutal enough in themselves, their adverse effects were multiplied by the maltreatment received by veterans upon their return home ...
>
> The purpose of the Vietnam Veterans Memorial is to recognize and honor those who served and died. It will provide a symbol of acknowledgment of the

136   Egalitarianism

> courage, sacrifice, and devotion to duty of those who were among the nation's finest youth.
>
> The Memorial will make no political statement regarding the war or its conduct. It will transcend those issues. The hope is that the creation of the Memorial will begin a healing process.[4]

It is important to note here that the expressed purpose of the Memorial is to "recognize," "honor," "acknowledge," and "heal." Thus the design of the Memorial "will make no political statement," a nearly impossible objective if one believes the communication theory axiom that "one cannot not communicate." To make "no political statement" is akin to making no statement at all, and even having no memorial at all would communicate, at least to some, a political point.

Perhaps the most stunning irony of the design process was the identity of the memorial designer, selected in an open national competition by a blue ribbon panel from among 1,421 entries. Maya Ying Lin was a 21-year-old Yale undergraduate, raised in Ohio, with only vague knowledge of the Vietnam War and little interest in politics in general. An apolitical young Asian-American female! What more poignant counterpoint to the seasoned vets, the political opportunists, and the cynical bureaucrats who populated the landscape of Scruggs' dream. If the design itself could make "no political statement," still the designer herself communicated an instrinsic messsage. At the very least, no one could fault the competition's openness. At best, Maya Lin's selection was the sort of "Only in America!" event that would foster the hoped for healing process.

Maya Lin had decided that "the way to build a memorial would be to cut open the earth and to have stone rise up as part of the healing—something that would be like two hands opening to embrace people."[5] At first she created an "architectural pun," a row of dominoes falling in front of a wall of names, a concept that satirized the "Domino Theory" of "communist aggression" used to justify intervention in Vietnam. In a later moment of frustration and cynicism she recalled another joking idea she had had—to leave the two acre memorial site empty, and every day at a set time a plane would fly over and drop napalm.[6] (Students everywhere should take heart: for Maya Lin's final design, which has been called "the great American work of art for this century," she received a grade of "B" in her Yale architecture seminar!)

The design competition committee was unanimous in its choice of Maya Lin's design. Jack Wheeler immediately declared it "a work of genius." But Jan Scruggs was not so sure. To the untrained eye, unaccustomed to visualizing three dimensional space from flat drawings, the design looked like:

> A big bat. A weird-looking thing that could have been from Mars. Maybe a third-grader had entered the competiton and won. All the Fund's work had

gone into making a huge bat for veterans. Maybe it symbolized a boomerang—the names of dead GI's bouncing back right in front of the White House and Congress—where it had all begun.[7]

Nonetheless, Scruggs put his faith in those whose judgment he had chosen to trust, and put his support behind the design.

Maya Lin's proposed memorial was designed for the two acre site at the foot of the Lincoln memorial that had been miraculously secured from Congress with the help of Senators Charles Mathias and John Warner. "The Wall" is a five hundred foot long open "V" of black granite panels, with "the angle formed solely in relation to the Lincoln Memorial and the Washington Monument to create a unity between the nation's past and present."[8] The panels diminish in height from the apex of the "V" as they taper outward, giving the impression that the wall descends into (or rises from) the earth. Carved into the wall, in chronological order, are the names of the more than 58,000 Americans who died in combat in Vietnam or are still listed as missing in action. Nothing more, nothing less.

Yet this simple notion provoked intense reactions pro and con. Most fell into the "work of genius" camp. "Totally eloquent." "Presents both solitude and a challenge." "Reverential." "It's easy to love it." "Understated brilliance." "Extreme dignity and restraint." "There's no escape from its power." "The most moving war memorial ever erected." But the design had its detractors, some of them very influential. "It's something for New York intellectuals." "A tribute to Jane Fonda." "A body count on the Mall." "A wound in Mother Earth." "Inane." "An erosion control project." "A wailing wall." "Orwellian glop." "A black ditch." "A black gash of shame and sorrow." This last comment, by Veteran Tom Carhart, received considerable press coverage and symbolized the heated struggle between those who wanted to kill the project and those who were committed above all else to its realization.

There were many bones of contention. Some vets thought that the names should be listed alphabetically for ease in finding them. Maya Lin argued that a chronological listing was essential to her design, which should read like an epic Greek poem. Maya Lin prevailed, preventing the wall from looking like a giant granite telephone directory. Also, the vets wanted an inscription; Lin was hard to persuade. After much consultation with dozens of people, it was decided the inscription would read:

> Prologue: In honor of the men and women of the Armed Forces of the United States who served in the Vietnam War. The names of those who gave their lives and of those who remain missing are inscribed in the order they were taken from us.

138   Egalitarianism

> Epilogue: Our nation remembers the courage, sacrifice, and devotion to duty and country of its Vietnam veterans. This memorial was built with private donations from the American people.

One interesting rhetorical feature of this inscription is the choice of the word "war" over "police action" or "conflict," a deliberate decision made after much discussion and debate. Vietnam, the war that was never officially a war, had been declared one at last.

Negotiation with the design's detractors eventually yielded two additions to the memorial: a representational sculpture of three GIs by Frederick Hart, and an American flag. In the process, Maya Lin herself became an opponent of the memorial. She said of Hart: "I can't see how anyone of integrity can go around drawing mustaches on other people's portraits."[9] Lin thus joined the powerful ranks of those who wanted to delay dedication, but the Vietnam Veterans Memorial Fund kept their single minded focus: every name would be on the wall by Veterans Day 1982. And so it was.

The Rhetoric of Ambiguity

> Son,
>   I didn't know what to expect or what my reactions would be at seeing this black wall. I just had to go . . .
>
>   The weather was unseasonably warm and sunny when we arrived in Washington, D.C. We got out of the car and started walking toward this Memorial. I could feel pulled toward this black wall and yet my feet didn't want to move. I was so scared. I was afraid I would find your name on this wall and yet I was afraid that maybe some mistake had been made and the name was left out . . .
>
>   Then I saw it. My heart seemed to stop. I seemed to tremble. I shook as though I was freezing. My teeth chattered. I felt as though I couldn't get my breath. God, how it hurt . . .
>
>   From the wall, like a mirror reflecting through my blurry tears, I seemed to see faces. Then I realized it was not the faces of the ones who had died, but of the living, who were here, like me, to find the name of a loved one[10] . . .

For a memorial with "no message," the wall certainly packs an emotional wallop. And from a rhetorical point of view, the message received by visitors to the wall and the way we relate to the wall as a representation of more than what it is are of special interest. On one hand, the wall may be the perfect "landscaped solution" to a design problem. Its harmony with and relation to the environmental context are worthy of note. But of more interest here is what and how the wall communicates with its viewers; its rhetorical power to teach, to please, to move.

Maya Lin saw her design as "visual poetry,"[11] a circle where "one part is the two arms of the wall. The final segment of the circle is the living person who visits and through his presence fills in the part of the circle that has been omitted."[12] This is precisely the structure of the enthymeme of classical rhetorical theory, wherein part of a chain of reasoning is supplied by speaker and part by the listener, completing the circle of communication.

Lin knew her design would communicate. "I never expected it to be passionless," she explained. "The piece was built as a very psychological memorial. It's not meant to be cheerful or happy, but to bring out in people the realization of loss and a cathartic healing process."[13] Earlier she had made an even stronger statement in explaining the evolution of the design concept: "I wanted to describe a journey—a journey which would make you experience death."[14] Not surprisingly, the memorial evokes almost universal feelings of great sadness. Even the several half-size plastic replicas of the wall on tour around the country under the aegis of the Vietnam Combat Vets of San Jose, California, have an enormous and surprising power to move the viewer. Most people cry.

Maya Lin anticipated this reaction. All during construction she believed that the vets did not know what they were really building. "They did not understand what it would really be. At one point, for example, Doubek asked her, 'What will happen when people first see it?' She swallowed and said something encouraging. She wanted to say, They'll cry."[15] Lin herself was not exempt from the spell of her own creation. "Later, when I visited," she wrote, " I searched out the name of a friend's father. I touched it and I cried. I was another visitor, and I was reacting to it as I had designed it."[16]

It is as if the memorial that communicates nothing in general communicates everything in particular about the tragedy of war and the profound sadness of human loss. That the wall does indeed communicate to the viewer who then participates in the creation of its message is best seen in the fact that so many people communicate back to the wall. Each day hundreds of mementos are placed along its length as if in atonement with the dead: flowers, medals, photographs old and new, letters and poetry, bits of uniforms, a ragged teddy bear, a model of that '57 Chevy he hoped to come home to. "Tokens of grieving, of greeting, and of letting go."[17] All of these artifacts are carefully stored and curated with the goal of documenting the legacy of the Vietnam era through them.

The intentional ambiguity of the message of the Wall sometimes leads viewers to very different opinions about its meaning and implications. Two studies of the memorial published in communication journals arrived at opposite conclusions regarding its rhetorical significance. Sonja K. Foss, writing in *Communication Quarterly* in 1986 concludes that "the memorial functions as an effective anti-war symbol."[18] On the contrary, Harry W. Haines, writing in *Critical Studies in Mass Communication* in 1986 argues that "the design's ambiguity allows for a wide variation in responses and simultaneously makes the Memorial vulnerable to political manipulation." Indeed, he asserts even that "the administrative attempt at co-opting the Memorial for political purposes is clear, and it is linked to the power strategies for future wars."[19]

It would seem that we have here the makings of a prima facie case in support of the success of the design's intentional ambiguity. Let's take a closer look at Foss and Haines in order to better understand their reasoning in support of apparently conflicting claims.

Sonja Foss aims to identify the characteristics of the Memorial that make it appeal to nearly everyone, and that "enable it to perform this function and thus to serve both as a symbol of opposition to the Vietnam War and as a symbol of honor to those who participated in it."[20] Foss begins by offering an interesting discussion of "the rhetoric of the visual image," wherein she distinguishes between "aesthetic" and "rhetorical" responses to art and other non-discursive forms of communication. She states that "visual works of art may be considered rhetoric in that they produce effects and are intentional and purposive objects."[21] The aesthetic response is more sensory; the rhetorical response more instrumental. Of course, most viewers have both aesthetic and rhetorical responses to the Memorial, which Foss distinguishes thusly:

> If a viewer responds primarily to the regularity and pattern of the names on the memorial, for example, the response is predominantly aesthetic.... But if the viewer attributes meaning to the names and they are used to consider the tragedy of war, the response has become a rhetorical one....[22]

Foss suggests that five major features account for the visual appeal of the Memorial. First, the Memorial violates the conventional form of war memorials because it does not provide any variant of the heroic "general on a horse" pseudo-realism." Also, because the Memorial focuses upon the specifics of the names, "our conventional expectations of a war memorial as abstract and general and thus lacking in capacity to involve its visitors personally in the war are violated."[23] So because conventional expectations about form are not fulfilled, more is demanded from the viewer to account for the work's meaning.

A second appeal of the Memorial, writes Foss, comes from its "welcoming stance." The Open "V" shape has been characterized as an "embrace," or "two open hands" that seem to safely envelop the viewer. The Memorial's "female sensibility" has been contrasted to more "phallic memorials that rise upwards." The Memorial seems secure and non-threatening partly because of its integral relationship with the earth from which it appears to rise and its harmonious balance between the Lincoln Memorial and the Washington Monument. We feel safe because the Memorial does not dictate to us, but rather supports whatever message the viewer chooses to attribute.

A third feature Foss finds significant is the Memorial's "lack of information," although I think she means here "lack of a specific message," because the Memorial certainly communicates a great deal of information. As Gregory Bateson wrote, "In the world of information, nothing can be a cause."[24] For instance, sometimes silence is the most powerful message of all. In communication as in design, "less is more." But what Foss seems to be actually saying is that it is the lack of a specific message that "allows supporter and protester of the war alike to see the memorial as eloquent."[25]

Fourth, the Memorial's focus on the dead rather than on the war itself strengthens its appeal by reminding us of the tragic human loss rather than reminding us of the deep divisions of opinion about the war itself. Writes Foss: "The repetitive form of name after name continually restates the message of waste and provides a common feeling and experience of sorrow in which all visitors share."[26] This is Maya Lin's "epic poem" read rhetorically.

Fifth and finally, Foss finds appeal in the Memorial's ability to generate multiple referents. The abstract form invites the viewer to attribute various meanings. For instance, the "V" shape can be seen as a peace sign or an index finger pointing in shame. The black color of the Memorial can signify shame, sorrow, or mourning. The submersion of the Memorial into the earth can be read as guilt or as healing.

Foss concludes that by prompting reflection upon the waste and loss of war without taking an ideological position, the Memorial functions as an effective anti-war symbol. She suggests that contemporary anti-war rhetoric should "avoid confrontative strategies," and "must communicate not that one group's view is right and that another is wrong, but that everyone is right to some degree and that all kinds of 'rightness' can be accorded room and value in the movement."[27] This highly debatable opinion goes a long way toward establishing Foss' point about the ambiguity of the Memorial's message. Foss also concludes, somewhat less controversially, that the Memorial indicates the need for new visual images and the effectiveness of focusing anti-war rhetoric not on ideology, but rather on the *essence* of war—death.

Harry Haines, in an essay at once somewhat deeper and more obscure than Foss' study, analyzes the role of the Vietnam Veterans Memorial in the "mediated struggle" to explain: "What did the war mean?"[28] Haines notes that "the struggle over the war's meaning now approaches the size of a major communications industry," including more than 750 books about Vietnam released in the decade following the end of the war. (And Haines writes pre-*Rambo* and *Platoon*.)

Haines proposes a very provocative thesis, stating that "The Memorial's brief history now reveals administrative powers' attempt to naturalize the Vietnam experience, incorporating the war's memory in a context similar to the memory of other, more successful, wars, a project with profound psychological implications for Vietnam veterans."[29]

Haines' analysis centers upon the evolution of the Memorial as a "sacred site," as it moves through MacCannell's five phases of sacralization once reserved for holy places and now also ascribed to tourist attractions. These phases are naming, framing, enshrinement, mechanical reproduction, and social reproduction.

The "naming" phase includes all the ways in which the Memorial came to be as it is, including the various rhetorical struggles cited earlier in this chapter. One of the outcomes of this, Haines writes, is that "Lin's design transcends the Vietnam debate through ambiguity, or rather her design mutes the debate, making it inappropriate in the shadow of the dead."[30] To name, but not to speak.

The "framing" and "enshrinement" phases came naturally to the Memorial because of its placement in the already hallowed national ground between the Lincoln Memorial and the Washington Monument. As Haines puts it, "The memory of Washington and Lincoln enshrine the memory of Vietnam."[31]

"Mechanical reproduction" is what authenticates the original, duplicating its presence in mediated culture. The Vietnam Veterans Memorial received extensive press coverage, including *Time* and *Newsweek* covers the same week. Much Wall memorabilia is available, from keychains, postcards, and T-shirts, to a commemorative postage stamp issued in November 1984. Most significantly, since Haines' writing several versions of a one-half size "Moving Wall" have been traveling around the country. These replicas, typically treated with great reverence by local veterans groups and visitors, are every bit as capable of eliciting a powerful response as is the "real" thing.

"Social reproduction," the final phase of site sacralization, is seen in the community of veterans who have become a "priestly group" that guards the wall and guides visitors to the names they seek. "For these veterans and many others like them," writes Haines, "The Wall is more than a sacred depository of memory; the wall is Vietnam."[32]

The social reproduction of the wall and the struggle for meaning that emerges from it is part of an inescapably political process. Even Maya Lin recognized that in addition to remembering the dead, "What is also memorialized is that people still cannot resolve that war, nor can they separate the issues, the politics, from it."[33]

Through the use of little known statements about The Wall by "administrative powers" such as Ronald Reagan and Caspar Weinberger, Haines tries to establish an establishment attempt to co-opt its symbolism in justification of future wars. For instance, Reagan avers "There's been rethinking on all sides, and this is good. And it's time we moved on, in unity and with resolve, with the resolve to always stand for freedom, as those who fought did, and to always try to protect and preserve the peace."[34] Thus the Vietnam War is "normalized"; we now remember to forget.

Haines comes to the conclusion that what he sees as the developing Vietnam consensus serves administrative power by signaling that the war and postwar debate are now closed, by requiring of ailing veterans a "strategic forgetting" in the service of reconciliation, and by allowing those in power to pursue future Vietnams.

Thus, it is precisely because of the Memorial's ambiguity that it becomes susceptible to political manipulation. Contrary to the popular myth that the Memorial places the Vietnam War beyond politics, its noncommittal message makes it especially vulnerable to exploitation. So it is that Haines is left with the impression that "The Memorial's profound meaning is not so much in how the dead are remembered by those of us who survived Vietnam at home or abroad, but in how that remembrance is used by power to explain—to justify—future sacrifices in future Vietnams."[35]

While Foss and Haines agree that the Memorial's rhetorical ambiguity is the source of the wide range of potential meanings attributed to it, they differ in their assessment of what sorts of meanings will predominate and possibly prevail. Foss sees the Memorial as primarily a potent anti-war symbol; Haines sees it as a highly co-optable potentially pro-war symbol. Which case is more convincing? By definition of the legitimacy of the rhetoric of ambiguity, both cases can be allowed to stand, although I personally think that Haines makes the stronger and more arresting case. Foss seems to suffer a bit more from wishful thinking in speculating that the Memorial can shape a whole new genre of anti-war rhetoric. On the other hand, Haines offers a dark view of administrative power that goes beneath and beyond the popular wisdom of the Memorial's "healing and reconciliation" theme to give fair warning about its potential for abuse.

The Paradox Of Remembrance

The realization of Jan Scruggs' dream in a short three and one half years was nothing short of miraculous. In a city where the process of monument building typically takes decades, America's most unpopular war was memorialized in an unconventional way in record time.

How can we explain such good fortune? While few seemed to object in principle to the idea of a memorial, Maya Lin's design itself had many powerful opponents, some of whom remained unreconciled even after the compromise that added Hart's statue. Also, the task of raising ten million dollars from scratch, supervised by the young and energetic Sandie Fauriol, was no minor venture. Against nearly impossible odds, Scruggs' Vietnam memories went from a nightmare to a dream.

Jack Wheeler, who was Chairman of the Vietnam Veterans Memorial Fund, has said that the "poetry of events" that characterized the process were miraculous enough to lead one to believe that it was "grace'" that created the perfect vehicle "to heal a nation." Wheeler saw themes of "surprise" and "economy" at work in the process. There was surprise at the designer's identity, surprise at the silence of the huge crowd that gathered for the dedication, surprise at the number of people who visit the memorial and who leave a part of themselves, surprise at the sight of one's reflection in the black granite and at the impulse to touch the names. And "economy:" at every step of the way just enough money and resources materialized. In every dark hour another major contribution or supporter appeared to keep the memorial alive.

What accounts for the Memorial's power? A power so personal it moves nearly all who experience it to tears and so great it has fostered what Haines calls a "cult of remembrance."[36] I think that three features of the Memorial are especially important: its chronological listing of the names of the dead and missing, its enthymemic structure that invites the viewer to participate in making its meaning, and its rhetorical ambiguity that confirms attribution of varied and even conflicting messages about the Vietnam War.

"The names have a power, a life, all their own. Even on the coldest days, sunlight makes them warm to the touch. Young men put into the earth, rising out of the earth. You can feel their blood flowing again."[37] It is said that no sound is so precious to a person as the sound of one's own name. Naming is a fundamental human activity; it is what distinguishes an object from its context, naming identifies this person as different from that one, thus validating the existence of the individual.

Jan Scruggs' most inspired contribution was his idea to include all the names of the dead and missing. Maya Lin's stroke of genius was to arrange the names chronologically on the memorial so that they take on a narrative structure. For instance all men lost in the same battle are listed together, buddies forever. The Wall thus tells the story of the war; it even rises in height just as the war escalated, athough the names start at the high midpoint, taper off on one arm, metaphorically encircle the viewer, and start from the end of the other arm to build to the war's conclusion. Thus does Maya Lin write the epic poem of the Vietnam War, etched in the blood of those who paid the ultimate price. It is a stunning story, and the names tell it all.

I mentioned earlier that the Vietnam Veterans Memorial expresses the classical rhetorical form of the enthymeme, which invites the viewer to participate in making its meaning. It does this discursively through the narrative of the names that leaves construction of the story of the war or of individuals involved in the war to the viewer. Non-discursively, the engulfing and encircling form of the Wall itself invites the viewer to share in its memorialization. Many have commented, too, upon the reflective quality of the granite, whereby the viewer sees himself and the world mirrored among the names of the dead. The eerily seductive appeal draws one into the horror and loss. It is thus not surprising that viewers reach out to touch the wall in completion of the circle of remembrance, and that they leave behind the myriad offerings that signify their part in the communication process.

The communicational structure of the Wall can also be seen as what Umberto Eco has called an "open text," which demands much from the reader in that it does not satisfy our "hunger for redundancy" the way a "closed text" (such as a traditional war memorial) would.[38] The Wall does not tell us what to think; it demands that we think for ourselves. Marshall McLuhan would no doubt term the Wall a "cool" medium, since it offers low sensory definition and thus invites a high degree of participation from the receiver. Said William Blake: "Wise men see outlines, so they draw them."

Finally, the Vietnam Veteran's Memorial rhetoric of ambiguity is consistent with the confused, contradictory, divisive, and unresolved character of that war. Jan Scruggs was arguing with an anti-war protester about the memorial when "The irony hit. People being memorialized usually did not do it themselves. Yet here were Vietnam vets building a memorial to honor service to a country that still seemed anxious to forget. "What the hell," he figured. "It had been that kind of war."[39]

It is precisely the Wall's ambiguity that confers its appeal and power. The appeal comes from its openness to all points of view about the war, and the power from the fact that it is the viewer who then constructs the personalized message in a process of self-persuasion. Haines writes that "Lin's achievement is a war memorial (perhaps, the first) which simultaneously comforts the visitor while evoking an interpretation of loss."[40] He might have added that the memorial also manages to simultaneously satisfy many conflicting message expectations in a way that a more polemic memorial could not.

And so we have the Vietnam Veterans Memorial poised on the edge of the paradox of remembrance: to remember the Vietnam War is unbearable; but to forget it is unthinkable. Peter Marin cautions against allowing the memorial to become an instrument of forgetting through its ability to mythologize the past, "making it a part of memory rather than thought, an object of sentiment rather than sentence."[41] There is something to this, for by selectively remembering the Vietnam War we can choose to conveniently forget its full meaning. By focusing exclusively on "healing and reconciliation" we can overlook the wounds that have yet to be opened. By seeing the Wall as the fnal chapter on Vietnam we can ignore the many thousands who suffer still and for whom the story is just beginning.

Marin shares similar concerns. What we owe the dead and ourselves, he argues, is serious contemplation of the ideas of moral value, conscience, generosity, solidarity, and community. "If the Vietnam memorial manages to remind us that this is what is missing and what must be begun," Marin writes, "this is fine. If not, then it will simply become—no matter how moving or lovely—simply another means by which, in the name of memory, we destroy the past."[42] We must not use the Memorial as a means of remembering to forget.

Combat poet David Collins is one of those for whom the Vietnam War has not yet ended. Reflecting on a visit to the "Moving Wall" in 1986, he wrote:

> *Up Against the Wall*
>
> *The boy I took to Vietnam*
> *Died and went to hell*
> *And this old man*
> *Brought his conscience home*
> *With a sad story to tell*
>
> *The draft is the cool breath of death*
> *On a napalmed peasant's funeral pyre*
> *And every day my heart grieves*
> *For the souls set on fire*
>
> *See the writing on the Wall?*
> *The words are the names*
> *Of those who served the call*
> *See the empty in America's eyes*
> *See the hollow in our lives*
> *Notice the scars on the heart*
> *If healing is coming, when does it start?*
>
> *That granite wall is but one chapter told*
> *Of the largest tombstone in the world*

Notes

1. Center for the Study of the Vietnam Generation. Report. Volume 2 (3), March 1987, p. 4.
2. Scruggs, J.C., and J.L. Swerdlow. *To Heal a Nation*. New York: Harper and Row, 1985, p. 7.
3. Ibid, p. xiv.
4. Ibid, p. 53.
5. Ibid, p. 54.
6. Ibid, p. 101.
7. Ibid, p. 64.
8. Swerdlow, J. "To Heal a Nation." *National Geographic*. 167(5). May 1985, p. 557.
9. Scruggs and Swerdlow, p. 121.
10. Ibid, p. 134.
11. Ibid, p. 59.
12. Ibid, p. 77.
13. Ibid, p. 147.
14. Ibid, p. 69.
15. Ibid, p. 11.
16. Swerdlow, p. 557.
17. Scruggs and Swerdlow, p. 159.
18. Foss, S.K. "Ambiguity as Persuasion: The Vietnam Veterans Memorial." *Communication Quarterly*. 34(3), Summer 1986.
19. Haines, H.W. "'What Kind of War': An Analysis of the Vietnam Veterans Memorial." *Critical Studies in Mass Communication*. 3(1), March 1986, p. 17.
20. Foss, p. 328.
21. Ibid, p. 329.
22. Ibid, p. 331.
23. Ibid, p. 333.
24. Bateson, G. *Steps to Ecology of Mind*. New York: Ballantine.
25. Ibid, p. 334.
26. Foss, p. 336.
27. Ibid, p. 338.
28. Haines, p. 2.
29. Ibid, p. 3.
30. Ibid, p. 6.
31. Ibid.
32. Ibid, p. 10.
33. Scruggs and Swerdlow, p. 133.
34. Haines, p. 14.
35. Ibid, p. 17.
36. Ibid, p. 13.
37. Swerdlow, p. 573.
38. Eco, U. *The Role of the Reader*. Bloomington: Indiana University Press. 1979.
39. Scruggs and Swerdlow, p. 19.
40. Haines, p. 7.
41. Marin, Peter. *Nation*. Nov. 27, 1982, p. 557.
42. Ibid, p. 562.

7

The Politics of Culture: Feminism and the Media

Muriel G. Cantor

From the beginning of radio and television broadcasting in the United States to the present day, different political and interest groups have made repeated attempts to control and change its content, especially television, through political action. Among these groups were feminists in the 1960s, the period now called the "second wave" of feminism, who paid particular attention to the fairness shown women by the media. Underlying the feminist political agenda of the time was the demand for a cultural change in the ways women were depicted as well as guaranteeing their equality in their economic and social roles. In addition to how women were portrayed in programs, feminist critics charged media owners and managers with sexism, supporting their claim with reports showing widespread discrimination against women in broadcast industry employment practices.[1] When a man and a woman applied for a job, most often the man was hired. And, if hired, the woman was probably paid a salary lower than that the man would have been given. In addition, the woman would have been on a slower promotion track, if at all.

In terms of portrayal, critics claimed that women were stereotyped and trivialized in programs and advertisements. However, it was not until the 1970s that these critics organized into groups to attempt through legal channels to have more women hired in decision-making positions and to change the ways women were depicted on the screen. Feminist activists working primarily through women's organizations, especially the National Organization for Women (NOW), adopted the methods that other "minority" groups had used to try to achieve more equal treatment in media presentations and equity in employment. To be specific, local NOW chapters, often in coalition with other community organizations, used the relicensing procedures of the FCC as opportunities to challenge the performance of particular broadcasters on issues of community responsibility and fair treatment.

Although other tactics are mentioned in passing, this chapter focuses on what I consider the most important tactic of the women's movement to reform the media: the license challenges. The first section will provide background and explanation for the growth and demise of the movement, followed by a review of the techniques used to try to convince broadcasters and the courts that women were not treated as equals in the media. The article closes with an assessment of the impact of these efforts. Although the material presented is "factual" in that I report actual events in which I had direct participation or witnessed, I will draw on sociological theory and insights as well as interpreting the significance of the events from a personal point of view.

Background and Rationale

During the 1970s and into the early 1980s at least 15 stations had their licenses challenged by women's groups at renewal time throughout the United States. Each of these "petitions to deny" failed in its primary goal because each station retained its license. However, at its outset, when the women's reform movement with NOW in 1972 petitioned the Federal Communication Commission to deny renewal of licenses to WABC-TV (New York City) and WRC-TV (Washington, DC), the tactic was considered the most potent weapon then available to influence the broadcast media.[2] Although others will hold a different opinion, in my view, the use of license challenges was not a successful strategy for the reform movement. However, it should not be seen as an absolute failure simply because the immediate and primary goals (of de-licensure) were not realized. In the short timeframe available, it is difficult to assess the final and eventual impact of any reform movement. The ostensible objective of the women filing the challenges with the FCC was to deny broadcast licenses to broadcasters who in their estimation were discriminating against women. However, there were other unstated goals that were less ambitious but could have had longer-term effects on society. What the reform movement actually accomplished will be discussed in detail in the conclusion. For example, because of my personal involvement with the WRC-TV challenge, I know that none of the women were so naive as to expect that an NBC owned-and-operated station could actually lose its license.[3] However, the NOW representatives also believed that forcing station-owners to respond to the challenge would itself require them to review and perhaps alter their policies on hiring and programming practices. As will be explained, the long-range effects of the WRC challenge were far more influential that those involved in the challenge would have anticipated. Thus, although the movement did fail at one level, it also did contribute to the growth and awareness of the many inside the women's movement and others who were active participants.

There is no question that the position of women in the broadcast industry differs today from what it was when the reform movement started in the early 1960s. How much of the change can be attributed to the license challenges is not measurable. In fact, it could be argued (as I will in my concluding remarks) that the license challenges may have done more for advancing the careers of the women involved in them than they did for the women employed in broadcasting. A great deal of effort went into these license challenges and large numbers of volunteers were involved in various aspects of the process necessary to carry out the FCC policies. At the same time as local NOW chapters were working on license challenges, national NOW and State affiliates were trying to get State legislatures to pass the Equal Rights Amendment (ERA). The decade was clearly one of action and excitement. Whereas it appeared that the ERA had a good chance of becoming the 27th amendment of the Constitution (it did not, of course), there were indications early on that the license challenge movement was doomed to fail. The questions then could be asked: Why was so much effort and time put into a movement which seemed to have so little chance of success? How and why did the movement start and what did it accomplish?

Historical Background

Since the mid-1960s women and minorities have insisted that over the air broadcasting is not diverse.[4] According to these groups, one just had to examine news, entertainment programs and advertisements to document that contention. Even "mere entertainment" was defined as a political issue requiring reform because the programs which stereotyped or defined group members negatively were creating psychological damage and possibly fostering economic inequity as well.[5] (Tuchman, 1978). Since publication of the *American Dilemma*,[6] Social scientists have grouped women with blacks as groups who shared similar structural and cultural problems in a society dominated by white males.[7] The emphasis in this chapter is on how women as political activists used political and legal tactics to change both their image and their power as workers in the broadcast industry. However, as will become clear, while it is possible to discuss minorities (especially the large black minority) and exclude women, it is impossible to discuss women as activists without including blacks and the civil rights movement as well.

Starting in the 1960s, social groups developed a new militancy that resulted in political action directed to eliminating media stereotypes and encouraging the employment of members in decision-making positions. Protesting negative images in the media was not new. For example, the Anti-Defamation League had been protesting anti-Semitic media images for decades. Blacks following that precedent denounced the television version of *Amos 'n Andy* in 1951. However, the methods used in the 1960s and beyond by these groups and others were new. Hundreds of organized groups, representing a large spectrum of political orientations, have employed various tactics to try to shape program content. When feminism was reborn in the mid-1960s, women's organizations and individual feminists joined forces to protest how women were portrayed in the media and their limited employment opportunities. In addition to taking political and legal actions, they often buttressed their cases with occasional research findings obtained from social scientists.

Although mass media research has flourished in the United States and elsewhere since the 1930s and 1940s, women and other minorities were not considered topics worthy of serious research interest. When and if included (which was rare), women were not perceived as having active roles in communication, as actual or possible communicators, gatekeepers, or opinion-leaders, but simply as passive members of audiences and consumers of others' messages, for example, on fashion.[8] It was assumed generally and correctly for the time that most communicators were men. As feminist scholars have charged, mass media research as all other social science research, was (and to a certain extent, still is) male-centered and -oriented. Although research was done on women in the audience, there was very little research on the status of women in the industry, or on the ways women were portrayed on the screen.

However, unlike most other areas of social science research, from its beginnings, mass media research typically included an applied or social policy component which in turn required that its findings be considered for implementation. Also, from its beginnings, the research that social scientists did on the mass media in general and on broadcasting in particular tended to focus on social issues and problems, such as crime and violence, racial discrimination, and how the media could influence the socialization of children.

Although most of the classic studies concentrated on either trying to measure the effects of the media on audiences or on the program contents themselves, these studies were often instigated by either the industries producing media content or by government agencies and foundations.[9] Throughout society, various groups and government leaders believed that the mass media were very powerful in shaping attitudes, beliefs and actual behavior as well. Of course, it was in the interest of the industry to have the studies they sponsored quiet fears about the power of the media, and the studies, especially those on the relationship between media and voting, found "personal" influence more important than the media, and that media, rather than directing values and behaviors, merely reinforced already established beliefs[10] (Lazarsfeld et al., 1944; Berelson et al., 1954; and Klapper, 1960).

However, the civil rights movement and the racial violence of the 1960s and the reawakening of the women's movement during the same period did shift the focus of research on the mass media. For example, the Kerner Commission Report (1968) charged that the mass media had contributed to the racial violence of the 1960s and proposed that the media recognize their responsibility in considering the effects their stories and portrayals might have on society and events.

Several analyses of television content had shown women to be stereotyped and underrepresented in primetime shows before Betty Friedan wrote *The Feminine Mystique* (1963).[11] Although Friedan used magazine short stories to show that women were trivialized, it was her analysis that pushed the portrayal of women in the media to the forefront as a topic for major feminist concern. Not only did the Friedan book provide much of the ideology for the feminist movement but her work inspired a series of studies and reports focusing on how women were being portrayed in the various media.

Soon after *The Feminist Mystique* was published, the President's Commission on the Status of Women released its report in which the mass media were again criticized for "projecting, intentionally or unintentionally, an image [of women] that contains old myths, misconceptions, and even distortions of true images." The Civil Rights Act of 1964 enacted shortly after the report was issued contributed to the scrutiny mass media were undergoing at the time.[12] Also in 1966, as a result of litigation pursued for two years by the Office of Communication of the United Church of Christ, the Court of Appeals issued a decision requiring the FCC to permit citizens to participate in Commission proceedings.[13] Following that decision, for the first time since the beginning of commercial broadcasting in the 1920s, there were societal supports (both legal and informal) which encouraged less powerful groups in society, particularly minorities and women, to conduct their own research on the role the mass media played in their lives and to use the research to try to achieve changes in public and social policy.

The Court of Appeal's decision also led to the formation of a number of broadcast reform groups. These groups, such as the Media Committee of NOW and the National Black Media Coalition (NBMC) were established because they believed their group members were underserved or excluded by television. Although not the only method used, the petition to deny became the primary tool. The electronic spectrum allotted for television signals can accommodate a limited number of broadcast stations, radio, and television. Although not all slots have been allocated, just a few television licenses are still available in medium or large markets areas. However, to start a station or to purchase one already broadcasting, especially in television, is far too expensive for disadvantaged groups to consider. This barrier to direct-ownership was as true in the 1960s as it is today. With just few exceptions, only those with extensive resources can afford to enter television broadcasting, so that rather than trying to start new stations, reform groups adopted the strategy of trying to change the status quo.

Every three years until 1984 when television was deregulated, broadcasters had been required to apply to the FCC for renewal of their broadcast licenses, and until 1964 when the United Church of Christ challenged the renewal of WLBT-TV's license, most were renewed without questions asked. That policy came under attack in 1964 when two black leaders in Jackson, Mississippi with the help of the United Church of Christ challenged the license of station WLBT in Jackson. With the aid of the church's Office of Communication, they charged that WLBT had systematically promoted segregationist views in its editorials and news coverage. The FCC dismissed the challenge, asserting that the members of the public had no "standing" before the Commission, that is, they could not participate in helping the FCC decide which broadcasters should have the privilege of retaining their licenses. The FCC dismissal was not upheld on appeal (leading to the 1966 decision from the Court of Appeals cited earlier) and the FCC was required to hear the case once more, this time allowing testimony from the Jackson men and the United Church of Christ. When the FCC still renewed WLBT's license in spite of their testimony, the United Church of Christ and the Jackson citizens returned to court.[14]

On June 23, 1969, the Court of Appeals reproved the FCC for shifting the burden of proof from the license to the challenger and denied the renewal, requiring the FCC to solicit new applications for the WLBT license. In 1971, the license was awarded to a local black group in Jackson.

Women Challenge TV Licenses

The activities of women's groups in reforming the broadcast media also started with "petitions to deny" station licenses. Partially because of the success of the challenge to the license of WLBT-TV, the National Organization for Women (NOW) with other feminist groups decided to use legal means to challenge two more stations, WABC-TV in New York and WRC-

TV in Washington, D.C.[15] Although in the end the station won the battle to retain its license, the WRC-TV challenge became a landmark case with far-reaching consequences. One of its results was the Court of Appeal's decision in the *NOW v. FCC* case in 1977 that the FCC could not allow stations to use the First Amendment as a defense for their biased portrayals of minorities and women. However that decision was the also the end of the movement because the WRC-TV license after five years of litigation and protest was renewed.

The WRC case became important in other ways as well because it provided the model that women's groups throughout the U.S. later adopted to use in similar challenges[16] (Lewis, 1985). It also led directly to the most comprehensive (now outdated) study on women and minorities in television, *Window Dressing on the Sets*[17] and *Window Dressing on the Sets: An Update*.[18]

On a legal basis, the challenges were based on three aspects of communication law and regulation: violations of the Fairness Doctrine; ascertainment of community needs; and discrimination in employment of women and minorities. The WABC challenge received more publicity in the beginning, but the WRC-TV challenge was better documented because systematic techniques had been used to gather data for it. For that reason, the WRC-TV challenge had also been cited more often in the research literature.

Because the FCC by necessity staggers its license renewals by year and month for different areas of the country, the petition for WABC-TV was filed first, on May 1, 1972, and that for WRC-TV on September 1st of the same year. The coalition challenging WRC-TV was chaired by Whitney Adams, then a law student, who decided to put heavy emphasis on using social science data for their petition to deny. For example, a project to monitor the broadcasts of the station was started, headed up by two social science researchers who had participated in the National Institute of Mental Health's $1 million project on television and children conducted in 1969 and 1970.[19] Because video taping was too expensive, the station's programs were recorded on audio tape and additional data were gathered by having the contents of programs coded from the screen by two observers. The coding forms were designed to collect data on the ratios of male to female actors and broadcasters in programs, news broadcasts and advertisements provided both by the local station and the network. The data obtained were used to document that women were often stereotyped, that is, presented primarily in non-working roles, romantic or domestic, and that women's issues were ignored by the station and network. The brief filed with the petition to deny renewal also criticized the adequacy of the survey that WRC-TV itself had conducted to ascertain community needs. Using a social scientist as a consultant, the NOW petitioners were able to claim that because of the way the station presented its survey, it was impossible to tell if the responses were statistically valid and reliable. In addition, the social scientist conducted a survey of women's groups not ascertained by WRC-TV.

Although ascertainment and monitoring were important, the legal bases on which most later petitions to deny were filed was on discrimination in employment or on equal opportunity employment violations. Employment regulations were adopted by the FCC in the early 1970s under the assumption that such policies would lead to more programming for minorities and would ensure that its licensees' programming fairly reflects the tastes and viewpoints of minority groups.[20]

I have claimed elsewhere that it is not possible to make a direct connection between the gender of the communicator and the content produced,[21] but from the earliest days of the media reform movement until just recently, the FCC has claimed that the connection exists.[22] It is understandable that the FCC would try to use indirect rather direct methods to influence programming. Although the FCC has monitored the types of programs a station may broadcast in the name of fairness or diversity, it has stayed clear of direct intervention into program content except when the content is considered unfair or obscene. Direct intervention would have brought up the issue of the First Amendment and censorship, both of which the FCC would prefer to avoid. Citizen groups using discrimination in employment as a legal basis for challenge have been helped by the data on employment that the FCC has required local stations to maintain to satisfy its requirement for affirmative action on women and minorities. Because each station was required to file reports on employees (Form 395) which social scientists could then use to study hiring practices, sociologists and economists were able to find out how many women and minorities were employed in what types and levels of jobs, and how their salaries compared among the various groups. Thus, later license challenges were usually supported by more and better data, collected more systematically from more sources, although more often by volunteer participants.

Of the fifteen license challenges examined by Lewis,[23] six had used some form of monitoring. Twelve had used data from Form 395 to analyze employment practices, and five had conducted other studies such as ascertainment and compilation of financial data on cross-ownership and media monopoly.[24]

By 1977, with its task unfinished, the feminist movement to reform the media lost momentum, and although women's organizations in several cities were still filing petitions to deny, the thrust was gone. Anne W. Branscomb and Maria Savage, writing in 1978, contended that the movement simply ran out of steam because the majority of organizations, feminist and other minorities, had run out of financial sources and resources to continue the effort. (From my own experience, I know how difficult it is to recruit and keep volunteers who are motivated and productive.) Also, according to Branscomb and Savage, small groups had found it difficult to change from *ad hoc* groups of committed volunteers to workers in established organizations. Even though the NOW Legal Defense and Education Fund (which took over the Media Project in 1979) continued to grow while its parent organization was in decline, it found it increasingly difficult to recruit volunteers to monitor television at the local level, and without volunteers, the chapters could not sustain the work involved. Research by NOW–LDEF during the 1980s was done in-house with little help from social scientists because it had decided that carrying out "scientific" studies was not worth the extra effort. Easier and smaller studies accomplished in-house, obtained similar results and were sufficient to get media publicity and public attention.[25]

The final blow to the reform movement took place when the Reagan administration took office in 1981. In the three years it took the FCC to deregulate television and radio, none of the few petitions to deny that were filed in those years were considered worthy of hearings. In fact, by that time, no organization could expect any kind of a redress from the FCC.

However, during the late 1970s and continuing to the 1980s citizen groups responded by using the petition or threat of petition as a tool to gain leverage. Most in the reform movement still believed that the petition was a useful weapon against broadcasters even though both parties knew that the petitions would be almost routinely rejected. The threat was sufficient to open up a path to negotiation and agreement because the broadcasters preferred to save the money and avoid the bother and adverse publicity of protracted legal hearings. Also, negotiating would preclude further investigation and scrutiny by the FCC into station practices.

Success or Failure?

The year 1963 marked the rebirth or "second wave" of the feminist movement in the United States. That year the Equal Pay Act passed and, possibly more important, Betty Friedan's book, *The Feminine Mystique*, was published. Most social historians and sociologists date the beginning of a modern feminist movement from publication of that book and passage of that Act. They, along with Title VII of the 1964 Civil Rights Act passed the following year, provided the conceptual bases for women's active participation in the political process to further the ideal of sexual equality (my definition of feminism). Also, the women's media reform movement could be dated as starting during the early to mid-1960s, beginning with the WLBT case. It was also a popular movement of amateurs and volunteers who under the guidance of charismatic, feminist leaders, organized themselves into effective and enthusiastic political action and research groups. In time, as its adherents aged or moved on into their own careers, the movement also aged, waned and eventually sputtered to a halt.

As noted earlier, analysts and critics differ on whether the movement had any lasting effects: No station that was challenged lost its license, and the FCC, instead of becoming more sympathetic to women's rights in the broadcast industry, has become less so. To support deregulation, both the government and the National Association of Broadcasters, principal lobbyist for the industry, had argued that the new technologies, such as cable and more independent UHF stations, had opened the marketplace to minority viewpoints, making further regulation unnecessary. There is no question that today the world of broadcasting is different from what it was when the women's reform movement started and different from what it was when the first license challenge was filed in 1972. Most of the changes can be attributed to the major demographic, economic, and political shifts which occurred over the past decades. However, there have been discernible changes in both content and employment in the broadcasting industry that might be attributed at least indirectly or as secondary effects to the political activism of women against the media during the 1970s. However, because the position of women in the labor force generally changed so dramatically in the last twenty years, it could be argued that the media industries would have changed whether or not women's organizations had actively worked toward reform. In fact, some recent studies suggest that although women did make some measurable gains in broadcasting during the past 20 years, as employees of both the networks and stations, they still lag behind women in other industries.[26]

Also there is no question that more women are on the air in both entertainment and news and information programs. These changes may not mirror exactly the extent of changes in the "real world" but none-the-less, viewers today see women in many more varied roles than were thought possible by the industry twenty years previously. However, the changes that occurred throughout the 1970s and 1980s seem to have occurred quite independently of the license challenges. For example, license challenges were directed to local stations, not to networks or the Hollywood production companies. A large increase of women employed at the local level took place in the early 1970s before feminists were actively involved in challenging licenses. In Hollywood, women did not make inroads in the production companies until the 1980s, long after the license challenge movement had died.[27] Although more women in the production companies and in positions of importance may make some difference, there seems to be little fundamental change in content to reflect the changing work roles in the industry. News personnel at the networks and in public television have changed as well. Although there are no women anchors on the networks at primetime, they are commonplace as replacements and weekend anchors at the national level and as regular anchors at the local level.

However, because no legal battles were won on the regulatory process, it is not clear to what extent the movement had any direct effect. In a presentation to the International Communication Association, Marilyn Fife compared the approach the women's movement took to that taken by black action groups to change broadcast regulations in their favor. Fife concluded that in general, the black groups were better organized and more sophisticated in their choice of strategies to increase black ownership and employment in the industry.[28]

In contrast, Lewis[29] concluded that to some extent they were successful in influencing broadcaster behavior, especially in the area of employment practices. Lewis also claims that they succeeded in placing the issue of women in television on the national agenda. In retrospect, the campaign to challenge license procedures was an effective tactic in modifying the practices and policies of some local television stations, and the views of those involved with the industry nationally, public, private, and government, to be more aware of feminist concerns.

In conclusion, it would be too simplistic to label the movement as either a success or failure. It never won a petition challenge but by raising the issue, it might also have raised the consciousness of sufficient station owners and managers to finally conclude: "Why *not* use more women in on-the-air and decision-making roles?" At one level, because no licenses were revoked and because the content of programs still do not portray women as they are in "real" life, the movement failed. However, at other levels, by putting the issue in the forefront for scrutiny and possible action, the activity and intrusion of ordinary citizens into the policymaking process probably did initiate a process with a number of positive although indirect outcomes. There were also probable personal gains for the women who had worked in the movement and on the license challenges. Women, mostly young and still not in the labor force, were given the opportunity to gain confidence and a sense of accomplishment, which contributed to their choosing and sustaining careers as professionals and managers. Also others, both men and women, made careers of the media reform movement, continuing to work as experts or consultants on license challenges and monitoring discrimination for various public and voluntary agencies.

Possibly the most important "effect" of the reform movement is that it contributed to a new focus in the research process. Its importance in that regard, although not usually recognized, cannot be over-emphasized. Whereas others also analyzed the content of television programs for gender role portrayals, the license challenge research generated media publicity in the national press and alerted feminists that it is possible to use research for political as well as for informational and educational purposes. The results of this new wave of activist research continue to be cited in the newest publications on the subject of women in media,[30] keeping the topic on the agenda in the classroom and among feminist researchers and scholars.

Although the women's reform movement had some beneficial effects, I would argue that the media changed less because of the activists and more because media generally reflects and responds to changes in political culture instead of leading it. The few who are left in the media reform movement essentially work to obtain more power for the women who work in the industry. More often than not the individual (sometimes class) law suit is used to gain equality for women in broadcasting. Underlying the motivation for reforming the practices of the media industries, whether in portrayal or employment, is the assumption that trickle-down would occur; placing more women in power roles in the industry would over time change how women are depicted, which, in turn, would change their role in society. The feminists who put so much effort and time into reforming the media did so because they believed that ultimately, the changes would increase the power of women in the marketplace and in the home. Instead, they found that even dedication, ingenuity, and long hours of work did little in the short run to alter the status quo. However, they did learn how power operates in a system in which decisions result from compromises among many interests, including those of the stations, the audiences, the networks, the production companies, advertisers, the FCC, and whoever is President at the time.

Notes

Author's note: I am especially grateful to Cherie Lewis and Marilyn Fife and those who shared their unpublished work with me for this article. Although now different in form and content, it is based on a report I prepared for the Benton Foundation (Cantor 1987a) for which Aliza Shapiro of the NOW Legal and Education Defense Fund provided valuable information, documents and editorial advice. This article is dedicated to my friend and colleague, Anne K. Peters, now deceased, who as an activist as well as contributing social scientist, understood the value of combining good research with active participation in the political process. Some comments in the article are drawn from her experience, as a member of the Coalition, in challenging the licenses of four stations in Los Angeles in 1974. Joel M. Cantor, my husband-colleague, as usual contributed his helpful editorial assistance and advice.

1. See Cherie Lewis (1985) and Butler and Paisley, (1980: 183-230) for specific citations concerning employment practices in the industry.

Feminism and the Media 161

2. See Sandman, et al. (1972).
3. See Cantor (1973).
4. The term "diverse" has many meanings. In this context it is used to mean diversity in types of programs broadcast during a broadcast day as well as diversity within presentations. For in-depth discussions of this term in broadcasting as it relates to women and minorities see Cantor (1987b), Jacklin (1978), Westin (1978), and Wilson and Gutierrez (1985).
5. See Tuchman (1978).
6. See Myrdal (1962).
7. See Hacker (1951 and 1974).
8. See Katz and Lazarsfeld (1955).
9. See Lazarsfeld and Stanton (1944). Paul Lazarsfeld, who was the "father" of broadcast research, worked exclusively as a consultant for the Columbia Broadcasting System (CBS). Frank Stanton, his co-editor, was head of research for CBS and later became president of the company.
10. See Ibid; Berelson et al (1954); and Klapper (1960).
11. See Smythe (1954).
12. There were several national conferences following the passage of the 1964 Civil Rights Act. These conferences advocated continuing efforts in working for the equality of women in the schools, family, and workplace. How women are portrayed in the media is a topic that recurs throughout the decade. Although there was not scientific evidence, most feminist critics believed as the author Marya Mannes (1968) did. In a speech to the Fourth National Conference on Commissions on the Status of Women, she asserted that women wanted an end to the sterotyping that she believed pervaded the media and especially television and newspapers. About television she stated:

Let's start with commercials. It must be completely apparent that the ladies who wash and wash and polish and polish and bake and bake are blithering idiots. . . . they talk of nothing but soap and peanut butter and laxatives—that's what they are pushing—it's that they talk like retarded third-graders.

In spite of the fact that well over a third of all women in the country have jobs, not one of these TV ladies ever works. Not one of them leaves the kitchen or living room. Not one of them is seen reading a paper or a book when she's not chasing doves or stuffing dirty socks in her washer. (Mannes, Marya. "To Break Attitude Barrier." in *1968: Time for Action*.)

13. Office of Communication of the United Church of Christ v. FCC (1966).
14. See Sandman et al (1972).
15. National Organization for Women (1972).
16. See Lewis (1985).
17. U.S. Commmission on Civil Rights (1977).
18. Ibid (1979).
19. I was in charge of the monitoring project and was aided by Heidi Hartman and Anne Peters. See Cantor (1973). Both Hartman and I were among those who participated in National Institute of Mental Health's Project on Television and Social Behavior, commonly known as the Surgeon General's Report on Television and Violence.
20. Butler and Paisley (1980), p. 187.
21. Cantor (1979).

22. See Cantor (1987b) for a complete discussion of how the FCC has recently changed its mind about the connection between women and owners and high-level decisionmakers and the content broadcast.
23. Lewis (1985).
24. See Ibid, Tables 2 and 3, pp. 98-102.
25. See Seaman (1986) and Stelson (1987).
26. Wachtel (1986).
27. See Cantor (1987a).
28. For example, she points out that it took women's groups almost two years following the ruling to get the FCC to rule that stations must meet EEO requirements for women as well as ethnic minorities. In May 1970 when the FCC adopted EEO rules for the broadcast industry, it required broadcasters to file reports on affirmative action programs on minorities but not women. Not until February 1972 were broadcasters required to include women workers' status in their affirmative action programs. This drive to include women was justified on the grounds that employment discrimination did exist. Also, implied in the policy was the belief that more women in larger numbers and higher position in the broadcast industry potentially would make a difference in programming and broadcast practices. See Fife, Marilyn (1984).
29. Lewis (1985). Lewis was cited earlier in this chapter for reviewing the history of fifteen license challenges by women's groups.
30. See Gunter (1986) and Signorielli (1985).

References

Berelson, Bernard, Paul Lazarsfeld, and William McPhee (1954). *Voting: A Study of Opinion Formation in a Presidential Campaign*. Chicago, Ill: University of Chicago Press.

Butler, Matilda and William Paisley (1980) *Women and The Mass Media*. New York, N. Y.: Human Science Press.

Branscomb, Anne W. and Maria Savage (1978) "The Broadcast Reform Movement: At the Crossroads" *Journal of Communication* 28, 4, 25-34.

Cantor, Muriel G. (1973) "A TV License Challenge—Women and Media Research" Unpublished paper presented at the Annual Meeting, Society for the Study of Social Problems. New York. August 25. (Available upon request from author.)

Cantor, Muriel G. (1979) "Would More Women Make a Difference" in Herbert S. Dordick (ed.) *Proceedings of the Sixth Annual Telecommunications Policy Research Conference*. Lexington, Mass: Lexington Books.

Cantor, Muriel G. (1987a) "Introduction" *The Hollywood TV Producer: His Work and His Audience*. New Brunswick, New Jersey: Transaction Books.

Cantor, Muriel G. (1987b) "Women and Diversity: A Report to the Benton Foundation" Unpublished Report (Available upon request from author.)

Fife, Marilyn (1984) "The Women's Rights Movement and Broadcast Policy: An Overview and Analysis" unpublished paper presented at the 1984 International Communication Conference. San Francisco, Calif.

Friedan, Betty (1963) *The Feminist Mystique* New York: Dell.

Gunter, Barrie (1986) *Television and Sex Role Stereotyping* London: John Libbey.

Hacker, Helen (1951) "Women as a Minority Group" *Social Forces* 30, 60-69.

Hacker, Helen (1974) "Women as a Minority Group: Twenty Years Later" *International Journal of Group Tensions*. 4, 122-132.

Jacklin, Phil (1978) "Representative Diversity" *Journal of Communication.* 28, 2, 85-88.
Klapper, Joseph (1960) *The Effects of Mass Media.* Glencoe, Ill: Free Press.
Katz, Elihu and Paul Lazarsfeld (1955) *Personal Influence: The Part Played by People in the Flow of Mass Communications.* New York: The Free Press of Glencoe.
Lazarsfeld, Paul and Frank Stanton (1944) *Radio Research 1942-43.* New York: Duell, Sloan & Pearce.
Lazarsfeld, Paul, Bernard Berelson, and H. Gaudet (1944) *The People's Choice: How the Voter Makes Up His Mind in a Presidential Election* New York: Columbia University Press.
Lewis, Cherie S. (1985) "Citizen Activism and the Broadcast Industry: Television License Renewal Challenges by Women's Groups" unpublished Ph.D. dissertation. Minneapolis, Minnesota: University of Minnesota.
Mannes, Marya (1968) "To Break Attitude Barriers" in *1968: Time for Action.* Highlights of the Fourth National Conference of Commissions on the Status of Women. Washington, D. C.: U. S. Government Printing Office.
Myrdal, Gunnar (1962) *An American Dilemma: The Negro Problem and Modern Democracy.* New York: Harper and Row. (Twentieth Anniversary Edition).
National Organization for Women (1972) *Women in the Wasteland Fight Back.* Washington, D. C.: NOW.
National Organization for Women v. FCC, (1977) 40 RR2d 679 (D. C. Cir.)
Office of Communication of United Church of Christ v. FCC, (1966) 359 F. 2nd 944 (D. C. Cir.)
Sandman, Peter M., David M. Rubin and David B. Sachsman (1972) *Media: An Introductory Analysis of American Mass Communications.* Englewood Cliffs, New Jersey: Prentice-Hall.
Seaman, Debbie (1986) "Voice-over Study Shouts Down Male-Superiority Notion" *Marketing Week* September 22, 55.
Signorielli, Nancy (compiler and editor) (1985) *Role Portrayal and Stereotyping on Television: An Annotated Bibliography of Studies Relating to Women, Minorities, Aging, Sexual Behavior, Health, and Handicaps.* Westport, Connecticut: Greenwood Press.
Smythe, Dallas (1954) "Reality as Presented on Television" *Public Opinion Quarterly.* 18, 143-156.
Stilson, Janet (1987) "Net Femmes Facing Upper-Level Block?" *Variety,* March 4, 83 and continued.
Tuchman, Gaye (1978) "The Symbolic Annihilation of Women in the Mass Media" in G. Tuchman, A. K. Daniels, and J. Benet (eds.) *Hearth and Home: Images of Women in the Media.* New York: Oxford University Press.
U. S. Commission on Civil Rights (1977) *Window Dressing on the Sets.* Washington, D. C.: U. S. Government Printing Office.
U. S. Commission on Civil Rights (1979) *Window Dressing on the Sets: An Update.* Washington, D. C.: U. S. Government Printing Office.
Wachtel, Edward (1986) "Television Hiring Practices 1980-1985: A Report on the Status of Minorities and Women." A report from the Office of Communication, the United Church of Christ.
Westin, Tracy (1978) "Barriers to Creativity" *Journal of Communication.* 28, 2, 36-42.
Wilson, Clint C. and Felix Gutierrez (1985) *Minorities and Media: Diversity and the End of Mass Communication.* Beverly Hills, Calif.: Sage.

Part V
Fatalism

Introduction

In his May, 1982 essay, "Conditions for Pluralist Democracy: Or Cultural Pluralism Means More Than One Political Culture in a Country" Wildavsky describes fatalism in these words (p.10):

> A culture of fatalism comes from a combination of weak group boundaries and many personal prescriptions. This is the culture of which it can properly be said that people have no control over the rules that run their lives. For fatalists there is no reciprocity, no mutuality, no sharing. Lacking power, fatalists believe in luck or in submission. People do not take risks for themselves or for others but because it is their fate.

Other characteristics of this political culture, Wildavsky explains, are as follows:

1. No leadership from within. Leadership comes from outside or external forces.
2. Little envy, since life is a matter of chance or luck.
3. Blame is not directed toward others but to bad luck or fate.
4. Inequality is the norm. Those with good luck are on the top of the mountain and those with bad luck are on the bottom, and there is little that can be done to change things.
5. Fairness is not an important consideration. For fatalists life is unfair and one has to make the best of things.
6. Obedience is connected to repression by those at the top since there is little else that can be done to fatalists, who have little and must be convinced that they should expect little.
7. Loyalty is not a value of fatalists. They have little; since they blame their situation on fate, they have no reason to be loyal to a given regime.

The egalitarians are interested in the fatalists and seek to better their lot. As Wildavsky explains:

> Whatever their circumstances, sects try to treat markets and hierarchies as if they were (that is, as they were responsible for producing) fatalists. Now these fatalists, being ruled from outside, subject to forces beyond their control, really lack the initiative to respond to a call for liberation. (If they could, they would be active, not passive, which is something else again.) This explains the

168   Introduction

> unrequited love of would-be sectarian liberators for the "masses" who so often fail to heed their call. (p. 42)

For one reason or another, fatalists reject dominant American political (and other) values such as individualism and the desire for achievement. Or, those who espouse traditional democratic values can, under certain circumstances, be driven into fatalistic stances.

Whatever the case, fatalism can pose severe problems to democratic societies. Fatalists, with little stake in society, are susceptible to being mobilized by undemocratic or authoritarian factions, especially when the economic system is in trouble and does not provide adequate rewards or "payoffs." The two essays included in this section, on graffiti by homeless youth, and on the Apple commercial "1984," both deal with fatalist elements in American culture.

8

Welcome To My Nightmare: The Graffiti of Homeless Youth

G. Cajetan Luna

> *... met with David at noon for coffee. He was upset, at times crying, his eyes were red, he said he hadn't slept the night before. His "partner" Josh had been stabbed in the chest and killed by a trick last night. In fleeing, Josh had "drown in his own blood." David sobbing: "he was a good kid, only tricked to get money for food, or to help out a buddy...." I wasn't sure why, but David wanted to show me the spot where his friend had died ... a three-story abandoned warehouse where a number of Seattle street youth crash. A path of blood was evident as we climbed two flights of stairs to an outer porch area. There were puddles of dried blood scattered all around. He pointed to the ground, "that's where he died right there, sixteen, shit...." Above one of the puddles of blood was a misspelled graffito: Welcome to my Nigthmare [sic].*

Graffiti contains profound social, psychological, and cultural information worthy of serious attention—not triviality to be ignored. Nowhere is this fact better illuminated than in the graffiti of homeless youth. During the past four years I have known hundreds of teenagers who are homeless. They live on the streets of Los Angeles, San Francisco, and Seattle. I interviewed and observed these youth on their own turf; often this meant entering the exploitive, violent social world in which they live.

I was surprised to find that the graffiti I encountered in the street environment so graphically displayed the antagonisms and sentiments that street youth, sometimes reluctantly, expressed verbally in interviews and informal conversations. Similarities in theme and content were evident in graffiti whether it was found in the alleys surrounding Hollywood or Santa Monica Boulevards in the Los Angeles area; on Pike Street in Seattle; or on the walls around Broadway, Haight, or Polk Streets in San Francisco.

For 6,000 years humans have been known to communicate through graphic imagery. Cuneiform characters on clay in Mesopotamia, writings on stone in Assyria, Babylonia, and Persia, and dendroglyphs on trees in Europe and North America provide specific examples. Generations of archaeologists have provided perspectives on the wall writings of the past back to the stylus of Pompei; social scientists have only recently focused on contemporary graffiti. Sociologists, for example, consider graffiti to be evidence of social change and unrest, a representation of shifting conditions of life. Psychologists believe it is a communicative process whereby people give form to their thoughts. It is also seen as a substitute for more violent actions. Herbert Kohl described the cultural significance of graffiti in the 1969 *Urban Review*:

> When one scrutinizes wall inscriptions discerning the recurrence of certain forms of expression and the energy and art with which they are inscribed, it becomes clear that graffiti does not represent attempts to deface walls. Nor is it a simple way of showing off. There are too many regularities in the forms in which graffiti manifests itself not to suspect that one is dealing with a complex cultural phenomenon.

Walls of graffiti serve as a means of communication among homeless youth—declaring their identities or relationships to others, and documenting that a community exists. *Community* is a word not often associated with people who live on the street. Homeless people are characteristically transient and in a constant state of flux. Descriptions frequently focus on a highly mobile population lacking any social framework. While violence is ever present and exploitation is rampant—especially the exploitation of youth by older adolescents or adults—among the youth themselves there is a street community which provides some semblance of security and comfort in an otherwise difficult environment.

A community of adolescent runaways, castaways, and drifters can be found in every major city in the United States. Certain cities attract particular types of youth. San Francisco, for example, long known for its liberal bent and large homosexual population, is a haven for gay youth. Los Angeles, the Hollywood area in particular, draws large numbers of gay teenagers, as well as those holding aspirations of fame and fortune. San Diego is the gateway to the north for Latino youth escaping political and economic oppression in Central and South America. Southern California also attracts North American youth searching for a carefree beach life.

Cities in the western United States, such as Seattle, draw youth mainly from their rural surroundings.

To understand the graffiti of street teenagers, we first have to understand the plight of homeless youth. Historically the nuclear family has been idealized as a supportive unit concerned with the development and welfare of its offspring. While a majority of Americans might believe that the nuclear family is the basic social institution, with the care and nurturance of children the primary responsibility of parents and other family members, for many young people this idealization conflicts with reality. Estimates are that more than one million American children and adolescents are homeless, struggling to survive, most without familial support.

Economic deprivation is the major cause of the large number of street youth outside the United States. Poverty and its social consequences take their toll on the family unit and are important causal factors which force children out of their families and onto the streets. Many of these youth are loved and wanted; but their families are unable to financially support them, and they have to survive on their own. In contrast, the reasons North American youngsters are homeless and on the streets are more insidious. Poverty is significant; general neglect and physical and sexual abuse are fundamental.

The street youth of today are not analogous to the Tom Sawyers of the past. The plurality of youth who leave their homes are not seeking adventure, nor are they necessarily in search of economic opportunity. Many were cast out of their homes or thrown away by parents or other family members. The vast majority who leave home do so because living there has become impossible for them. They flee turbulent households racked by conflict, violence, indifference, and, in a large number of cases, sexual abuse.

Many are battered youth escaping brutal, pathological parents or violent homes. Often they display objective evidence: abrasions, bruises, and similar remnants of recent beatings. Others are from households in which parents are frequently absent and the youth are generally left to care for themselves. After prolonged indifference or neglect, these latch-key children drift away. Increasingly, large numbers of youth are identifying themselves as homosexual in adolescence. As a result of coming out at an early age, gay youths often leave home in order to escape negative sexual labeling among peers, or to flee rejecting fundamentalist parents. Still others are leaving behind experiences of rape, molestation, and incest.

It is estimated that well over 100,000 children are sexually abused annually in the United States. Pediatrician Mary Rimsza of the University of Arizona has explained that when we hear about sexual abuse in childhood, we assume the child is a girl. Recent studies from police agencies report approximately 45 male victims for every 100 females. Rimsza estimates that up to 90,000 boys are victims of sexual abuse annually in the United States, and she indicates that this is a low estimate. Sexual abuse has a significant effect on adolescent development, especially in terms of gender role identification and the formation of future relationships. Sexually abused children often show an exaggerated interest in sexual activity and self-destructive behaviors. These behaviors include substance abuse, promiscuity, prostitution, and, most significantly, runaway behavior:

> Dressed in tattered blue jeans, a soiled down jacket, and a pair of well worn Adidas sneakers, Chris watches people as they pass on Market Street in downtown San Francisco. Occasionally, he hustles a quarter, bums a cigarette, or nods at others who are doing the same. Most of the time he stares at nothing in particular. At sixteen Chris is streetwise. I would learn that his stepfather and uncle had sexually abused him when he was twelve; the stepfather had thrown him out of his Denver home twice. . . . In the past year he has lived in Seattle, Los Angeles, and San Diego. During this time he has had syphilis, hepatitis, pneumonia, and numerous kidney and liver disorders. . . .

The majority of runaways—often twelve or thirteen years of age—are unable to find means of financial support other than through prostitution, drug dealing, and crime. Youth are drawn to the fast life on the streets, easy access to drugs, and a variety of interesting companions involved in exciting and illicit activities. Street companions may provide friendship and the acceptance and understanding previously lacking at home or in foster placements.

For the most part, the lives of street youth are characterized by unstable haphazard shelter; poor nutrition; and emotional and health-related problems, including the possibility of HIV infection and the development of AIDS. Shelter ranges from sleeping in abandoned buildings and public parks, to rented hotels or apartments derived from pooled monies from the youth themselves. Still others take refuge under stairs and in doorways or sleep on sidewalks.

Prostitution can provide street youth with the economic means necessary to remain independent and to obtain shelter for themselves. According to Dr. Robert Deisher of the University of Washington Medical Center, in the 1982 *Pediatric Annals*, after a life of negative self-image and/or abuse, prostitution can even provide an illusion of success for street youth. Similarly, in my interviews with kept youth supported in part or in full by older nonrelated adults (sugar daddys), the majority believed they were better off than they were in the past, were more secure than street prostitutes, and were with people who cared for them. In the sexual marketplace, homeless youth may find a relatively satisfactory survival modus vivendi. It is a short-term life-style, as temporal as is adolescence.

Homeless youth easily succumb to the destructive situations and lifestyles present in some street subcultures. Their eagerness to be accepted, and their relative openness translates to vulnerability. Paradoxically, they are avoided, ignored, or overlooked; invisible to many, their lives are a mystery to most people. Yet there are accessible, identifiable, publically visible signs illuminating their struggle and life situation in their graffiti.

The graffiti of street youth present an unobstrusive glimpse of street life. Their meanings are associative, the graffiti captures the essence of the runaway, castaway, homeless youth experience. These graffiti have the capacity to unfold, revealing layer upon layer of inner meaning. This urban iconography is usually ignored. Nevertheless, we best understand a culture or social organization within its ecological setting and with reference to the milieu in which it operates. The graffiti of street youth are the most graphic expressions and by-products of the culture of the street. We confront what street youth reveal about their lives in the marks they leave. Marks that are angry, poignant, violent, vulnerable, often tragic, and illustrative of lives which are these things and more.

9

1984—The Commercial

Arthur Asa Berger

There is only one way left to escape the alienation of present-day society: to retreat ahead of it: *every old language is immediately compromised, and every language becomes old once it is repeated. Now, encratic language (the language produced and spread under the protection of power) is statutorily a language of repetition; all official institutions of language are repeating machines: school, sports, advertising, popular songs, news, all continually repeat the same structure, the same meaning, often the same words: the stereotype is a political fact, the major figure of ideology. Confronting it, the New is bliss (Freud: "In the adult, novelty always constitutes the condition of orgasm"). Whence the present configuration of forces: on the one hand, a mass banalization (liked to the repetition of language)—a banalization outside bliss but not necessarily outside pleasure—and on the other, a (marginal, eccentric) impulse toward the New—a desperate impulse that can reach the point of destroying discourse: an attempt to reproduce in historical terms the bliss repressed beneath the stereotype.—Roland Barthes,* The Pleasure of the Text

Synopsis: Important Elements of the Commercial

The commercial opens with "1984" appearing on the screen. It cuts to an extreme longshot of vaguely perceived figures marching through a tunnel joining gigantic structures, then to another longshot of figures marching.

The marcher's heads are shaven and they wear dull uniforms. Their faces are expressionless. There is a closeup of their heavy boots.

A quick cut shows a blonde woman wearing a white jersey and red shorts, running. We see her only for an instant, and then the camera cuts back to the dull, expressionless figures. Next cut, the blonde is being pursued by helmet-clad storm-trooper figures. Here the commercial cuts back and forth between the blonde woman and the troopers pursuing her. We see another extreme longshot of the inmates of this institution sitting in a huge room, watching a gigantic television set. A figure wearing glasses addresses the inmates, who sit staring at the television image as if in a hypnotic trance. He talks about their being free, united, etc.

The blonde woman, who is now carrying a sledge-hammer, enters the room. She hurls the sledge-hammer at the television screen, causing a huge explosion that resembles the explosion of an atomic bomb. The inmates stare, dazed and open-mouthed, at the screen. A message from Apple computers then appears on the screen, informing viewers that Apple will be introducing a new computer—The Macintosh—shortly.

The Background

This commercial, directed by Ridley Scott, was shown only once—during the 1984 Superbowl—although it was also aired, as a news item, by a number of news programs. The commercial was created by Apple's advertising agency, Chiat/Day, of Los Angeles. It cost $500,000 to make and $800,000 for air time. Apple was hesitant to use it and only decided to do so at the very last minute. They actually called to England to stop production of the commercial, but by the time they called the commercial had already been shot.

It is a remarkable text. The actors in the commercial were skinheads from England, who were recruited to play the roles of the prisoners. The commercial has a much diffferent look from the average commercial and takes a much different approach to the matter of marketing a product than we find with most commercials. The director, Ridley Scott, is a distinguished figure in the film world, (*Alien, Blade Runner*) and the commercial has his signature; its look, its narrative structure, its message, all suggest an art film rather than a commercial.

I believe that many "creative" people in the advertising industry could create aesthetically interesting and artistically pleasing works (and sometimes they do) were they not prevented from doing so by the companies whose products they are advertising. A great deal depends on the nature of the product being sold and the nature of the company selling the product.

In the remainder of this chapter I will examine some of the most important images from the commercial and speculate about how they generate meaning, what that meaning is, and how viewers might be affected by these images. It is often held that there is no minimal unit to deal with in a television text (unlike film, which has the frame). I do not think this is a major issue, for one can always isolate and analyze important images and scenes, so that even if one does not have frames, one does have "shots" or images, which serve the same function.

1984

The title of this commercial brings to mind George Orwell's novel, *1984* and the text of the commercial is based on the idea of dystopia. The world of the commercial is that of a perverted utopian community, a total institution, in which every aspect of people's lives is controlled—and, in particular, their minds. We see 1984, the commercial, in terms of *1984*, the book. Here we have an example of what is known in semiotic literature as "intertextuality;" we "read" one text in terms of another. The events in the commercial would have much less significance if we did not know about Orwell's classic novel.

The title is also connected to a great deal of speculation about Orwell and his predictions that occurred in the year 1984. Thus, merely *seeing* the title generated ambivalent feelings, and raised questions: Would it be about the year 1984 or about the novel *1984*? (Many social commentators had mentioned that the year 1984 did not bring the kind of society that Orwell imagined.) The title created suspense.

The Total Institution

The first shot resolved any questions that might have been generated by the title. We see an extreme longshot of gigantic structures, connected by a tubular tunnel, in which we can dimly perceive marching figures. The scene's scale is terrifying; the figures are minute and seemingly irrelevant when contrasted with the huge buildings in which they are incarcerated. One almost thinks of blood flowing through veins.

Thus, the spatiality of this scene and the image of control and conformity generated by the columns of figures, tells us immediately that the commercial, "1984," is indeed about an Orwellian world. This is reinforced in the next shot—a longshot of the prisoners, all with shaven heads and heavy, ill-fitting uniforms, sullenly marching in columns in the tunnel.

The Boots

An important shot occurs with the closeup cut of the prisoner's boots. The heavy, thick-soled boots, shown moving in unison, reflect the degree to which the inmates are under their master's control. (This is an example of metonymy, which confers meaning by association. And, in particular, it is an example of synedoche, in which "a part can stand for a whole.") The shot of the boots is meant to intensify the message. (We may even recall the famous shot of the boots in *The Battleship Potemkin*, thought the situation was somewhat different.) Uniforms suggest depersonalization and, in the context of the commercial, dehumanization. The shot of the boots, moving in common, strengthens this message by emphasizing one part of the human being and isolating it from the image of the whole human being.

The uniformity of the prisoners feet as they march, the rather sullen and lethargic nature of their marching, suggest that these inmates have been reduced to the status of automatons. It is the same kind of reductionism that occurs when we talk about young people being "college material" or football players as "horses," though it is much more intensified here.

The Blonde

Into this scene of marching zombies, of dehumanized and depersonalized bodies, there appears, for just an instant, an image of a beautiful blonde woman, wearing a white shirt and red shorts, running down a corridor. We can see her breasts heaving as she runs directly at us, the viewers, on the Z-axis of the screen. This figure appears for perhaps a second or two, and then we return to the marching bodies and scenes of totalitarian control.

Who is she? We do not know—but the fact that she exists tells us that there is resistance in this totalitarian society, that not all are enslaved. We see, shortly, that she is being pursued by a troop of policemen who look terribly menacing in their helmets with glass facemasks. Her color, her animation, her freedom, even her sexuality, serve to make the situation of the inmates even more obvious and pathetic. Her image functions as a polar opposite to the enslaved men and even though we only see her the first time for a second or two, her existence creates drama and excitement.

The Brainwashing

We have a longshot of the inmates, sitting in rows, gazing at a gigantic television screen in the front of the auditorium, where a Big Brother figure is shown speaking to them. They are mute, expressionless, and seem to be almost hypnotized by the figure on the television screen. The message we get from this image is that mind-control is an important element in the operation of this totalitarian society. By implication, of course, control of the media (the gigantic television screen reflects this) is vital for control of the minds of the inmates—and perhaps everyone. Is this scene a metaphor for contemporary society, in which we, like the inmates, gaze in a hypnotic stupor, at figures who "brainwash" (or try to, at least) us? Is the distance between the world of the "1984" commercial and American society less that we might imagine? These questions are raised by this image. Are we "like" these prisoners and are we "mind controlled" the way these prisoners are? We may not wear their uniforms, have shaved heads, or be prisoners (or recognize that we are prisoners, that is) in some kind of a total institution, but could that be because the control is more subtle, the indoctrination less apparent? That there may be more control over us than we imagine is one of the matters raised by this image.

Big Brother

We see little of the Big Brother figure—only a few shots in which we see him spouting gobbledy-gook to the inmates. The choice of the actor to portray this character is very interesting. He looks like a clerk or minor bureaucrat from some organization. He is in his fifties or sixties, wears glasses, and is definitively bland and un-charismatic. He speaks in a low, rather monotonous voice. Indeed, for all we know, he may only be a minor functionary in whatever vast organization runs this society.

The message we get from a figure like this is that totalitarian institutions are essentially bureaucratic, held together not by charismatic individuals but by drab, conformist, bureaucratic types who do their jobs in a routine matter and do whatever they are told to do. They are not that different from the inmates in many respects, although the control exerted over these figures may be less overt.

The Message

Following is a transcript of the message that the Big Brother figure gives to the inmates. He speaks it, but it is also shown in captions running across the bottom of the screen.

> Today we celebrate the first glorious anniversary of the information purification repentence. We who created from out of this time in all history a garden of pure ideology, where each worker may loom secure, from the test of purveying contradictory thoughts. Our communication is enormous. It is more

powerful than any fleet or army on earth. We are one people with one will, one resolve, one cause. Our enemies shall talk themselves to death and we will bury them with their own confusion. We shall prevail . . .

At this point television screen is shattered.

The first thing we notice is that this rhetoric is somewhat garbled and confusing. He talks about events we know nothing of—although we can imagine what might have transpired. The language has the ring of indoctrination, there is a "glorious revolution" being "celebrated." The language contrasts, starkly, with the scenario in which it is being used. There is talk in this futuristic, oppressive hyper-urban setting of a "garden of pure ideology" and the "security" that the workers should feel from all this.

Communication is given the major role here—it is a more powerful force than the military, it unites the workers/inmates/prisoners into a collectivity (or is it mass society) with "one will, one resolve, one cause." And then there is that wonderfully comic line about the enemies of this society "talking themselves to death." It is the rhetoric of persuasion, and we have the sense that the inmates of this society have been exposed to this kind of talk almost endlessly. That is, they have been brainwashed by this doubletalk.

The language, with phrases such as "information purification repentence," is that of mind-control and psychic domination, and the commercial does a wonderful job of imitating it (and perhaps, in a sense, of parodying it). The goal preached is escape from "contradictory thoughts," which leads to "one will." In other words, the essentially human function of considering options and alternatives is to be obliterated (or has been already?).

The Explosion

There are several scenes in which we see the blonde woman twirling a sledgehammer as she prepares to throw it at the screen, the police racing toward her. She launches the sledgehammer and it smashes into the gigantic television screen. There is an explosion and we see, briefly, an image vaguely similar to that produced by an atomic bomb.

The explosion, which destroys the screen—and by implication the domination by the mass media of the inmates/workers—is the most significant act in the commercial. With this act a great blow is struck for freedom, and we are led to imagine, in our own minds, what might follow. We are shown very little. Implicit in this scenario is the notion that once the control of people's minds by a totalitarian regime is broken, the destruction of that regime more or less follows automatically. This does not have to be spelled out. It is like lancing a boil—when the system of pressure is punctured, healing can take place. The exploding screen signifies, then, the destruction of the totalitarian order that generates mind-controlling images on that screen.

The Response

After the explosion we cut to a scene in which the inmates are shown open-mouthed, staring in disbelief at what has happened. They are, relatively speaking, emotionless and display no affect other than bewilderment. They have been so brainwashed, we are led to believe, that they are incapable of any kind of response—at least, in the immediate present. We hear a low hissing sound, as if air is escaping from the gigantic television apparatus in the front of the room. The camera pans the inmates as the announcement from Apple rolls onto the screen.

The Announcement

We see the following announcement:

> On January 24th, Apple Computers will introduce Macintosh and you will see why 1984 won't be like "1984."

The brevity and simplicity of this announcement, which takes but a few seconds, contrasts with the excitement and visual richness of the commercial. In this situation the understatement "shouts" and creates a great deal of interest. Apple Computers announces that it is introducing a new computer, but also that this new computer has enormous political and social implications—it will save us from ending up as victims of a totalitarian state.

There had been a great deal of material about the Macintosh computer in the press and computer fanzines, so those interested in computers already knew about it. When the Macintosh computers went on sale, Apple sold about 17,000 the first day—a figure far beyond what they had anticipated. People from Chiat/Day talk about the phenomenon as if it was the commercial that sold all those computers—an assumption that is very questionable.

The Heroine as Mythic Figure

The blonde heroine of this micro-drama calls to mind several different heroic figures from our collective consciousness. First, there is something

182   Fatalism

of "David and Goliath" in this story: a small, seemingly weak, and in this case female, character brings down a Goliath figure, by hurling a stone (sledgehammer) at it. In the commercial there are some close-ups of the Big Brother/Goliath figure, which simulate the size relationships between David and Goliath. A missile to the head that does the job in both cases. And with the destruction of Goliath, of course, the forces of good can prevail. Here we find how intertextual readings can enrich an event and give an image a great deal of cultural resonance.

In addition, the woman is an Eve figure; the fact that the Apple symbol is an apple with a bite out of it implies that. But the blonde heroine also functions like Eve—for ultimately she leads us to knowledge of good and evil in a reverse Garden of Eden. Before she shattered the image, the inmates were brainwashed and had but "one will, one resolve, one cause." What information these poor souls had was "purified." Their state is vaguely analogous to Adam before he ate of the apple. It is the tasting of the fruit, which led to Adam and Eve's "eyes being opened"—and the beginning of human history, one might argue.

Thus, the blonde herione is an Eve who brings knowledge of good and evil, and by implication, knowledge of reality, to the inmates. We do not see their transformation after the destruction of the Big Brother figure—and their immediate reaction of awe and stupefaction—but ultimately we cannot help but assume that something important will happen. It is quite possible that this beautiful blonde figure may also represent, in our psyches, the Apple corporation. We know that corporations have different images in peoples' minds, often based on symbolic figures in advertisements and commercials. On the basis of this commercial one might guess that the corporate image we have of Apple is that of a beautiful woman (who liberates men from political and psychological domination and ignorance). Much of this would be at the unconscious level, no doubt. In any case, it's probably a good image for a computer company to have, since one of the biggest problems computer manufacturers have is fighting anxiety about the difficulties of computer operation—Macintosh's very reason for being, as a matter of fact. If people see Apple computers as beautiful blondes, so much the better for the corporation.

From a psychoanalytic standpoint, the heoine is an ego figure who mediates between a monstrous and perverted superego figure, Big Brother, and the deenergized and devastated ids of the inmates. We see this in the chart that follows:

As an ego figure, the heroine has to mediate between the inmates, whose ids have been weakened and drained of energy and the brainwasher, whose superego has become monstrous and distorted. One might see vague elements of an Oedipal conflict, in which a young female and an older, per-

ID	EGO	SUPEREGO
inmates	blonde	Big Brother
perverted	normal	perverted
no energy	strong	no heart

haps even "fatherly" figure have a (to put it mildly) very difficult relationship.

The Mediator

One function of the mythic hero or heroine is to mediate between opposing forces in an attempt to resolve some basic opposition. The text of this commercial is very binary and the blonde heroine serves to identify and highlight the oppositions found in it. There are, in essence, three characters in this text. First the inmates, who function as one character. Then Big Brother and the police who are part of him. Finally there is the blonde heroine. Her function is to revolve the oppositions, one way or another—and she does.

In the chart that follows I will contrast the inmates and the Big Brother figure. Here we are eliciting the paradigmatic structure of the text, which according to Levi-Strauss, tells us its real meaning (as opposed to the surface meaning, which we get with a syntagmatic or linear narrative analysis).

The blonde heroine, with her vitality, her energy, her force, resolves the dialectic by destroying Big Brother and making it possible (we imagine) for the inmates to regain their humanity. She also makes us aware of the depths to which the inmates have sunk, for unlike them she resists, she has a mind of her own, she accepts danger. Thus she contrasts with both the inmates and with Big Brother, who she destroys. The inmates and Big Brother are reverse images of one another—both drab, depersonalized and locked into

INMATES	BIG BROTHER
obey	commands
uniforms	regular clothes
hairless	hair
listen	speaks
brainwashed	brainwasher
look at	is looked at
mindless	calculating
dehumanized	dehumanizing
alienated	alienating
emotionless	heartless

a slave-master relationship that defines each character and on which both may turn out to be independent.

Alienated Proletariat

The inmates, workers, automatons—whatever you wish to call them—reflect with terrifying clarity, the way modern bureaucratic states can destroy humanity and lead people into a state of radical alienation. We have here a classic case (even if somewhat oversimplified and parodied) of a mindless proletariat being manipulated by a heartless bourgeois. This bourgeois rules by virtue of its control of the media and the manipulation of the consciousness of the proletariat. The situation in the commercial is one in which the horrors of a capitalist society are shown pushed to their logical conclusion, where workers are now enslaved and the society in which they live has become totalitarian.

The blonde heroine's actions symbolizes revolution: She stands for the role of progressive forces (pushed underground in this society) in leading a stupified proletariat out of its chains. Since the inmates have been brainwashed, they are incapable of action and are perhaps, even reactionary. Hence they remain passive while the revolution takes place—and can only stare in open-mouthed wonder at the destruction of the power structure than enslaves them.

In this scenario, the power of the media is shown as central, and when it is put out of action, the rest is almost automatic. Interestingly enough, this message is not too far removed from the overt message of the Apple corporation—that access to user-friendly computers will prevent a totalitarian society from coming into being. Apple is a "revolutionary" force in the quasi-totalitarian world of hard-to-use computers where power will be held by those who know how to function in the information society. The Macintosh will prevent society from splitting into two groups: those who have access to computers and are part of the information society and those who know nothing about computers, are condemned to menial jobs, and form a class of workers which will have little economic power and little status.

Apple is the blonde who will prevent the evolvement of a rigid information-based class system and, by implication, a "totalitarian" or totalitarian-like society. The Macintosh brings knowledge of good and evil to man- and womankind—all it takes is a bite (or is it byte?).

The Big Blue

It is not too far-fetched, I would argue, to suggest that the totalitarian society shown in this commercial is an indirect representation of IBM

Corporation. Apple sees itself as a small, humanistic, open corporation battling a gigantic, super-powerful, and highly bureaucratic IBM. There are two readings to which this insight leads: First, the whole story is about IBM. The Big Brother figure is the corporate leadership and the inmates are the IBM workers who are controlled (white shirt and tie, etc.) by IBM. IBM has a reputation for being rather strict about the way its workers and salespeople dress and this commercial may be alluding to this regimentation. The second reading suggests that Big Brother is IBM and the inmates, the American public, which is duped and controlled by IBM—but is about to be liberated by Apple and its Macintosh computer.

The battle resolves down to one between the beautiful blonde heroine fighting against the monolithic monster-bureaucratic corporation full of faceless nobodies mindlessly following rules and regulations, "enslaving" the multitudes. The Macintosh—a user—freindly machine which will, democratically, make computing available to all—is the sledgehammer which Apple throws at IBM. Apple is now trying to sell the Macintosh to businesspeople, a group in which IBM seems to have a lock on the market. How well it will succeed is questionable since there is not a great deal of business software yet available for the Macintosh and Apple's "blonde" image may, in fact, work against it.

Conclusions

Although the "1984" commercial cost a great deal of money to produce (perhaps three or four times as much as a typical high-budget commercial) and air, due to the notoriety it attracted, it ended up being a very good buy. We must remember that although it aired only once, it was the subject of a great deal of media attention and fascinated the huge audience that was watching the Superbowl. As someone in the creative department at Chiat/Day explained to me, "good campaigns end up being relatively inexpensive." A good commercial (and campaign) may cost a great deal to produce and air, but if its impact is sufficiently strong, on attention per-thousand basis it might work out to be relatively cheap.

Chiat/Day (and Apple) took an unusual approach with this commercial. In the un-Cola genre it focused attention *not* on the benefits to be derived from using a Macintosh but, instead, on the dangers inherent in not using one. The commercial was not selling a specific product in a direct manner—it used indirection and suggestion to build an image for Apple and Macintosh and, at the same time, cast aspersions on its main rival, IBM. In the course of sixty seconds it created a memorable micro-drama that worked subtly and indirectly. Like many commercials, it was highly compressed, with neither a beginning nor an ending. (Many commercials do not have a beginning but do show a "happy" ending, with someone using the product or service advertised.)

The ending implied in the "1984" commercial focused on the avoidance of something hateful rather than the gaining of something desirable. In its own way, there is an element of conditioning involved here; we have a condensed form of aversion therapy. The argument, like the commercial, is very binary. If there are only two possibilities, Apple and IBM, and IBM (and all that it and its imitators stand for) is shown to be horrible, one is led to choose Apple. One acts not so much to gain pleasure (though that beautiful blonde attracts us) but to avert pain (Big Brother and the dystopian world that he represents).

The "1984" commercial launched the Macintosh brilliantly. Apple continued to attack conformity in the business world in its 1985 commercial, which showed blindfolded businessmen jumping off a cliff, like lemmings. But this ad lacked the polish and aesthetic complexity found in "1984" and it was followed up by a rather meager event—Apple announcing a few minor items in its campaign to get businessmen to purchase Macintoshes for their offices.

What will happen in the future remains to be seen. Some think that Apple is now fighting for its life and that if it does not penetrate the business market, it will become a minor player in the computer-sales wars. Others argue that Apple's penetration of the school market and the individual or non-office market is so great that it will remain IBM's major competitor. Whatever the case, its "1984" commercial was a fascinating and extremely rich text.

References

I would like to express my gratitude to John Minzer of the Media Production Center at the Annenberg School of Communications, The University of Southern California, for his invaluable assistance.

Barthes, Roland, *Mythologies*. New York:Hill & Wang. 1972.
Berger, Arthur Asa. *The TV-Guided American*. New York: Walker & Co. 1975.
Berger, Arthur Asa. *Television as an Instrument of Terror*. New Brunswick, New Jersey; Transaction, Inc. 1980.
Berger, Arthur Asa. *Signs in Contemporary Culture: An Introduction to Semiotics*. New York: Longman, Inc. 1984.
Berger, John. *Ways of Seeing*. New York: Penguin Books. 1977.
McLuhan, Marshall. *The Mechanical Bride*. New York: Vanguard. 1941.

Name Index

A.K. Daniels, 163
Aggarwala, Narinder, 72
Arnold, Edward, 121
Arendt, Hannah, 40
Arterton, F. Christopher, 95
Attali, Jacques, 82

Ball, Terrence, 44
Banning, Lance, 44
Barfield, Claude E., 46
Barker, James, 77
Barnes, Samuel H., 35, 44
Barth, Fedrik, 127
Barthes, Roland, 113, 175, 186
Bateson, Gregory, 141
Becker, G.S., 23, 45
Benet, J., 163
Benjamin, Gerald, 95
Berelson, Bernard R., 39, 44, 153, 162, 163
Berger, Arthur Asa, 17, 175, 186
Berger, John, 186
Blake, Frederick, 43, 44
Blake, William, 145
Bloomgarden, Kathy, 36, 44
Blumler, Jay G., 77, 96
Bogart, Leo, 1, 6, 7, 8, 17, 50, 51
Bose, Subhas Chandra, 53
Brady, Henry E., 29, 44, 45
Branscomb, Anne W., 156, 157, 162
Brizola, Leonel, 104
Burnham, David, 88
Burt, Ronald S., 44
Butler, Matilda, 162

Caan, James, 122, 127
Calhern, Louis, 127
Canning, George, 77
Cantor, Joel M., 160
Cantor, Muriel G., 6, 13, 14, 132, 149, 162
Capra, Frank, 121
Carhart, Tom, 137

Carvalho, Elisabeth, 120
Chaves, Aureliano, 117
Chong, Dennis, 33, 42, 45
Cimino, Michael, 134
Clair, Janete, 115
Cleveland, Harlan, 82, 95
Collins, David, 146
Conover, Pamela Johnson, 30, 34, 44
Cook, Timothy E., 40, 44
Cotgrove, Stephen, 44

DaMatta, Roberto, 108
Danziger, James N., 96
Doubek, Bob, 134, 135
Douglas, Mary, 4, 17, 23, 35, 44
Downs, Anthony, 79, 96
Dreisher, Robert, 172
Duff, Andrew, 44
Dutton, William H., 6, 8, 9, 50, 79, 96

Eco, Umberto, 13, 145, 147
Elkin, Stephen, 40, 44
Elkins, David J., 35, 44
Ellis, Richard, 31, 44
Ellul, Jacques, 95

Feldman, Stanley, 31, 34, 44
Fife, Marilyn, 159, 160, 162
Fonda, Jane, 137
Forester, Tom, 90
Foss, Sonja K., 13, 139, 140, 141, 147
Franco, Wilton Tupinamba, 111
Friedan, Betty, 14, 153, 157, 162

Gaudet, H., 163
Geertz, Clifford, 35
Goodenough, Ward, 35
Goulart, Joao, 103
Gramsci, A., 27
Gray, Jerry, 120
Gross, Jonathan L., 31, 44

Gulager, Clu, 127
Gunter, Barrie, 162
Gutierrez, Felix, 163

Hacker, Helen, 162
Hagen, Michael G., 29, 45
Haines, Harry W., 13, 139, 141, 142, 143, 147
Halfoun, Eli, 120
Hamill, Ruth, 43, 44
Harrison, J. Richard, 42, 44
Hart, Frederick, 138, 144
Hartley, Keith, 41, 44
Hawks, Howard, 122
Herz, Daniel, 120
Hirsch, Paul M., 101, 111, 116, 120
Hitler, 65
Holm, John, 45

Jacklin, Phil, 162
Jackson, Karl, 44
Jaffe, Sam, 127

Kalt, Joseph B., 36
Kalt, Joseph P., 45
Katakis, Michael, 133
Katz, Elihu, 163
Kehl, Maria Rita, 120
King, John, 89
Klapper, Joseph, 153, 163
Kling, Rob, 96
Kohl, Herbert, 15, 170
Kottak, Conrad Phillip, 2, 6, 10, 11, 17, 100, 101
Kraemer, Kenneth L., 89, 96

Lancaster, Burt, 128
Lane, Robert E., 42, 45
Lauber, Volkmar, 45
Laudon, Kenneth, 83
Lazarsfeld, Paul R., 39, 44, 153, 162, 163
Lemmon, Jack, 121
Lenin, V.I., 63
Levi-Strauss, Claude, 35, 183
Lewis, Cherie S., 160, 163
Lewis, Jerry, 118
Liberato, Augusto, 110
Lichter, S. Robert, 36, 45
Lin, Maya Ying, 13, 136, 137, 138, 139, 141, 142, 144
Lindblom, Charles E., 21, 24, 45

Lodge, Milton, 43, 44
Luna, C. Cajetan, 6, 15, 169

MacBride, Sean, 52, 73, 77, 78
Maluf, Paulo, 117, 118
Mann, Anthony, 122
Mann, Michael, 12, 122
Mannes, Marya, 163
March, James G., 24, 41, 42, 44, 45
Marin, Peter, 146, 147
Marinho, Roberto, 112, 114
Marvin, Lee, 127
Marx, Karl, 40
Massing, Herta Herzog, 10
Mathias, Charles, 137
McCloskey, Herbert, 42, 45
McClosky, Herbert, 33
McLuhan, Marshall, 53, 82, 145, 186
McPhee, William N., 29, 44, 162
Meadow, Robert, 96
Merton, Robert, 40
Michael, R.T., 23, 45
Milbrath, Lester W., 45
Minzer, John, 186
Miranda, Ricardo, 120
Mondale, Walter, 58
Montenegro, Fernanda, 117
Morrison, Patt, 120
Mouse, Mickey, 63
Murdoch, Rupert, 67
Myrdal, Gunnar, 163

Newcomb, Horace, 120
North, Oliver, 89

Oakeshott, Michael, 40
Olsen, Johan, 24
Orren, Gary R., 29, 45
Orwell, George, 15, 177

Paisley, William, 162
Papandreou, George, 59
Parenti, Michael, 116
Parker, Edwin, 82
Pateman, Carole, 43, 45
Pavarotti, Luciano, 63
Pereira, Carlos Alberto M., 120
Peters, Anne K., 160
Ping, Deng Xiao, 63
Pipe, Russell, 78

Name Index

Ploman, Edward, 65, 77
Pool, Ithiel de Sola, 82, 95
Pye, Lucian W., 2, 3, 17

Ramos, Roberto, 120
Rappeport, Michael, 77
Rayner, Steve, 31, 44
Reagan, Ronald, 58, 90, 118, 127, 143
Rimsza, Mary, 171, 172
Roach, Colleen, 78
Robinson, John, 42, 45
Roosevelt, Franklin D., 116
Rothman, Stanley, 36, 45
Rubin, David M., 163

Sachsman, David B., 163
Sandman, Peter M., 163
Santos, Silvio, 11, 109, 110
Savage, Maria, 156, 157, 162
Schambra, William A., 46
Schiller, Dan, 90
Schreider, David, 35
Schwarz, Michiel, 22
Scott, Ridley, 15, 176
Scruggs, Jan, 13, 134, 135, 136, 143, 144, 145, 147
Seaman, Debbie, 163
Shafir, Michael, 45
Shapiro, Aliza, 160
Siegel, Don, 127
Signorielli, Nancy, 163
Simeon, Richard E.B., 35, 44
Simon, Herbert, 21
Smith, Howard K., 134
Smythe, Dallas, 163
Sniderman, Paul M., 29, 30, 44, 45
Stanton, Frank, 163
Stevenson, Robert L., 78
Stewart, James, 122
Stigen, Wayne Douglas, 133

Stilson, Janet, 163
Stimson, James A., 29, 45
Stourdze, Yves, 82
Straubhaar, Joseph D., 120
Sussman, Glenn, 36, 45
Swerdlow, Joel L., 135, 147

Tavola, Artur da, 102, 113, 120
Tetlock, Philip E., 29, 45
Thatcher, Margaret, 90
Thompson, Michael, 22, 41, 45
Treille, Jean-Michal, 78
Tsetung, Mao, 65
Tuchman, Gaye, 151, 163
Tunstall, Jeremy, 78
Tylor, Edward Burnett, 2, 17

Ugboajah, Frank, 78

Verba, Sidney, 27, 45

Wachtel, Edward, 163
Wagley, Charles, 120
Warner, John, 137
Weinberger, Caspar, 143
Westin, Tracy, 163
Wheeler, Jack, 134, 136, 144
Wildavsky, Aaron, 4, 5, 6, 11, 12, 17, 21, 32, 39, 43, 44, 46, 49, 50, 99, 100, 121, 131, 167
Wilder, Carol, 6, 12, 132, 133
Wilson, Clint C., 163
Winner, Langdon, 83
Wolin, Sheldon S., 40, 46
Woolgar, Steve, 84

Yu, Frederick T.C., 76

Zajonc, R.B., 27, 28, 46
Zupan, Mark A., 26, 45

Subject Index

1984, 177
'1984' the commercial; alienation in, 16; background, 176, 177; IBM (International Business Machines) and, 184-86; id, ego and superego elements in, 16, 182, 183; mythical heroine and, 181-83; Orwell's novel *1984* and, 15, 177; significant images in, 177-81; synopsis, 175, 176; use of aversion conditioning in, 186
Advertising; internationalization of, 69; in United States, 69; media content and, 69
AIDS (acquired immune deficiency syndrome), 172; risk and, 37, 38
Alien, 176
All My Sons, 121
American Dream; *Thief* and, 12, 122, 123
American Political Science Association, 5
Amiga, 103, 113, 114
Amos 'n Andy, 152
AP (Associated Press), 71
Apple Computers; Macintosh commercial and, 15, 16
Arab League, 64
Articles of Confederation, 34
ASEAN, 64
Atlantic City, 128
AT&T (American Telephone and Telegraph Company), 90
Audimarket, 106

Bandeirantes television network, 108
BBC (British Broadcasting Corporation), 90, 91
Blade Runner, 176
Brainwashing, 178, 179
Brazil; 1984 presidential campaign, 116-18; censorship and political reporting, 104; Globo television network, 10, 11; Manchête television network, 11; presidential elections in 1984, 11; SBT (Brazilian television network), 11; social classes in, 107, 108; telenovelas, 10, 108, 110; television audience, 114-16; television in, 10, 11, 101-20

Cable television, 89-92
Capitalism; cinema and, 121-28
Censorship, 102-5
Civil Rights Act of 1964, 153
Communication Quarterly, 139
Competitive individualism; characterized, 25-27; equality of opportunity and, 99; loyalty and, 99; new knowledge and, 100; ostentation and, 99; prescriptions and, 99; risks and, 99; *Thief* and, 12; uncertainty and, 99; weak boundaries and, 99
Conservatism, 30
Conservatives, 33
Constitutional Convention, 34
Control of new media; democratic marketplace view, 80; pluralist view, 81; reinforcement politics and, 81; technocratic view, 80, 81
Critical Studies in Mass Communication, 139
Cross-national research; into news, 74; into values, 74
Cultural hypothesis, 28, 29; institutionalized moral judgments and, 4; preference formation and, 28
Cultural imperialism; domination by advanced states, 73; national cultural distinctiveness and, 69, 70
Cultural theory; heuristics and, 29, 30; ideology and, 31; left-right distinction and, 33; liberal and conservative division and, 33, 34; risk and, 31; schemas and, 30, 31
Culture; codes and, 35; definitions of, 2; politics and, 8; politics of, 13, 14; risk and, 35-38
Cultures; subcultures and, 7
Culture theory, 1; basic axioms of, 24, 25; group boundaries, 25-27; prescriptions, 25-27

Dallas, 10; world audience of, 65
Deregulation, 90
Desert heuristic, 30

'Ecology of games' metaphor, 90, 91
Economics; preferences and, 23, 24
Economist, 67
EEC (European Economic Community), 64
Egalitarianism, 6; Armageddon complex and, 132; characterized, 25-27; control of envy, 131; equality of result and, 131; fairness and, 131; few prescriptions and, 131; problem of leadership and, 131; rejection of authority and, 131; system blame and, 131
Equal Pay Act of 1963, 157
ERA (Equal Rights Amendment), 151

Fantastico, 108, 109
Fatalism, 6; belief in luck and, 167; characterized, 26; egalitarians response to, 168; lack of leadership and, 167; lack of loyalty and, 167; many personal prescriptions and, 167; unconcern with fairness, 167; weak group boundaries and, 167
FCC (Federal Communication Commission), 86, 160
FCC (Federal Communications Commission), 150-57
Feminism, 149-63; media and, 13; television and, 13, 14

Gallup International, 56, 105
Gatekeepers; censorship by, 101, 102; levels of control by, 101, 102
Gentlemen Prefer Blondes, 122
'Global village,' 53, 82
Globo television network, 101, 103, 106, 107-15, 117, 118; cultural imperialism and, 113
Gomer Pyle, 110
Gong Show, 110
Good Housekeeping, 67
Graffiti; as signs of lives of homeless youth, 173; cultural significance of, 170; functions of, 170; homeless youth and, 15; messages in, 169
Group boundaries; four political cultures and, 25

Harper's Bazaar, 67
Heuristics; preferences and, 21
Hierarchical collectivism; characterized, 25-27, 49-50; inequality and, 49; leadership and, 49; loyalty and, 49; risk and, 49; scarce resources and, 49; *Thief* and, 12; uncertainty and, 49
'High Culture;' popular culture and, 102
Hill Street Blues, 105
Homeless youth; criminality of, 172; economic deprivation and, 171; search for community by, 170; sexual abuse of, 171, 172

IBM (International Business Machines), 184-86
IBOPE (Brazilian Statistical Public Research Group), 11
IBOPE (The Brazilian Statistical Public Opinion Research Institute), 105, 106, 107, 114
ICA (International Communication Association), 159
Ideological constraints; social interaction and, 29
Ideologies; preferences and, 21
Ideology, 35
Impossibility theorem; four political cultures and, 25
Indiana Jones and the Temple of Doom, 104
Individualism; two kinds of, 32-35
Individualism. *See* competitive individualism
Information technology. *See* new media, 79-95
Information utilities, 88
Interests; as preferences, 22, 23
International Association for Mass Communication Research, 55
International Commission for the Study of Communication Problems, 52

Kerner Commission Report, 153

Liberalism, 30
Liberals, 33

Macintosh computer, 181, 182
Manchête, 113
Manchête television network, 108, 113

Subject Index 193

Mass communications; world opinion and, 51-76; world public opinion and, 6-8
Mass media; apartheid and, 73; difference in systems, 66; impact on culture, 8; inhibitions of developing nations and, 74; international influence of, 66-72
Mass media research; male centered aspects of, 152; neglect of women, 152, 153
Miracle on 34th Street, 121
Missing, 121

Name That Tune, 109
NATO, 56, 64
NBMC (National Black Media Coalition), 153
News media; bureaucracies and, 88; control of; 80, 81; democratic impact of, 82; elitist impact of, 82, 83; governmental institutions and, 86-89; hierarchies and, 95; interests served by, 81-84; national sovreignty and, 95; neutral impact of, 32, 81; political campaigns and, 84-86; public telecommunications networks and, 89-92; use in Santa Monica, California, 87
News; about developing countries, 72, 73; philosophies of, 70; radio, 71; television, 71
Newsweek, 56, 67
New technologies; elections and, 9, 10; governmental communications and, 9, 10; political campaigns and, 9, 10; politics and, 8, 9; public telecommunications and, 9
New World Information Order, 8, 53, 72-75
Nielsen, 105
North Dallas Forty, 121
NOW Legal Defense and Education Fund, 157
NOW (National Organization of Women), 156; television challenges and, 149-51; WRC-TV renewal application and, 14
NOW vs. FCC, 155

O Globo, 112, 113
O Jornal da Brasil, 117
OPEC, 64
Opinion Research Corporation, 59
Opinions; cultural values and, 61-66; culture and, 7; information and, 57; national character and, 7; national cultures and, 7, 8; self interest and, 58; shared information and, 59; two-way communication and, 66; volatility of, 63
Os Giganes (The Giants), 115

Pan African Congress, 64
PANA (Pan African News Agencies), 71
Parents, 68
Pediatric Annals, 172
Platoon, 141
Playboy, 67
Political culture, 1, 21-46; defined, 2, 3; four political cultures and, 4; power and, 3; preferences and, 4, 5; uses of, 3, 4
Political cultures; left versus right, 32-35
Political institutions; as cultural creations, 63; impact on culture, 63
Politics; definitions of, 40; values and, 40
Polls; ingroup and outgroup positions and, 7; marketing and, 6; politics and, 6; public opinion and, 55, 56; topics dealt with, 6
Popular culture, 8, 114
Popular Mechanics, 67
Power; as a social phenomenon, 26
Preferences; calculations of, 38-40; endogenous not exogenous, 23, 24; first order, 4; four political cultures and, 38-40; institutions and, 21, 22; interests and, 24; interests as, 22, 23; political cultures and, 21-46; second order, 4; social relations and, 40, 41
Prensa Latina, 71
Prescriptions; four political cultures and, 25
Public opinion, 1; collective behavior and, 1; in Communist countries, 55; literacy and, 60; political systems and, 54, 55; polling and, 1; relation to political thought, 51, 52; subcultures and, 62
Public opinion research; apathy and, 61; ignorance and, 61

Qube, 87

Radio Free Europe, 57
Rambo, 141
Readers Digest, 57
Reuters, 71
Riffifi, 127

Risk, 35-38

SBT (the Brazilian television system), 108-10
Schemas; preferences and, 21
Scientific American, 67, 68
SECOM (Brazilian government press agency), 112
Sinal do Alerta (*Danger Signal*), 114
Social issues, 34
Society magazine, 10
Star Wars, 108

Tass, 71
Telenovelas. *See* Brazil
Television; as government mouthpiece, 101; Brazil and, 10, 11; Globo television network, 10, 11; government control and, 101; propaganda and, 101; propaganda role of, 101. *See also* Brazil, 101-20
Tevê, 113
The Asphalt Jungle, 127
The Battleship Potemkin, 178
The Deer Hunter, 134
The Killers, 127
The People on TV, 110, 111
The Right to Be Born, 113
The Stunt Man, 105
The Twilight Zone, 104
Thief, 121-28; American Dream and, 12, 122, 123; and political culture, 11, 12; capitalism and, 121, 122; competitive individualism of hero, 122; craftmanship and, 126; hierarchical collectivism and, 124

Thunder Bay, 122
Time, 67, 68
Two-Step flow of communication, 39

UNDP (United Nations Development Program), 72
UNESCO, 6, 71; world public opinion and, 6
United Church of Christ (Office of Communication), 154
Urban Review, 170
USA Today, 67

Variety, 67
Vietnam Veterans Memorial; ambivalent meanings of, 143; as anti-war statement, 1, 13; as epic Greek poem, 137; as means of political manipulation, 13; as open text, 13, 145; as sacred site, 142; creation of, 134-38; description of, 137; enthymemic structure of, 138; female sensibility of, 140; impact on people, 139; rhetorical analyses of, 138-46

WABC-TV, 150, 151-54
Wall Street Journal, 67
Warsaw Pact, 64
Wired cities, 92, 93
WLBT-TV, 158, 151-54
World Association for Public Opinion Research, 55
World opinion; non-existence of, 75. *See also* mass communication and, 51-76
WRC-TV renewal application, 14, 150, 151, 154, 155